Roman Martin

Azores

The finest coastal and mountain walks

105 walks on nine islands in the middle of the Atlantic

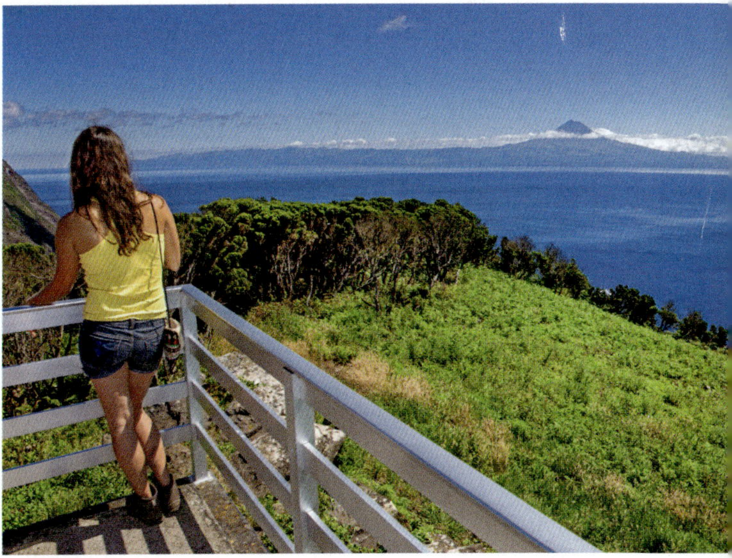

PREFACE

Everyone has heard about the Azores High – here is its home. The nine islands of the Azores are scattered like tiny specks in the middle of the Atlantic, just over two hours from the Portuguese mainland – an archipelago on the westernmost edge of Europe. Five centuries after their discovery, they now face the growing challenge of mass tourism. In the 16th and 17th centuries, the islands became the port of call for all trading ships crossing the new route to America and the old seaway to India, providing a hub between three continents. The wind-torn islands became Portugal's main source of grain. In the 18th and 19th centuries, the orange trade and whaling flourished – but these times are long gone. Harpoons belong to the past – nowadays, tourists with cameras are chasing whales during the whale-watching trips.

The people of the Azores are proud, cosmopolitan and eager to please. They live with one foot on the land and the other in the sea. The forces of nature and poverty caused many to flee westward – over a million Azoreans live in Canada and the USA – three times the population of the Azores itself; many, however, have returned. On the Azores, the sky reigns as master – doling out sunshine, spraying rain or covering the island in shrouds of thick clouds. Not without reason, the archipelago guarantees unspoiled natural scenery including an undreamed of spectrum of species. Many endemic plants have found a niche here. Flower-clad islands just wait to be explored. The blue sky is mirrored time and again in countless crater lakes and only stops to do so when it dips into the ocean and disappears. The mild Gulf Stream provides the motor for a year-round temperate climate. In a place where pineapple and tea grow, the landscape must still be unspoilt.

But today, even paradise has its dark side. Tourism has long since conquered the Azores: during the peak summer months, São Miguel's infrastructure is hopelessly overbooked. During winter, the islands have become a popular destination for cruise ships: 200 stops per year and up to 6,000 visitors a day have brought tourism on the island to an entirely new level. Budget airlines now fly to the islands, there is a lack of parking spaces and if you want to go to a restaurant, you have to book several days in advance. If you want to avoid the crowds, go between September and May or visit one of the lesser frequented islands. Quo vadis, Azores? Please lend your hand to keep this a paradise!

All walks in this guide have been brought up-to-date. Nevertheless, new construction projects, road work or landslide may change a route temporarily or even make it impossible to walk. If you should come upon such a change, we would appreciate if you could inform the publisher.

Summer 2025   Roman Martin

Lighthouse on the Ponta do Arnel (São Miguel).

CONTENTS

Preface..3
Top Walks...8
Important notes for the walks 10
    Grades...10
    GPS tracks and coordinates of the starting points........................11
    Symbols..12
General information 13
    Climate tables...14
    Sports and other activities..24

The Azores 26

Santa Maria – Ilha do Sol 36
#	Time	Walk	Page
1	2.00 hrs	Baía do Tagarete	40
2	3.15 hrs	Circling Santa Bárbara (via Norte)	42
3	3.00 hrs	Circling Santa Bárbara (via Pico)	45
4	2.40 hrs	Circling the Pico Alto	47
TOP 5	3.40 hrs	From Santa Bárbara to Praia Formosa	49
6	3.50 hrs	From Santo Espírito to Santa Bárbara	52
7	4.20 hrs	From Santo Espírito to Maia	54
8	4.50 hrs	From Maia to Praia Formosa	56
TOP 9	3.20 hrs	From Vila do Porto to Praia Formosa	60
10	5.00 hrs	From Anjos to the Baía do Raposo	62
11	4.40 hrs	From Anjos to Vila do Porto	65

São Miguel – connecting to the Western World 68
#	Time	Walk	Page
12	2.00 hrs	Circling the Pico de Mafra	74
13	5.30 hrs	Circular walk around the Caldeira das Sete Cidades	76
TOP 14	2.20 hrs	Lagoas Empadadas	79
15	1.20 hrs	Ponta da Ferraria and Pico das Camarinhas	82
16	2.00 hrs	Rocha das Feteiras	84
17	2.10 hrs	Rocha da Relva	86
18	1.40 hrs	Nascentes de Santo António	88
19	2.10 hrs	From Calhetas to São Vicente Ferreira	90
20	1.45 hrs	Pico Queimado	92
21	2.40 hrs	From Caldeiras to the Salto do Cabrito	94
TOP 22	2.30 hrs	Janela do Inferno	97
23	5.15 hrs	From Água d'Alto to the Lagoa do Fogo	100
24	2.40 hrs	Circular walk along the Lagoa das Furnas	103
25	2.40 hrs	From Ribeira Quente to Povoação	106
26	2.50 hrs	From Faial da Terra to the Pico dos Bodes	108
27	5.20 hrs	From Faial da Terra to Água Retorta	111
28	1.45 hrs	Around Água Retorta	114

29	1.40 hrs	Fajã do Araújo	116
30	2.00 hrs	From Lomba da Fazenda to the Ribeira do Guilherme	118
31	3.00 hrs	Pico da Vara	120
32	1.45 hrs	From Achadinha to the Ribeira dos Caldeirões	122
33	2.40 hrs	Alminhas de Achadinha	124
TOP 34	2.45 hrs	From Fenais da Ajuda to the Ribeira da Salga	126
35	1.40 hrs	Moinhos da Ribeira Funda	128
36	2.30 hrs	From Lomba da Maia to Maia	130
37	2.15 hrs	Around Maia	132
38	1.15 hrs	Chá Gorreana	134
39	2.00 hrs	Porto Formoso – Ladeira da Velha	136

Pico – the whalers' island 138

TOP 40	3.00 hrs	Zona do Verdelho	142
41	3.00 hrs	From the Furna de Frei Matias to Madalena	144
TOP 42	6.00 hrs	Montanha do Pico, 2351m	146
43	5.00 hrs	Circling Santa Luzia	148
44	1.15 hrs	Loop around São Roque do Pico	151
45	4.30 hrs	From the Lagoa do Capitão to the Baía de Canas	153
46	3.15 hrs	From the Lagoa do Capitão to Cais do Pico	156
47	2.00 hrs	From the Miradouro da Terra Alta to Santo Amaro	158
48	3.50 hrs	From the Miradouro da Terra Alta to Piedade	160
49	7.00 hrs	Pico's highland lakes	163
50	4.00 hrs	Ponta da Ilha	166
51	3.10 hrs	Around Calheta de Nesquim	170
52	3.00 hrs	From the Parque Florestal de São João to Silveira	172

Faial – a sailors' paradise 174

53	1.30 hrs	Monte da Guia and Monte Queimado	178
54	3.40 hrs	Circling Ribeirinha	180
55	4.15 hrs	From the Caldeira to Ribeirinha	183
56	2.30 hrs	Circular walk around the Caldeira	185
57	5.15 hrs	From the Caldeira to Cedros	187
58	2.40 hrs	From Capelo to Praia do Norte	190
59	4.50 hrs	From Praia do Norte to Norte Pequeno	192
TOP 60	4.20 hrs	Ponta dos Capelinhos	195
61	1.10 hrs	Morro de Castelo Branco	198

São Jorge – a paradise for the cheese gourmet 200

62	3.40 hrs	Ponta dos Rosais	204
63	4.40 hrs	Fajã de João Dias	206
TOP 64	2.50 hrs	Fajã de Além	208
65	2.15 hrs	Fajã da Ribeira da Areia	210
66	3.45 hrs	Fajãs do Norte	212
67	4.45 hrs	Via Pico da Esperança to Fajã do Ouvidor	214

	68	1.50 hrs	From Biscoitos to Fajã Grande 217
TOP	69	3.40 hrs	From the Serra do Topo to the Fajã dos Cubres 219
	70	3.10 hrs	Portal – Fajã dos Vimes 222
	71	6.00 hrs	Serra do Topo – Fajã dos Vimes – Fajã de São João 224
	72	2.40 hrs	São Tomé – Fajã de Saramagueira – Fajã de São João 228
	73	2.50 hrs	From São Tomé to Topo 230

Terceira – the Holy Spirit island 232

	74	3.45 hrs	Fajãs and Mata da Serreta 236
	75	2.45 hrs	Pico da Lagoínha 238
	76	2.00 hrs	Vinhas dos Biscoitos 240
	77	2.30 hrs	Baías da Agualva 242
TOP	78	2.10 hrs	Místerios Negros 244
	79	5.10 hrs	Malha Grande – Biscoitos 246
	80	3.20 hrs	Rocha do Chambre 250
	81	2.50 hrs	Algar do Carvão – Furnas do Enxofre 254
	82	2.00 hrs	Passagem das Bestas 256
	83	2.45 hrs	Rota da Água 258
	84	3.00 hrs	Monte Brasil 260
TOP	85	2.30 hrs	Fortresses of São Sebastião 262
	86	2.15 hrs	Relheiras de São Brás 264

Graciosa – island of windmills 266

TOP	87	2.40 hrs	From Bom Jesus to the Barro Vermelho 270
	88	4.30 hrs	From Praia de São Mateus to Fontes 272

89	3.15 hrs	From the Serra Branca to Praia de São Mateus	274
90	3.50 hrs	From Praia de São Mateus to Carapacho	276
91	2.50 hrs	Volta à Caldeira	278
92	1.00 hrs	Baía da Folga	280
93	2.30 hrs	Ascent from Beira Mar to the Serra Branca	282

Flores – the flower island 284

TOP	94	5.00 hrs	From Costa to Fajã Grande	288
	95	2.40 hrs	Circling Fajã Grande	292
TOP	96	3.10 hrs	From the Lagoas to Fajã Grande	295
	97	4.30 hrs	From Fajã Grande to Ponta Delgada	298
	98	2.30 hrs	Trilho das Barrosas	302
	99	3.20 hrs	From Ponta Ruiva to Fazenda de Santa Cruz	305
	100	2.10 hrs	Fajã do Conde	308
	101	1.20 hrs	Ponta da Caveira	310
	102	1.35 hrs	Porto da Lomba	312
	103	3.20 hrs	Fajã de Lopo Vaz	314

Corvo – remote and lonely in the Atlantic Ocean 316

| TOP | 104 | 2.00 hrs | Caldeirão | 318 |
| | 105 | 2.30 hrs | From the Caldeirão to Vila Nova | 320 |

Geographical dictionary: Portuguese – English 322
Index 323

View from Miradouro das Cumeeiras across the giant crater of Sete Cidades (Walk 13).

TOP WALKS

From Santa Bárbara to Praia Formosa (Santa Maria)
Crossing the island takes you through various altitude zones and different landscapes to the island's prime sandy beach *(Walk 5, 3.40 hrs)*.

From Vila do Porto to Praia Formosa (Santa Maria)
The scenic coastal walk leads to the island's longest sandy beach *(Walk 9, 3.20 hrs)*.

Lagoas Empadadas (São Miguel)
The most popular walk in the west passes the top viewpoint at the Sete Cidades crater *(Walk 14, 2.20 hrs)*.

Janela do Inferno (São Miguel)
Popular family trip across aqueducts and to some old water collection points *(Walk 22, 2.30 hrs)*.

From Fenais da Ajuda to the Ribeira da Salga (São Miguel)
This easy beginners' walk takes you to a remote headland and some hidden waterfalls *(Walk 34, 2.45 hrs)*.

Zona do Verdelho (Pico)
This beginners' walk leads through Pico's UNESCO-protected wine-growing region *(Walk 40, 3.00 hrs)*.

Montanha do Pico, 2351m (Pico)
Scaling Portugal's highest mountain rewards you with panoramic views, however, you must book your places weeks in advance in the summer *(Walk 42, 6.00 hrs)*.

Ponta dos Capelinhos (Faial)
The Capelinhos volcano resembles a barren moonlike landscape contrasting with the green volcanic cones *(Walk 60, 4.20 hrs)*.

Fajã de Além (São Jorge)
The challenging footpath winds its way up endless stone steps to secluded gardens and weekend cottages *(Walk 64, 2.50 hrs)*.

From the Serra do Topo to Fajã dos Cubres (São Jorge)
This classic walk in the north of the island that leads to an idylic sea lagoon is a must for every visitor *(Walk 69, 3.40 hrs)*.

Místerios Negros (Terceira)
A challenging nature trail winds along black lava mounds and lakes leading to a massive lava tunnel *(Walk 78, 2.10 hrs)*.

Fortresses of São Sebastião (Terceira)
On a historical trip along the coast, you pass century-old fortifications *(Walk 85, 2.30 hrs)*.

From Bom Jesus to the Barro Vermelho (Graciosa)
An adventure walk through the wine-growing region and along the wild northern coast of Graciosa *(Walk 87, 2.40 hrs)*.

From Costa to Fajã Grande (Flores)
An ancient mule path connects the villages on the western side of Flores *(Walk 94, 5.00 hrs)*.

From the Lagoas to Fajã Grande (Flores)
An old shepherds' path leads from the picturesque highland lakes to the village of Fajã Grande *(Walk 96, 3.10 hrs)*.

Caldeirão (Corvo)
The descent into the giant crater of Corvo is the busiest walk on the island *(Walk 104, 2.00 hrs)*.

IMPORTANT NOTES FOR THE WALKS

Grade
Many of the walks presented in this guide follow good trails and distinct paths; some walks, however, require sure-footedness, a good head for heights as well as physical fitness. Wherever orientation becomes difficult when away from marked trails, this is noted in the text.
The walk numbers are colour-coded to indicate the grade of the walk:

GRADES

■ = Easy
These walks are ideal for beginners or families with children. All trails are distinct, sufficiently wide, sometimes tarmac and mostly marked. They can be walked without any great difficulty even during periods of poor weather.

■ = Moderate
Some sections of these walks follow narrow, sometimes precipitous stretches of path that are also steeper and maybe slippery when wet. A certain degree of sure-footedness and a good head for heights is required. Some sections may also demand a higher degree of orientation skills.

■ = Difficult
These trails demand a high degree of sure-footedness and well-developed orientation skills. Furthermore, longer stretches may be very precipitous and could lead through open country without a distinct trail or over long stretches of scree, sometimes even requiring scrambling with the use of hands.

Walking times
All listed walking times are measured using a moderate walking speed and do not include breaks, photo sessions or alternative excursions. Poor weather may also create slippery trails and increase the walking time needed.

Height notations
The routes of all walks were several-times controlled using GPS data. Despite barometric height measurements, the data given here may not be completely exact. The listed differences in height are to be understood in terms of the altitude that must be negotiated and also includes intermediate descents and ascents.

Getting there
If there is a direct bus service to the start of a walk, it will be indicated in the text. Still, the easiest approach will always be by personal vehicle or

Trail boards show height profiles and the course of the hiking trails (Walks 70/71).

rental car. If you do not want to return by foot to the starting point during a lineal walk, you should arrange a taxi in advance or ask for one in a bar. Permanent taxi stands are only found in the cities but elsewhere, the few local taxi drivers are usually known to all and sundry.

Refreshment, inns and accommodation

You will not encounter any mountain huts serving refreshments on the Azores. Food and accommodation is only available in the settlements where you will usually find a corner shop and a bar. Away from these, you must depend on carry-along provisions. On many costal walks, we used

GPS TRACKS AND COORDINATES OF THE STARTING POINTS

On **gps.rother.de**, GPS tracks and coordinates of the starting points are available for free download which can be accessed by scanning this QR code.
5th edition, password: 481805azh
The GPS tracks can be imported into the **Rother App**. The app tells you exactly where you are and where you are going when you are on the move. You can find instructions on **rother.de/gps**
As possible changes and errors can never be ruled out completely, we advise you to never entirely rely on GPS data for orientation, but to assess the conditions on the ground.

SYMBOLS

Symbols in the tour headings
- 🚌 accessible by bus
- ✘ refreshment en route
- bathing spot

Symbols for height profiles
- settlement offering refreshment
- restaurant, inn, bar
- bus stop
- car park
- harbour, boat landing
- bathing spot
- † summit, peak
- church, chapel
- ruin
- lighthouse
- wind farm
- △ campsite
- picnic site
- windmill
- watermill
- ∩ cave
- viewpoint
-)(bridge
- waterfall
- spring, fountain

local springs and waterfalls for a welcome thirst-quenching drink of water and never suffered from digestive problems.
If you are planning a lineal long-distance walk, you should first investigate the availability of accommodation at the end of the daily stages.

Trail network and markings

Nowadays, there are about 90 marked trails on all of the nine islands which are numbered and signposted (for the international marking symbols, see below). Circular walks always begin with the prefix PRC, long-distance trails with GR. At the starting point, you will find an information board with an overview map and more specific details on the route.

The local *turismos* sometimes provide additional leaflets with basic information for the individual routes. Rother walks do not always follow the signposted trails. It is essential to be aware that some stretches of trail may nevertheless be more difficult and toilsome to walk due to construction projects, landslips or poor maintenance, since the clearing crews only do their duty sporadically or the community does not want to spend money.

■ Information concerning the *turismo* routes is also available through the internet and includes the required GPS tracks: https://trails.visitazores.com.

right way	wrong way	change in direction
═	✖	➡ ⬅

GENERAL INFORMATION

Best time to visit

Thanks to the temperate Gulf Stream, relatively constant temperatures are enjoyed year-round. With mild winters when temperatures during the day seldom drop below 14 °C and the summer months when there are up to 250 hours of sunshine with temperatures up to 27 °C, the Azores merit a visit any time of the year. Nevertheless, up until now, only the stable months of summer have attracted tourists. Due to the cooling breezes from the Atlantic, it is never unpleasantly hot or cold. Depending on humidity, however, the sensory effects of temperatures can fluctuate considerably – the humidity varies between 70% and 90% here. The weather is usually stable in mid-summer but even in July and August, there is no guarantee as far as sunshine is concerned and cloudless blue skies are few and far between. During seasonal changes starting in May and June as well as the entire autumn months stretching into December, temperatures remain relatively mild during the day. In the winter months from January until April, the risk of longer periods of bad weather increases, with heavy rain and powerful storms. The average annual precipitation currently measures between 1000 and 1600mm. Generally, the weather is quite changeable, so even on a summer day starting off with sunshine, you should expect a short rain shower. In the higher altitudes, periods of fog, lasting for days, can obscure everything any time of the year. You can forget the maxim 'all four seasons in a single day' for despite the fickleness of the weather in general, it is at best a mixture of sunshine, showers and fog. Often the

Many hiking trails have now been marked (Walks 55–57).

Coffee in São Jorge is simply delicious.

sun is waiting for you just beyond yonder mountain. The best holiday timeframe we can recommend to the walker is May until November, although in July and August, most of the available accommodation, hire cars and flights are often booked out months in advance. The bathing season lasts from July until November. Water temperatures vary between 16 °C in spring and 23 °C in late summer. The actual weather forecast is televised every evening at the end of the regional newscast on RTP Açores and can also be read as teletext on all of the RTP programmes.

■ On the internet, you can find the weather forecast at www.ipma.pt. A number of live weather webcams can be viewed with the APP SPOTAZORES.

CLIMATE TABLE WESTERN ISLANDS, STATION SANTA CRUZ

	Jan	Feb	Mar	Apr	May	June	July	Aug	Sept	Oct	Nov	Dec
Maximum temperature °C	16.4	16.0	16.7	17.3	19.2	21.5	24.2	25.1	23.9	21.2	18.9	17.3
Minimum temperature °C	11.1	10.5	11.2	11.9	13.6	15.7	18.0	18.9	17.8	15.6	13.8	12.2
Water temperature °C	16	16	16	16	17	19	22	23	22	21	19	17
Hours of sunshine hrs	77	79	111	132	166	162	205	213	157	113	79	65
Rain mm	214	200	142	114	107	87	58	93	126	154	199	221

CLIMATE TABLE CENTRAL ISLANDS, STATION HORTA

	Jan	Feb	Mar	Apr	May	June	July	Aug	Sept	Oct	Nov	Dec
Maximum temperature °C	16.3	15.9	16.3	17.2	18.9	21.2	23.9	25.1	24.0	21.3	18.9	14.2
Minimum temperature °C	12.1	11.4	12.0	12.6	14.0	16.1	18.3	19.4	18.6	16.5	14.6	13.1
Water temperature °C	16	16	16	16	17	19	22	23	22	21	19	17
Hours of sunshine hrs	91	95	120	155	182	174	232	238	178	145	103	83
Rain mm	112	98	81	65	56	49	35	54	90	101	115	120

CLIMATE TABLE EASTERN ISLANDS, STATION PONTA DELGADA

	Jan	Feb	Mar	Apr	May	June	July	Aug	Sept	Oct	Nov	Dec
Maximum temperature °C	17.0	16.8	17.3	18.1	19.7	21.8	24.3	25.6	24.7	22.1	19.6	17.9
Minimum temperature °C	11.6	11.0	11.6	12.1	13.3	15.4	17.2	18.4	17.8	15.9	13.9	12.6
Water temperature °C	17	16	16	16	17	19	22	23	23	21	19	18
Hours of sunshine hrs	97	103	120	141	174	163	208	213	175	142	109	93
Rain mm	133	107	100	72	53	37	30	38	86	113	131	127

Getting there

SATA Azores Airlines offers direct flights to São Miguel from Portugal (Faro, Lisbon, Porto, Madeira), Germany, France, the UK, Italy, the Canary Islands, Cape Verde and Spain as well as from the USA and Canada. Some direct flights also serve Terceira. International flights are mostly seasonal and do not fly daily. TAP operates year-round with a stopover in Lisbon. From this hub, there are daily flights to Faial, São Miguel and Terceira as well as several times a week to Pico and Santa Maria. For all other islands, a layover is usually required. In 2024, there were seasonal flights from other airlines to Belgium, Germany, the UK, the Netherlands, Switzerland, the Czech Republic and the USA.

If you fly via Lisbon, make sure you allow enough time as your luggage may not arrive in the Azores until one or two days later. It is recommended to have all flights booked on one ticket. Don't forget to check your flights in advance as there may be last-minute changes, especially with TAP.

Unfortunately, there is no ferry service at all from any country to the Azores.

SATA Air Açores operates daily flights connecting all nine islands with small propeller planes.

Taking care of the environment ...

When we are out hiking, we also leave an ecological footprint, however, being in harmony with the environment is not that difficult!

PREPARATION AND GETTING THERE
- Before you go, find out what you can do to protect the nature and the environment in the hiking area you are visiting.
- Wherever possible, use public transport such as busses and trains as well as hiking busses.
- If you travel by car, share the ride with others.
- If it's a long drive to the starting point, plan multi-day trips or find a local guesthouse from where you can do several walks.
- Try to limit air travel as much as possible and offset it by contributing to climate protection projects.

CLOTHING AND EQUIPMENT
- Buy environmentally friendly and fair-trade outdoor gear and use your clothes as long as possible.
- You can also buy second hand equipment or use rental gear.
- Fix broken things rather than buying new equipment.

FOOD
- Make sure you buy organic food as well as regional and seasonal products.
- Stay in huts and guesthouses that offer local products.
- Bring your own water bottle and sandwich box instead of buying disposable bottles or food that is wrapped in plastic.

ACCOMMODATION
- Book your accommodation directly with the locals, so they can benefit.
- Save electricity and water in huts and other places you stay in.

WHEN WALKING
- Use designated trails and avoid shortcuts.
- Respect closed trails and conservation areas.
- Don't pick flowers or take plants home with you.
- Respect forest fire warnings.
- Take your rubbish with you and dispose of it at home.
- If possible, avoid going to the toilet in the open.
- Avoid noise.
- Put your dog on a leash.

Travel within the Azores

Flights
SATA Air Açores services all of the islands via the hubs at Faial, São Miguel and Terceira. Some flights operate several times per day. The airports are small and easy to get around. Check-in and boarding is usually quick and uncomplicated.
■ Flight schedules can be found at azoresairlines.pt/en.

Atlânticoline ferry operating in the central island group.

Ferry service
Atlânticoline provides reliable ferry connections year-round between Faial, Pico and São Jorge (the *Triângulo*) extending to Graciosa and Terceira in summer. In autumn and winter, services are more limited. Since 2020, there are no more ferry connections between the island groups.
■ Ferry schedules can be found at atlanticoline.pt.

Car hire
Hire cars are available on all of the islands except Corvo. There are two rates to choose from: a basic fee with the kilometres driven being charged separately or an all-inclusive rate with unlimited mileage. As a rule, all rates include a partially comprehensive. Full comprehensive insurance (CDW) with excess must be arranged separately but is not required. If you are over 23 years of age and have had a driver's license for over one year, you may hire a car here. During the months of July and August as well as during the major holidays, be sure to make a reservation for a car hire well in advance.

Public transport
There is bus service offered on all the islands except Corvo; the service is tailored, however, to the needs of the inhabitants. The remote interior and the mountainous regions are not serviced. Good connections can be enjoyed on São Miguel and Terceira. Also on Faial, Graciosa, Pico and Santa Maria, bus service is sufficient. Often, there are only a few bus lines with infrequent service and the routes can be somewhat difficult for tourists to grasp. Several starting points for walks are therefore not easy to reach by bus.
The busses are modern and fares are incredibly low. When service allows, you can take a round-trip of the island by bus. You usually pay your fare to the driver when you get on – most drivers only speak Portuguese.
■ Bus schedules are available at horarios.visitazores.de.

Aldeia da Cuada – a 19th century holiday experience (Walk 95).

Taxis
Taxis can be hired on all of the islands except Corvo. On Faial, there is a taxi service central for the entire island. In Ponta Delgada, there are two centrals. APP Taxilink operates on both islands. The price per kilometre is still less than € 1. The distance driven will be recorded on the metre. For certain routes to tourist attractions, the price may be already fixed. For a day trip, a fixed price should be negotiated with the driver. Many taxi drivers are excellent sources of information concerning the countryside and its inhabitants and are even better versed than some guides, however, not all of them speak English!

Accommodation
Throughout the archipelago, there is a wide choice of accommodation offered to fit every possible budget. Generally there are two categories. Hotels are classified from two to five stars. However, all premises are of a manageable size, modern and are equipped according to international standards. There are also some *quintas*, some of which are still operating farms. They range from grand manor houses to farm stays. The prices for this kind of accommodation are usually higher than the average price of a hotel room but indeed the flair is well worth the difference. The entire private rental market – from apartments and holiday homes to small complexes – falls under the category Alojamento Local (AL). There are now over 4000 such accommodations, including several hostels, mostly in larger villages. For a truly individualist's sojourn, we recommend a holiday home. Here you usually have to provide for yourself and a hire car for many locations is a certain necessity due to the distances involved. Basically, every rental must be registered and certified. Renting out rooms without registration is illegal.

For backpackers, there are camping sites to choose from; camping in the wild is not permitted. Many of these campsites have been modernized in the recent past. Indeed, accommodation can be tailored to every wallet.

Useful information

Addresses and telephone numbers
■ **Tourist information**
Direcção Regional de Turismo dos Açores; Rua Ernesto Rebelo, 14; P-9900-112 Horta; tel +351 292 200 500, visitazores.com/en
Turismo de Portugal; info@visitportugal.com, visitportugal.com/en
■ **Embassies and Consulates**
Great Britain: British Embassy; Rua de São Bernando, 33, 1249-082 Lisbon; ppa.lisbon@fco.gov.uk
USA: US Embassy; Av. Príncipe de Mónaco, 6-2 F; 9500-237 Ponta Delgada; ConsPontaDelgada@state.gov
Canada: Honorary Consul; Rua d'Água, 28; 9500-040 Ponta Delgada; lsbon.consular@international.gc.ca
■ **Internet**
visitazores.com/en: the official website of the Tourist Office provides basic, multi-lingual information.
whatson.azores.gov.pt: event calendar for the Azores
gps.azoren-online.com: detailed maps for Garmin devices
trails.visitazores.com/en: official website for marked walking trails by *turismo*.

Visa information
As on the Portuguese mainland, a valid identity card or passport is sufficient for EU citizens. A visa is not required for stays of up to 90 days for travelers from the UK, the USA and Canada, but ETIAS will be needed from 2025.

Holidays
Bank holidays: January 1, Shrove Tuesday, Good Friday, Easter Sunday, April 25 (Freedom Day), 1st of May, Whitsun Sunday, June 10 (Portugal's national holiday), Corpus Christi, August 15 (Assumption), October 5 (Founding of the Republic), All Saints' Day, December 1 (Independence Day), December 8 (Immaculate Conception), December 25.
In addition, every settlement has at least one local celebration to honour their patron saint and a Holy Spirit Celebration as well.

Currency
On the Azores, the legal tender in use is the Euro. Cash machines are available in all of the major settlements from which up to € 200 in

Sanjoaninas in Angra do Heroísmo.

cash can be withdrawn using debit or credit cards. Credit cards are now widely accepted in shops.

Opening hours
Shops are usually open from 9.00 until 12.30 and from 14.00 until 18.00 Saturdays, most shops close at 13.00. The larger supermarkets are usually open all day until late in the evening and sometimes are even open on Sunday. Banks: 8.30 until 15.00; post offices: 9.00 until 18.00.
Many museums and restaurants are closed on Monday.

Medical
No special inoculations are needed to visit the islands. If you have been injured or become ill, you will find a medical clinic in every town to provide you with the assistance you need; in Ponta Delgada, Lagoa, Angra do Heroísmo and Horta, there are also major hospitals with specialists trained at European standards. At every medical facility, an international health insurance card suffices for receiving treatment. It is nevertheless a good idea to have traveller's medical insurance. Pharmacies can be found in all of the major settlements (with emergency service).

Clothing
Light clothing is usually sufficient during the summer. Although temperatures are normally moderate, because of the high humidity, you 'feel' con-

Carpet-weaving on São Jorge (Walks 70/71).

siderably warmer and you may easily begin to perspire. In spring and autumn, you will definitely need warmer clothing, since temperatures drop drastically starting early in the evening. In winter, a jumper should be packed. At any time of the year, you should be sure to bring rain and wind gear with you. Wearing some sort of head covering is advisable since the gentle Atlantic breezes make the sun's rays seem less intense than they really are.

Religion

Most of the inhabitants are strict Catholics. Every settlement has its own church, usually disproportionately large, as well as additional chapels. These are usually open to visitors during the day; the times for mass are posted at the entrance.

Packaging tea in Gorreana (Walk 38).

Crime

The Azores are still a very safe place for travellers. In recent years, theft and car break-ins have been restricted to the areas around the popular tourist attractions on São Miguel. The locals usually do not even bother to lock their doors. Women travelling alone can feel perfectly safe on any of the islands.

Souvenirs

You can find local handicrafts on all of the islands to bring home with you as souvenirs. On São Miguel, you can purchase basalt jewelry as well as hand-made pottery and ceramics. Faial offers whalebone carving (*scrimshaw*), handicraft made from fig tree pith (*miolo de figueira*) and artificial flowers and jewellery from fish scales (*camas de peixe*). On Flores, you can find handicrafts made from hydrangea pith (*miolo de hortênsia*). São Jorge is famous for its wool blankets (*colchas*) produced in Fajã dos Vimes. On Santa Maria, you will find wicker weaving (*trabalhos em vime*) and baskets (*cestos*). All of the islands offer embroidery (*bordados*). In addition, there are local wines, excellent cheese, pineapple products and, on São Miguel, Europe's only tea plantation.

Power supply

The Azores are provided with a 230 volt network. Plugs types C and F fit the system.

Ocean acrobats: short-beaked common dolphins riding the waves.

Telephone and internet
The country code for the Azores is +351. From the Azores to Great Britain, use the prefix 0044, USA and Canada – 001. In the meantime, the mobile phone network is very well developed on all of the nine islands. In isolated areas and especially in the mountains, you can still expect 'dead spots' with no reception. For longer sojourns, we recommend buying a pre-paid mobile telephone card which you can recharge at the post office.

Internet cafés are few and far between. On many islands, free Wi-Fi is now available in urban areas and popular hotspots. A number of restaurants also provide free (Wi-Fi) hotspots.

Tips
Normally, service is included in the price. For an appropriate tip, about 5–10% is the usual rate. In restaurants, as a rule, you round off the bill and leave your money on the table.

Drinking water
Water from the public plumbing system is reputed to be drinkable but does not always taste especially good. In any case, to be absolutely certain, we recommend buying spring water that is available in 5 litre containers in the supermarkets for a very low price.

Time difference
The time difference to the Greenwich Mean Time (GMT) is always minus one hour.

Books and maps

Maps
We reccomend the 2019 2-map set 'Azoren' by Freytag & Berndt (ISBN 978-3-70791-794-9) at a 1:50,000 scale covering all roads and walking trails as well as a road map of the same name and same scale. Kompass also offers a 2019 'Azoren' walking map set (ISBN 978-3-99044-267-8) at the same scale which is perfect for walkers. Another great option is the 'Azores Tour & Trail' map (2023, ISBN 978-1-7-8275-085-7).
For basic orientation, you can also get folding maps including useful maps of the towns, free of charge, at the local *turismo*.

Azores travel guides
By far the best companion to this walking guide is the newly revised 'Azores' (2024) by David Sayers which is part of the Bradt Travel Guides series (ISBN 978-1-8046-9173-1). A great alternative is the 2024 edition of Moon 'Azores' (ISBN 978-1-6404-9994-2).

Plant Guide
For more information on the flora of the Azores, the excellent 'Flora of the Azores' by Hanno Schäfer (ISBN 978-3-82361-792-1) is highly recommended.

At the Mercado da Graça in Ponta Delgada you can find many regional products.

SPORTS AND OTHER ACTIVITIES

Bathing
Long stretches of sandy beach are rare on the Azores. Golden sandy beaches are only found on Santa Maria. Especially on São Miguel, but also on Faial, Graciosa and Terceira, there are sandy beaches of volcanic origin with black-coloured sand, but the sand is often washed away by autumn storms. In addition, you can dip into the sea at the natural bathing pools. Some bathing areas are watched over by lifeguards in the summer months and are marked by blue flags. Aside from lifeguards, you can find showers and changing rooms. On São Miguel there are also thermal pools with hot spring water. Especially from April until June, watch out for the Portuguese man-of-war; this species of jelly fish can be seen from afar on the waves because of its large crested air sac and can lead to circulatory collapse (see photo p. 32).

Bicycle touring
Cycling tourism is still in its infancy since the numerous ascents that must be made are fairly tiring for most cyclists. In the meantime, mountain biking and downhill trails have been developed. E-bikes are also available. As offers are very scarce, cycling holidays are only possible to a limited extent.

Deep sea fishing
Azorean waters are a paradise for the deep sea sport fisher since the variety of fish is immense. Swordfish and tuna as well as barracuda can be found just about anywhere. Record catches are made quite often. There are many services to choose from, especially on Faial but also on Santa Maria, São Miguel and Terceira.

Diving
Apart from Corvo, each island has a Clube Naval where you can get help and find a contact person. On Faial, Graciosa, Pico, Santa Maria, São Miguel and Terceira are also diving schools offering equipment. The steeply plunging coastlines continue underwater and present an untamed submarine seascape, a habitat for countless marine life. A splendid area is around the uninhabited Formigas between Santa Maria and São Miguel. In the *Triângulo*, there are also underwater volcanic cones, protruding from the waves as rock needles, however these should only be tackled by experienced divers.

Geocaching
Scattered throughout all of the islands, you can locate hundreds of geocaches. Many of these are linked together as a series along the walking routes.

Golf
Dark-green fairways amidst gentle hills surrounded by flower-blanketed meadows and views of the deep-blue sea – all to be found at the three lovingly cared-for and marvellously situated 18-hole golf courses on São Miguel and Terceira.

Mountaineering
There are no established via ferratas on the Azores. The greatest challenge for a mountaineer is the volcanic cone of Pico, at 2351m above sea level.

Sport fishing
The coastal regions are teeming with fish. At every harbour as well as secluded spots on the seashore, you will see locals surf fishing. For sport fishing in the interior, you need a temporary fishing permit for tourists; this is only locally available at the area's forestry administration offices.

Horse riding
You can experience the splendid countryside very well on horseback. Large riding stables can be found on Faial, Graciosa, Santa Maria, São Miguel and Terceira. Organized riding holidays have become increasingly popular and are also offered by some of the *quintas*.

Whale-watching
From June until September, an unusual number of whales plough the waters here, so rich in marine life. In the spring, sometimes the blue whale makes an appearance, in summer, mostly the sperm whale and smaller species. Pico and Faial are the centres for whale-watching but also, São Miguel offers successful excursions. Many agencies only operate from May to October.

Walking
In recent years, many trails have been marked and numbered. There are info signs at the entry points. A collection of walking suggestions is also published in compact brochures, available at the local tourist offices.

The old whaling village of Lajes do Pico is sheltered in a wide bay.

THE AZORES

Each of the nine inhabited islands differs from all the others. Because of this, a successful sojourn on the archipelago begins with of choice of the most suitable. A complete selection of touristically interesting information can be found in the introductory sections for the various islands.

Inhabitants

Azoreans are Portuguese but indeed not quite the same. Many of the original settlers came from Alentejo and Algarve. Many Flemish settled in the central islands and during the occupation of the 16th century, some Spanish remained. The native languages of these settlers are reflected in place names and dialects. Their native architectural styles are apparent in the building details right up to the chimneys.

The century-long seclusion in the mid-Atlantic had a deep impact on the people here. Life on the Azores can hardly be compared to that of Central Europe and is further stamped by the individuality of islanders in general. New arrivals notice this at first in the spoken language; local dialects are not always easy to understand even for those versed in Portuguese. An Azorean is always friendly to others despite an initial wariness; in no time at all, they will also receive tourists with hospitality and a welcome hand. Only a few words of Portuguese can break down barriers and win you instant kindliness and support which has become rather rare elsewhere.

A common denominator for all of the inhabitants is fixed in their religion; also binding are relationships with family members, even those who have emigrated to the USA or Canada. Three times more Azoreans than the 237,000 on the archipelago itself live with their descendants in North America. In the years from 1965 to 1975 alone, 100,000 Azoreans expatriated. These emigrations present one of island's most serious problems. Especially on the marginally-inhabited smaller islands, the population is declining even more. Natural catastrophes, a lack of future perspectives and the desire to reunite with departed family members are to blame.

Holy Ghost Festival in Lajedo on Flores.

History

With the discoveries of Santa Maria and São Miguel in 1427, the first Portuguese disembarked on the Azores which had been uninhabited until then. The islands were named by the first settlers after the buzzards that still circle the islands today; they mistook the birds for hawks (Port. açor). As a nation of seafarers, Portugal recognized the strategic importance of the archipelago.

Since the earliest days, life on the Azores has been characterized by farming, raising livestock and fishing. The extensive cultivation of grain lead to large-scale land holding which has remained in existence even today. Starting in the middle of the 16th century, the exportation of plants for dyes to far-away Flanders became yet another corner post for a flourishing economy.

Spanish bulwark in Angra (Walk 84).

In 1580, the Spanish conquered Portugal; on the Azores, a long battle against Spanish rule began. In 1582 the defeated Portuguese King António moved into exile on São Miguel. In the same year, the Spanish put down insurgents near Vila Franca. Spanish rule lasted until 1642 on Terceira. During this time, numerous bastions were built against pirates and buccaneers attracted by booty since in the 16th and 17th centuries numerous ships were making the Azores their port of call on the way between the Old and the New Worlds. Raids, pillaging and sea battles occurred time and again.

Around 1700, plants for dyes became unprofitable and a new niche was established in the extensive cultivation of oranges which led to a second economic boom in the 18th and 19th century; prosperity reigned once again. Most oranges were shipped to England. Grape-growing also began to flourish; Pico wine would be delivered even as far away as the court of the Czar. Starting in 1765, American whalers began to stop over in Azorean harbours. Young workhands were recruited and the foundation was laid for the ever-increasing emigration to America. In the middle of the 19th century, disease decimated the vineyards and orange plantations within only a few years. The once flourishing economy quickly came to a halt and was followed by a great wave of emigration.

In 1846, the first steamship line began service between the Azores and the European mainland; the operation quickly fell into the hands of the Bensaúde group which prospers even today. Beginning in 1893, Horta became the centre of telecommunications for the Atlantic. All of the major telegraph companies laid their cables across the Atlantic Ocean via Faial

Holy Ghost Festival in Ponta Delgada.

and established their central switchboards there. In the year 1900, the first network for electrical power started operating in Vila Franca. The first seaplane landed offshore from Horta in 1919 on its way across the Atlantic and Lufthansa began flights to Faial starting in 1936. During the World Wars of the 20th century, the islands served as a base and stopover point for the Allied Forces.

After the Carnation Revolution of 1974, the Azores were given wide-sweeping autonomy with self-government. In 1976, the new constitution was put into force and Ponta Delgada became the official state capital while Parliament was seated in Horta. In the 1980s, whaling was banned; one of the last traditional economies came to an end.

Festivities

The Portuguese love to celebrate. Because of this, the calendar is replete with bank holidays. Preparations begin weeks in advance. Streets are strung with decorative lighting. The annual highpoint for every community is the local celebration of the patron saint. This usually goes on for days, ending with a procession on a Sunday. Every day there is dancing and brass bands playing until late in the evening. Aside from these popular local festivities, from May until August, the Holy Spirit is the focus for celebration – a special tradition kept on the Azores. On São Jorge, Pico, Graciosa and especially on Terceira, bullfighting on the streets is staged in the summer, the *tourada à corda* – an interesting, albeit dangerous spectacle where carelessness can be rewarded with an emergency trip to the hospital!

Gastronomy

A typical Azorean meal is simply prepared but very tasty. Grand culinary trumps and Nouvelle-Cuisine are out of place here. In contrast, generous portions are most usual. Depending on certain established standards, food is offered in restaurants, snack bars, *casas de pasto* and cafés. On a typical menu (*ementa*) you will find a good selection of superb quality meat dishes and freshly-caught fish which are presented in a cooled, glass display case changing daily in variety. In addition, there are stews and daily soups which can be a full meal on their own. Vegetarian meals are still hard to find. Most desserts are very sweet, the homemade *pudims* and cakes are calorie-rich feasts on their own. A delicious delight is the pineapple from São Miguel. In summer, there are also melons from Santa Maria and Graciosa, and in winter, the local oranges provide a culinary contrast. Unfortunately, more dishes are often offered on the menu than what is truly on hand.

Liquid refreshment is standard European. There are local beers and good regional wines which have become overpriced. It is very rare to be served the simple locally produced wine, *vinho de cheiro* which can be a challenge for your taste buds. To complete a meal, drinking a *café solo* (*espresso*) or a *galão* (*latte macchiato*) is a must. Local specialities are the *cozido das Furnas* stew on São Miguel, *amêijoas* (clams) on São Jorge, *alcatra* (a stew made with marinated meat) and *telha* dishes (served in hot clay tiles) on Terceira as well as *lapas* (molluscs), which are offered throughout the islands. Typically Azorean is the cheese that is made locally in home production or cooperatives. In all restaurants, meals are preceded by a place setting with bread and cheese which will be added to the bill if consumed. Breakfast *(pequeno almoço)* is usually served beginning at 7.30 am, lunch *(almoço)* between 12.00 and 14.00 and dinner *(jantar)* for the Azoreans usually not until 20.00; the kitchens in most restaurants close at about 22.00 in the evening.

Culture

Only a few buildings in their original form dating back to colonial times have been spared by the frequent earthquakes that have occurred. Between the 16th and 18th centuries, the Azores developed a unique style of Baroque. Especially worth a visit is the city of Angra do Heroísmo on Terceira with an

Fresh from the grill. *Fisherman with a moray eel.*

old town centre boasting many churches, palaces and fortifications; in 1983, the town was added to UNESCO's World Heritage list. Today, a number of art history and anthropological museums present an overview of the history and the life of the islanders. They give you an insight into the traditions and customs of the Azores and exhibit sculpture and painting as well. Also worth seeing are the windmills which differ from island to island as well as the numerous churches and their treasure troves of religious and secular art.

Language
The official language of the island is Portuguese but includes numerous local dialects. Many Azoreans also speak English. In the countryside and also when dealing with many of the taxi drivers, one should have mastered some basic Portuguese to be understood.

Economy
The Azorean economy is quite simple to understand. Within the EU, the Azores are considered a peripheral region and thus enjoy generous subsidies, which in recent years have had a noticeable impact, particularly in the construction industry. Recently, there has been a strong focus on tourism, often pushing beyond local capacities. Milk production and livestock are the main cornerstones for the agricultural sector. Dairy industries can be found on all of the islands; São Miguel also boasts tobacco, tea and pineapple plantations. On Santa Maria and Graciosa sugar melons are successfully cultivated. On Faial, Graciosa, Terceira, Pico and São Miguel, commercial viniculture is being actively pursued. Yet another economic pillar is fishing and specifically tuna fishing is a popular large-scale commercial venture. Most fishermen, however, operate small boats heading out to the sea daily regardless of weather conditions.

Evening milking on São Jorge.

Nature and the environment

Landscapes
The Azorean landscape is the very picture of extremity. Enchanting forests fuse with heavenly rolling hills, deep-blue crater lakes and steaming sulphur springs. The cliffs and the numerous tiny islets lying offshore are ideal nesting grounds for many bird species. The cultivated parcels near the coasts, often difficult to reach, are incredibly fertile thanks to their individual microclimates and have been lovingly tended with great toil for generations.

Extinct volcanoes with crater lakes tower to the sky. Countless deep valleys have been cut through the easily eroded volcanic stratum. From a multitude of scenic overlooks, one can gather breath-taking views of volcanic craters, lakes, the hilly countryside or the bizarre coastline. Additional attractions are fumaroles and hot springs as well as thermal bathing pools. These are impressive witnesses to the ever-present volcanic activity of the archipelago. Lava tunnels can also be found on the islands and a few have been opened to tourists in the meanwhile.

Vast areas of the nine islands, especially along the coastline, enjoy special protective regulation and are designated natural and environmentally important reserves or zones of communal interest. Corvo, Graciosa and Flores have been classified as World Biosphere Reserves by UNESCO in the meantime.

Geography and geology
The Azores are located in the Atlantic Ocean between Europe and the Americas at about the same latitude as Lisbon and are about 1500km away from mainland Europe. The archipelago is made up of nine islands and subgrouped into three sets: Corvo and Flores (western islands); Graciosa, Terceira, São Jorge, Faial and Pico (central islands) as well as São Miguel and Santa Maria (eastern islands). Corvo and Santa Maria are about 600km apart. The largest islands are São Miguel, Pico and Terceira; Corvo, the smallest island, boasts only a single settlement. The highest point in the Azores is the volcano Pico (2351m), and the highest in Portugal as well.

The Azores are not only of volcanic origin but indeed a volcanically active area even today. Three tectonic plates converge directly below the archipelago. Since the first settlement in the 15th century, over 30 major volcanic eruptions have occurred, the last one in 1957/58 off the coast of Faial. Combined with this activity are also frequent earthquakes, sometimes with disastrous consequences. During the last two major quakes of 1980 and 1998, entire villages were destroyed in the central islands. Even today, some of the damage remains. Longer series of earthquakes occur from time to time. However, most earthquakes are not felt.

Beware – Portuguese man-of-war.

Fauna
Straight off: on land, there are no dangerous or poisonous animals on the Azores. The variety of feathered wildlife is especially striking. The rarest species, only found on the Azores and numbering around 1000 surviving specimens, is the priolo (*pyrrhula murina*), a type of bullfinch whose habitat is located around the Pico da Vara on São Miguel in an especially protected reserve with limited access. In addition, there are buzzards, canaries, blackbirds, serin (finch), grey wagtails, robins, blackcaps, sparrows, chaffinches, harriers, crested grebes, wood pigeons and kingfisher species. Many migratory birds use the archipelago for their winter quarters, as a stopover or for nesting. Especially the isolated coastal regions cut off by rugged cliffs provide countless nesting areas. The eerie-sounding cacophony from skyward in spring and summer, when twilight begins at the coast, is caused by cagarros, nocturnal birds which can be observed in large flocks on the ocean waves during the daytime.

On the ground and to the delight of hunters, countless hares and wild rabbit abound on the islands, but indeed, when it comes to Azorean four-footed creatures, nothing can compete with the ever-present bovine.

The aquatic wild life is also very diverse; crater lakes are replete with trout and carp. In the ocean waters off the Azorean shores, hundreds of species of fish and shellfish can be found. Prominent visitors to the waters around the archipelago are varieties of dolphins and whales. For two centuries, the sperm whale was hunted here from small boats and only using harpoons. Since the ban on whale-hunting from the 1980s, harpoons have been replaced with the cameras of whale-watchers.

Flora
Vegetation on the Azores has changed significantly since the first settlements. Due to the encroachment of settlers, much of the original flora has disappeared or has been seriously decimated to make room for cultivation and pastureland. Other plants, on the other hand, have been introduced from far-off lands and have changed the landscape considerably. One of the most striking is certainly the hydrangea, as well as the prolific wild ginger lily and the Japanese cedar, first introduced around 1860, which has taken over almost half of the available woodland. Nearly two-thirds of the flora found here has been brought in from foreign lands. On the Azores, about 60 endemic species of flora can be found, including juniper *(juniperus brevifolia)*, tree heather *(erica azorica)*, bilberry *(vaccinium*

cylindraceum), bay laurel *(laurus azorica)*, pau branco *(picconia azorica)*, the redwood tree and the tamujo tree. Many other species have been imported and have spread considerably during the course of centuries: Japanese cedar *(cryptomeria japonica)*, blackwood *(acacia melanoxylon)*, hydrangea *(hydrangea macrophylla)*, blue lily *(Agapanthus praecox)*, azaleas *(rhododendron indicum)*, camellia *(camellia japonica)*, wild ginger lily *(Hedychium gardnerianum)*, belladonna lily *(brunsvigia aethiopica)*, arum lily *(zantedeschia aethiopica)*, and the frankincense tree.

Depending on the altitude, the spectrum of flora appears in different forms. The coastal regions are dominated by varieties of grass. At the middle elevations starting at 500m above sea level, one encounters, above all, the bilberry tree, juniper and bay laurel, leftovers of the original vegetation, still found in part only on Faial and Pico. 1000m above sea level, one mostly encounters heath as well as moss and ferns. Around 1300 species of flora can be counted, including 400 different types of moss, nine of which are endemic. Many plants were imported to the islands in the 18th and 19th centuries by well-to-do families as they landscaped their wonderful gardens with flora from all over the world; many of these gardens still exist. On São Miguel, you can also find pineapple, tobacco and tea plantations.

■ Additional information can be found at azoresbioportal.uac.pt.

Hydrangea.

Azorean bellflowers (endemic).

Azorean bilberry (endemic).

Santa Maria – Ilha do Sol

- population: 5400
- capital: Vila do Porto, 3000 inhabitants
- area: 97km²
- length: 16km, width: 10km
- coastline: 76km
- highest point: Pico Alto, 587m

There is nothing very spectacular to discover on Santa Maria. All points of interest can be easily taken in on a day's circular drive around the island with a personal vehicle or a taxi. Nevertheless, the island is attractive due to its lovely, bright sandy beaches. Pleasant water temperatures in summer combined with the most hours of sunshine in the entire archipelago make Santa Maria a bather's paradise. During the winter months, tourists disappear completely. In summer, on the other hand, life returns to the tiny villages as countless relatives living in the USA come back for month-long visits.

The Portuguese seafarer Diogo de Silves came upon Santa Maria in 1427, making it the first Azorean island to be discovered. Gonçalo Velho Cabral followed in 1432 and initiated the first settlements on the island. In 1472, Vila do Porto was the first town in the Azores to receive a town charter. On his return in 1493 from his first voyage to America, Christopher Columbus made the island his stopover and was at first mistaken for a

Wild Azorean bellflowers below the lighthouse at Ponta do Castelo (Walk 7).

pirate. In the 16th and 17th centuries, pastel and woad were exported to dyeing works in faraway Flanders. The American Armed Forces established the immense military airport on the western side of the island in 1944. This became the most important supply base in the Atlantic and served as a stopover for flights on the way from the US to Europe.
More than half of the island's inhabitants emigrated during the last 50 years. Today, about 5400 persons are living on the island. Very little industry exists here. The population lives off agriculture and especially from cattle breeding. The most recent product to be cultivated is the muskmelon and you really should be sure to try one! In the meantime, the fruit counts as an island speciality and could provide a solid economic base for the future, at least for a part of the population.

In the capital **Vila do Porto**, life is quiet and unhurried. The village offers some sites worth seeing: the parish church of Nossa Senhora da Assunção hales back to the 16th century, the city hall is housed in the former Franciscan monastery Nossa Senhora da Vitória from the 17th century and in the tiny fort of São Brás at the harbour, the old cannons, even after 400 years have gone by, still point their muzzles at the ocean waters. Almost all shops, restaurants and public buildings are lined up like a spring of pearls along the main street. The lower district of the town is also the oldest. Some buildings here, however, have been abandoned and have fallen to ruin.

Sheltered seawater swimming pool in Maia (Walks 7 and 8).

In geological terms, Santa Maria is the oldest island of the Azores. On the slopes of Figueiral on the southern coast, it is even possible to find rare fossils from the Tertiary period. On the northern island, the ancient clay quarries of Faneca which appear as a small, red desert, lie hidden behind the dense forest.

Volcanoes have been inactive here for a very long time. The entire western island around Vila do Porto, Almagreira and São Pedro is mostly flat and not very scenic. In summer, this extensively arid region changes into a yellow-brown, withered prairie landscape with agave and cactus.

Anjos is a small seaside resort that seems completely abandoned in winter. The chapel of Nossa Senhora dos Anjos as well as a monument commemorate Columbus' landing here in 1493. The highest point on Santa Maria is the centrally-situated Pico Alto with a futuristic display of transmitters as a crown. A thick band of heather trees, laurel and juniper covers the mountain slopes and stretch all the way down to the villages below.

The eastern side around Santa Bárbara and Santo Espírito is more hilly. Little villages are scattered far and wide here, bedded down in luscious greenery – a picturesque setting where one can easily find some peace and quiet. Near Santo Espírito, the local recreation area of Fontinhas offers numerous barbecue pits. Its counterpart, Valverde is near the forestry administration at the gates of Vila do Porto. On the eastern coast, the villages of São Lourenço and Maia are set apart in seclusion by the sea; near Maia, the prominently-situated lighthouse Gonçalo Velho perches on a small hillock. Santa Maria's mostly sheer coastline is only accessible in a few places via zigzagging footpaths. In the meantime, some stretches of coastline have become protected zones. A few of the most beautiful sites are the viewpoints at Fontinhas, Lagoínhas, Macela and Espigão.

About 35km north of Santa Maria lie the largely unknown and uninhabited Formigas, a group of islets only a few metres above the surface of the ocean, the undoing of many a ship's captain. The protected undersea reserve here provides a veritable paradise for divers.

SANTA MARIA

Getting there
From Lisbon, SATA operates one flight per week. SATA provides service with at least one flight per day from São Miguel to Santa Maria. The airport is situated only a few kilometres outside of Vila do Porto. Ferries no longer operate on this route.

Bathing
Lovely, golden sandy beach at the Praia Formosa and a small stretch of the same in São Lourenço. Seawater swimming pools in Maia and Anjos.

Festivities
Holy Spirit Celebrations in late spring. Festa de Santo António (Vila do Porto), mid-June. Festa de São João (Vila do Porto), end of June. Festa de Nossa Senhora da Assunção (Vila do Porto), August 15. Music festival Maré de Agosto (Praia Formosa), mid-August. Festa do Emigrante (Maia), end of August. Festa das Vindimas (São Lourenço), beginning of September.

Medical services
Hospital in Vila do Porto, tel +351 296 820 100.

Tourist information
Turismo de Santa Maria has a counter at the airport, tel and fax +351 296 886 355, pt.sma@azores.gov.pt, cm-viladoporto.pt.
Free Wi-Fi at the harbour in Vila do Porto and at the airport.

Cultural activities
Centro de Interpretação Ambiental and Casa dos Fósseis in Vila do Porto. Ethnographical museum Museu de Santa Maria in Santo Espírito. Artistic handicrafts cooperative in Santo Espírito. Centro de Artesanato in São Pedro.

Public transport
The quick-to-grasp bus network is useful for tourism only to a limited extent. If you don't have a hire car, you can explore the island using taxis without any problem. The central taxi rank is located in Vila do Porto, tel +351 296 882 199.

Accommodation
The handful of hotel complexes on Santa Maria are more than sufficient to satisfy the demands of tourism. In addition to these, a selection of private, typical country homes are available for rental. A youth hostel has been established in Vila do Porto. The campsite is located on the southern end in Praia.

1. Baía do Tagarete

Santa Maria ↗ 270m | ↘ 270m | 5.9km
2.00 hrs

Excursion to some abandoned watermills and a small cove for bathing

Most of the ancient watermills on Santa Maria are tumbledown today and lie hidden away from all walking routes. This walk leads you to two lonely ruins located on the secluded northern coast. A tiny cove can also be found here, only known to insiders. The descent is rewarded by a marvellous view taking in the rugged northern coastline. This is a walk reserved for sure-footed adventurers!

Starting point: ER 2, the turn-off to Lagos at km10.3, 225m (bus stop Lagos).
Grade: a steep descent and ascent along a little-used path leading into the cove. A high degree of sure-footedness is required.
Refreshment: nothing en route.
Linking tip: Walk 2.
Bathing: the Baía do Tagarete has a gravel beach and some rock pools to bathe in.

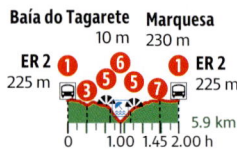

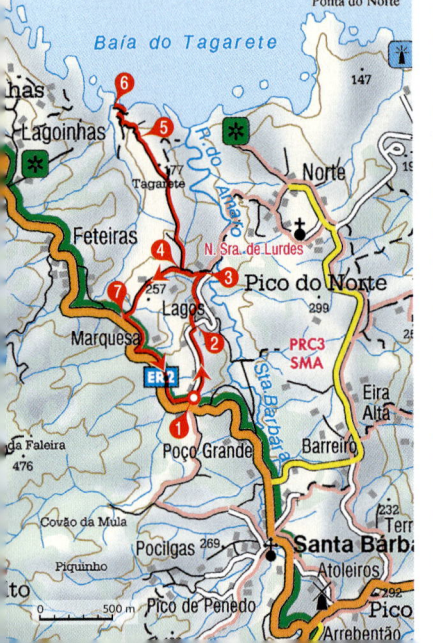

Begin the walk from the bus stop at Lagos on the **ER 2** ❶ and at first follow the slightly ascending narrow road northward. Not quite 10 mins later, beyond a right-hand bend, turn left onto a descending **concrete trail** ❷ across from a power pylon with a transformer. This immediately meets up again with the narrow road; turn left here and follow the road until it ends, passing the ruins of an old schoolhouse. At the end of the road take a sharp left onto a concrete **secondary trail** ❸ which ascends rapidly.

After a short ascent, turn right past a solitary standing house onto a **concrete road** ❹ and continue. By the mound of earth that follows and while bearing right, reach a high plateau that is being used as pastureland. After a total of 40 mins, the concrete trail ends at a car park.

A wonderful place for a rest – you can recharge your batteries on the swing at the Baía do Tagarete.

Behind the car park, you will reach a **picnic spot and a viewpoint** ❺. From here, a footpath continues, descending along the stone wall on your right-hand side.
Now the real descent begins along a footpath that becomes more slippery underfoot as it zigzags downward. Halfway down, pass a terraced area with cultivated vineyards and beyond this, bear to the left. Along this stretch, there are a number of alternative paths. From one turn in the trail to another, however – to provide some orientation – the distance between them is never more than 20 metres.
In any case, your destination is the watermill ruins that can be seen ahead perched on a little promontory. After a 15 mins descent, finally reach the bottom. To the right, a broken-off path leads to the little sheltered bathing cove **Baía do Tagarete** with a rough gravel beach. To the left, reach the ruins of the old **watermills** ❻, a secluded spot for a picnic.
To return, ascend at first along the same trail as the approach route. You return to the first houses of Lagos via the high plateau from where you follow the concrete path to the right until you reach the main road in **Marquesa** ❼. At the **ER 2**, turn left to return in another 15 mins to the **starting point** ❶.

Santa Maria ↗ 330m | ↘ 330m | 10.8km

2 Circling Santa Bárbara (via Norte)

3.15 hrs

Excursion into the sparsely-settled north-east part of Santa Maria

The secluded houses of the community of Santa Bárbara stand out in the landscape like little white brush-strokes on a canvas of greenery. This walk, one of the island's classics, leads in a circular course through the further-most north-eastern end of the island and guarantees surprising views of the bays at São Lourenço and Tagarete.

Starting point: Santa Bárbara, church, 215m (bus stop Santa Bárbara/Centro on the main road, 70m away).
Grade: a pleasant walk along easy trails. Just before the Ribeira do Amaro, often a very marshy stretch for a few metres.

Refreshment: bar Pôr do Sol at the church in Santa Bárbara; nothing en route.
Alternative: Ponta do Norte (3km, an additional 1 hr): before Norte, at the point where you meet up again with the road, turn right and descend to continue. Soon pass the ruins of an old radar station. After 20 mins, the road ends near some more ruins. Passing between the two buildings, a footpath continues, crossing pastureland (watch for red/white waymarkers). Continue pathless along the lower edge of the pasture until you reach the small beacon at the Ponta do Norte. Remain along the lower edge of the pasture and soon, after you traversed a ridge, you will enjoy a marvellous view of the sweeping Baía do Tagarete. Past this, veer inland, heading towards a hut, built from undressed stone, behind which an ancient mule track begins an extremely steep ascent. 5 mins later, this becomes a country lane and ascends, as an ancient cobbled trail at the end, to reach the road in Norte. Turn right to get to the cul-de-sac.
Linking tip: Walks 1, 3, 5 and 6.

Past the church in the town centre of **Santa Bárbara** ❶, follow the ER 2 southward and, after 200m, turn left onto a concrete trail (sign: Atoleiros). This ascends over the slope and ends at two tumbledown **wind-**

A view of the bay at São Lourenço from the Miradouro dos Alagares.

mills ❷ on the road to São Lourenço. Here, continue to the left. 250m on, before descending again, a footpath leads to the right behind the last residencial building with a palm tree on a descending hollow path. Reach the **stone quarry ❸** on the Pico Vermelho (with a little lake) and follow the country lane to the main road (to the left, a path ascends at the car park to the summit, which boasts a lookout). On the other side, a narrow road continues to Terra Velha, which merges with the road to Norte after 20 mins. Follow this road to the right. You immediately pass the viewpoint **Miradouro do Barreiro ❹** with a picnic table.

15 mins later, exactly in the hollow, a **country lane ❺** turns right (sign: Alagares). This soon hooks away to the right; continue following it. The country lane ends at a meadow, 200m on. Continue straight ahead along a mule path and after 150m turn right to leave the washed-out gully. The

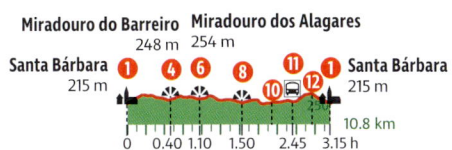

The old quarry on the Pico Vermelho.

traces of a path lead onto the hillock just in front of you. Past a gate, continue along the stone wall to reach the marvelous **Miradouro dos Alagares** ❻ with a view of the bay at São Lourenço (1.10 hrs).

Now return to the spot where the country lane hooked away and turn right to continue along the somewhat overgrown, ancient mule track. The track sometimes leads in the woods as an old hollow way that is tumbledown in places. Afterwards, reach a narrow road (the Alternative turns right), and turn left onto it to ascend. 100m further on, turn right to continue to **Norte** where, at a **cul-de-sac** ❼ the road ends (1.40 hrs).

At first, follow the right-hand gravel trail downhill to where it stops at a meadow. Behind the cattle gate, continue descending some metres more to enjoy a lovely view ❽ of the Baía do Tagarete.

Afterwards, return to the **cul-de-sac** ❼ and turn right onto the concrete road (sign: Bananeiras). This hooks off immediately to the right and then sharp left. Exactly at this point, a **grassy trail** ❾ with ancient cobblestones continues straight ahead downhill. A 150m-long stretch follows that even in summer is sometimes marshy; the best way to negotiate this is by hopping from stone to stone. Now continue over a wooden bridge spanning the Ribeira do Amaro and, along a grassy trail, to the **cul-de-sac** ❿ in Lagos. Starting here, remain on the road and pass the ruins of the old schoolhouse. 100 metres past this, ascend steeply to the right on a concrete trail. Once above, meet up again with the road and turn right here to continue to the **ER 2** and the **bus stop** ⓫ (2.45 hrs).

Here, turn left and immediately after you have passed the sign for the village of **Poço Grande**, turn sharp right again onto a steeply ascending roadway whose surface is initially concrete. After 20 mins, when the trail starts to slightly descend again, turn left at the **fork** ⓬. Passing some pastures, the path, now deeply cut, descends again. Soon, at the first houses of **Santa Bárbara**, the trail is concreted again. The street leads straight ahead to the town centre and the **starting point** ❶.

↗ 450m | ↘ 450m | 8.4km   Santa Maria

3.00 hrs

Circling Santa Bárbara (via Pico) | 3

Walking on the old connecting paths around the farming village of Santa Bárbara

Above the centre of Santa Bárbara, the houses of the individual parts of the village are scattered across several ridgelines. You first reach the highest point of the island, Pico Alto, via an old connecting path. The trail then follows a wide loop through the hamlet of Forno and finally takes you back to the broad valley of Santa Bárbara.

Starting point: Santa Bárbara, church, 215m (bus stop Santa Bárbara/Centro on the main road, 70m away).
Grade: challenging ascent starting on an old connecting path. It can be muddy and slippery when wet. Boots are recommended. The middle section of the walk is mostly on the road.
Refreshment: bar Pôr do Sol at the church in Santa Bárbara. Nothing en route.
Linking tip: Walks 2, 4, 5 and 6.

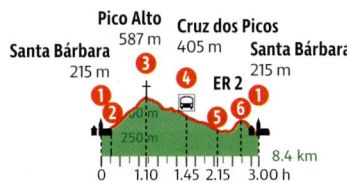

Before the church in **Santa Bárbara** ❶, cross the bridge over the water canal and immediately turn right after the first house. Just 10m ahead, follow the steep concrete path to the left at the fountain (sign: Boavista). It quickly turns into a country lane. Five mins later, the country lane turns into an old **mule track** ❷ that steadily ascends through the forest. Eventually, you'll reach another country lane, turn left for a few steps, and immediately follow a deep ravine uphill. The path continues to climb along the ridge, sometimes

A wonderful view: across the pastures near Santa Bárbara, life is still as it should be.

through the forest, sometimes in the open. After 10 mins, pass the Piquinho. Another 10 mins later, reach a crossroads. Here, take a left and soon reach the road leading to the summit. A few steps to the right, just before the iron gate, you'll see stairs leading up to the north peak of **Pico Alto** ❸ (1.10 hrs). Continue along the access road on the eastern side of the mountain ridge for 30 mins before you reach the main road. Turn left here, and you'll soon arrive at the large bus stop at **Cruz dos Picos** ❹. After that, follow the side road to the right of the stone board (sign: 6.5 t) and continue straight ahead. After 30 mins, you'll arrive at the hamlet of **Forno** ❺ (2.15 hrs).
Cross the village street and walk straight down the narrow concrete path. Behind a solitary house, the footpath continues and leads to the Ribeira do Salto. Heading downstream, the path veers left. After 5 mins, you have to cross the stream again by hopping over stones before the old mule track ascends again. In some years, this section is so wet that it's better to walk along the pasture.
The path eventually ends up in a road, which you follow to the right. At the **main road ER 2** ❻, turn right again and, after 150m, turn left at the ruins of the windmills onto the concrete path. Follow this path downhill to **Santa Bárbara** and return to the **starting point** ❶.

↗ 370m | ↘ 370m | 7.1km   Santa Maria

2.40 hrs

Circling the Pico Alto   4

A walk around the island's highest mountain

The Pico Alto is the dominant mountain range on the island and, since recent times, its slopes boast a dense network of trails where walkers and mountain-bikers are made to share some of the sections. At first, the route descends northwards over the mountain ridge. The return trail keeps constantly through the forest, following old connecting trails from days gone by.

Starting point: the entrance gate at the end of the road to Pico Alto, 566m (next bus stop Casa dos Picos on the main road, 2km away).
Grade: mostly along pleasant walking trails. The descent to the forestry houses is boggy and muddy when wet. Boots recommended. Sure-footedness is required. Due to numerous intermediary ascents, this route should not be underestimated!
Refreshment: nothing en route.
Alternative: from the bus stop on the Cruz dos Picos (2.1km to Pico Alto, 2.6km return; 1.15 hrs): at the central intersection on the Cruz dos Picos, at first head 150m towards Vila do Porto (sign) and then turn right onto the narrow road for Pico Alto. 30 mins after the main road, reach the northern summit. Along the return route to Cruz dos Picos, at waypoint ❼, keep to the footpath heading straight on above Alto do Nascente. 25 mins later, pass under electric cables; afterwards, reach the ER 1. Here, turn left to ascend, passing the Miradouro dos Picos, then along the road to return to the starting point.
Linking tip: Walks 3 and 5.
Note: do not follow the tempting mountain-bike tracks – this mountain is a Mecca for the mountain biker!

The summit of the Pico Alto is richly decorated with radio masts.

The starting point is the **entrance gate** ❶ on the northern summit of Pico Alto. Here, a number of steps immediately begin to climb up to the aerial-crowned peak. 30m away from the stepped trail, follow the right of the two paths that leads

into the forest (sign: Bananeiras). After a few mins, continue straight at the fork. Now keep steadily along the ridge trail towards north. Without many openings for views, the trail runs mostly through dense forest, later traversing a bushy terrain while steadily descending. Pass a **shelter** ❷ and, after 30 mins along the wooded ridge, reach a **double bend** ❸. Keep right at the fork. 5 mins later, take an excursion by turning left to climb up the **Pico da Caldeira** ❹ (50 mins).

Back at the main trail, turn left to continue. The footpath winds around to circumvent the mountain and then ends at two **abandoned forestry houses** ❺ (1.20 hrs).

Once you have directly passed the two ruins at a small clearing, follow the slightly dropping footpath downhill. 20m below at the fork, turn left back to the continuation of the footpath which runs up-and-down through the forest, dodging over numerous watercourses. A good 10 mins later, reach a stretch cut into the rock. Five mins after that, the trail clearly begins

to ascend. Soon afterwards, reach the end of the forest. At a **water reservoir**, get to the houses of **Alto do Nascente** ❻ (1.50 hrs).

Just where the concrete street begins, at the first lamp post, turn left onto the footpath. The ancient, sometimes rock-hewn path, winds up the slope, following a gully. After 15 mins, take a sharp left-turn at a **trail sign** ❼ (the Alternative continues straight ahead) and ascend to the summit of the Pico Alto. In a depression at the top, pick up a gravel trail. At first, turn right to reach the southern peak crowned with a striking radar dome. Then turn back, passing the commemorative plaque for the aviation accident in 1989 and continue straight on to the **starting point** ❶.

↗ 435m | ↘ 640m | 9.4km   Santa Maria   **TOP**
3.40 hrs
                    # From Santa Bárbara to Praia Formosa   **5**

Traversing the island across its highest mountain to the bathing paradise in the south

The scattered houses of the farming village of Santa Bárbara are nestled idyllically in a small valley. This walk takes you across the island's highest peak, Pico Alto, and along a deeply cut hollow path through dense forest to the south coast to the small summer resort of Praia Formosa with its long sandy beach. This walk is a classic island crossing.

Starting point: Santa Bárbara, church, 215m (bus stop Santa Bárbara/Centro on the main road, 70m away).
Destination: beach in Praia Formosa, 8m (bus stop Praia).
Grade: leisurely walk almost exclusively on old footpaths. The area around Pico Alto can be muddy when wet. Descent to Praia on a rocky path which partially leads across bare rock.
Refreshment: in Santa Bárbara and Praia Formosa. Nothing en route.
Bathing: sandy beach in Praia Formosa.
Linking tip: Walks 2, 3, 4, 6, 8 and 9.

Hidden in the rolling hills, the village of Santa Bárbara is nestled in the landscape.

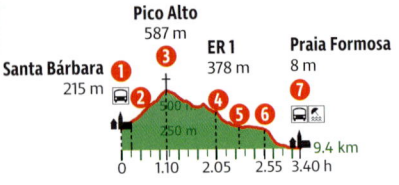

Before the church in **Santa Bárbara** ❶, cross the bridge over the water canal and immediately turn right after the first house. Just 10m ahead, follow the steep concrete path to the left at the fountain (sign: Boavista). It quickly turns into a country lane. Five mins later, the country lane turns into an old **mule track** ❷ that steadily ascends through the forest. Eventually, you'll reach a country lane, turn left for a few steps, and immediately follow a deep ravine uphill. The path continues to climb along the ridge, sometimes through the forest, sometimes in the open. After 10 mins, pass the Piquinho. Another 10 mins later, you reach a crossroads. Here, take a left and soon reach the road leading to the summit. A few steps to the right, just before the iron gate, you'll see stairs leading up to the north peak of **Pico Alto** ❸ (1.10 hrs).

Below the summit, follow the roadway through the gate, keep right at the monument, behind which you take the forest path downhill on the

The old hollow path above Almagreira.

right, exactly in the dip. 75m on, keep right. After 15 mins, you reach a crossroads where you turn left. 30 mins later, a power line crosses the trail. Beyond that, the path joins the **main road ER 1** ❹.

On the other side, a footpath continues. The old cobbled path is heavily eroded in many places. After 10 mins, a deep hollow trail starts with roots climbing impressively up on both sides. Eventually, a wooden bridge crosses the Ribeira da Praia, and the path soon widens and turns into a country lane. It merges with a **crossroads** ❺ at the edge of Almagreira at the end of a concrete road (2.35 hrs).

Turn left here and follow the dirt path. After a good 5 mins, turn right uphill at a fork. A quarter of an hour later, the dirt path ends at a **natural stone ruin** ❻. From here, a footpath continues and the steep descent along the ridge toward Praia begins immediately.

The old mule track reaches the valley floor and crosses a stream. Beyond a residential house, the trail is paved again and merges with the main road. Follow it downhill to the left, and after 150m, just before the bridge, turn right onto a concrete trail leading to the stream. From there, follow the creek downstream all the way to the sea. Once there, turn left at the road. After 5 mins, you reach the wide beach of **Praia Formosa** ❼.

An old shepherds' path leads to Praia Formosa.

Santa Maria ↗ 480m | ↘ 580m | 11.8km

6 From Santo Espírito to Santa Bárbara

3.50 hrs

A stroll through the eastern part of the island

The east of Santa Maria is dotted with numerous scattered settlements. During this stage, old connecting trails link up many of these hamlets. The starting point in Santo Espírito has a museum, which is worth a visit. Halfway through, reach the beautiful bay of São Lourenço, where it's worth going for a dip. An exhausting and arduous ascent on an old path takes you to your destination, the farmers' village of Santa Bárbara.

Starting point: Santo Espírito, church, 315m (bus stop Santo Espírito/Centro 100m to the west).
Destination: Santa Bárbara, church, 215m (bus stop Santa Bárbara/Centro on the main road, 70m away).
Grade: mostly along pleasant walking trails and remote side roads. Some of the sections can be slippery and earthy when wet. Steep ascent from São Lourenço.
Refreshment: restaurants/bars in Santo Espírito, São Lourenço, Santa Bárbara.
Bathing: sandy beach and salt water pool in São Lourenço.
Linking tip: Walks 2, 3, 5 and 7.

Go left behind the church in **Santo Espírito** ❶ and follow the Rua do Museu. At the crest, go left to join a country lane that turns into a walking trail just ahead of a radio mast. After a good 10 mins, reach the **road** ❷ to Almas. Follow it shortly downhill to the right, and just before you get to the bus stop shelter turn immediately left into the Caminho do Pico. Just where the tarmac section of the road ends, continue straight down a country lane. After 50m, reach a derelict house. Continue straight on the deep hollow path until you reach a chapel and the hamlet of **Santo António** ❸. Continue left on the main road (30 mins).

After 15 mins, turn right at the power pylon with a transformer and **bus stop shelter** ❹ to join a secondary road (sign: Forno de Cal) that leads past the stretched-out settlement of Azenha. After another good 15 mins, the road veers to the left. Shortly afterwards, turn right to join a concrete trail (sign: Forno de Cal). Where the trail dips, follow the narrow walking trail along a stream towards your right and head for the coast. A stepped trail leads down to the remote spring of **Fonte Clara** ❺ (1.10 hrs).

Ascent above São Lourenço.

Return to the concrete trail and after 30m, you reach a restored lime kiln (Forno de Cal). From here, a footpath continues. After 10 mins, cross a small stream. Beyond the stream, the mule path ascends again and merges with a road. Go right here, and after 200m keep right again at the junction with traffic island. After 75m, it's well worth taking a little detour to your right to the **Miradouro do Espigão** ❻ above the wide bay of São Lourenço.

Return to the main road and follow it until a wide footpath turns off to the right after a good 5 mins. At the bottom, this broad old cart track merges with the road again. Go left for about 50m and follow the grassy trail on the other side leading up the valley. You cross the stream several times walking along ancient overgrown terraced fields. After 20 mins, you reach the end where several **waterfalls** ❼ plunge down into a valley basin (2.10 hrs).

Back on the main road, the route continues towards the left. At the next junction, go straight ahead and follow the road down to São Lourenço. 75m after the opening of the bay, leave the main road to the right and walk down concrete stairs with steel railing. The trail continues as farm road descending straight through the vine terraces. At the coast, turn left, and once you are back on the road, follow the promenade in **São Lourenço** ❽ along the sea (2.50 hrs).

In the back part of the bay, turn left at the two prominently growing araucaria and walk up a narrow roadway (sign: Fajãzinha). This is where the arduous steep ascent over stone steps starts. You pass the first viewpoint with a bench. Once you are all the way up, turn left onto the road, pass the **Miradouro do Barreiro** ❾ and turn left again shortly after (sign: 6.5 t). Behind the first residential house, turn right onto a country lane, which leads to a road after a good 5 mins. Follow this road straight ahead. Once you reach the bottom, turn left at the main road and continue to the centre with the church in **Santa Bárbara** ❿.

Santa Maria

7 From Santo Espírito to Maia

↗ 570m | ↘ 570m | 13.6km
4.20 hrs

Panoramic descent in the remote south-eastern island

Only a few paths on the island are so well preserved as the descent trail to Maia, a village stretching all along the coastline. It starts off at Santo Espírito via dirt trails at the edge of a high cliff. Then an old, sometimes steeply descending path crosses through terraced vineyards to reach the coastal settlement of Maia with its hidden waterfall. Continuing on and going by the lighthouse Farol de Gonçalo Velho, pass the ruins of a whale-processing plant. On the return route, take in yet another marvellous viewpoint.

Starting point: Santo Espírito, church, 315m (bus stop Santo Espírito/Centro 100m to the west).
Grade: sometimes a steep descent on a broad path to Maia. The return route sometimes follows the reasonably quiet main road.
Refreshment: snack bars in Santo Espírito and Maia.
Linking tip: Walks 6 and 8.
Bathing: a seawater pool in Maia offers a great bathing opportunity.

Behind the church in **Santo Espírito** ❶, follow the Rua João Freitas Pereira (sign: São Lourenço). 10 mins later, the concreted **Caminho do Reque** ❷ forks off to the right and immediately forks again. Bearing left to continue, reach the ruins of a tumbledown windmill. Immediately past this, look for the traces of a path, at first very indistinct, that hooks off to the right and follows a row of bushes along a fence to soon enter a wood. After 150m, reach a gate and an abandoned fountain (dated 1931).
Past the fountain, continue across the pasture without a distinct path, following the barbed wire fence to reach the residential buildings on the other side; here, behind the cattle gate, join a dirt trail. Turn right here and, 100m on, turn right again at the **roadway** ❸. Descend along this dirt trail for 10 mins until reaching the **second street lamp** ❹ at the forest's edge (slightly before, a concrete path forks off to the left). At this point, a footpath turns left to disappear into the forest, passing a washing site and immediately meets the concrete road that leads through **Lapa de Baixo**. Continue by turning right and, past a tumbledown house, the road becomes a mule path and finally hooks left at a stream. After a few mins, reach the edge of a **drop-off** ❺ (50 mins).
Here cross over the stream and immediately come to the steep cliff above Maia. Enjoy a splendid view back to the waterfall on the Ribeira

A steep descent to Maia.

do Aveiro. The path that follows is very exposed but always sufficiently wide. At the end, the path descends steeply via stone steps and 25 mins later, reach the street in **Maia** ❻.

Now turn left and continue to a bridge just before the street ends. A footpath ascends left to a basin that was shaped by the waters of the **Ribeira do Aveiro** ❼ crashing down from high above (sign: Foz da Ribeira). The picnic tables are perfect for a break (1.25 hrs).

Afterwards, go back again along the street, pass the harbour and then the seawater swimming pool. At the first **hairpin bend** ❽, take a shortcut from the street by keeping straight ahead on the stepped trail. Past the last house, continue for another 10m and then ascend via steep stone steps on an old winegrowers' path to the street. Continue left until reaching the next junction at a **memorial** ❾. Turn left to climb down to the lighthouse Gonçalo Velho. At the lowest point, turn off to the right onto a broad serpentine path that leads to the tumbledown ruins of the old **whale-processing plant** ❿ (2.25 hrs).

Now return again to the main road ER 1 and ascend further. Soon, an access trail follows which descends and ends at the viewpoint at the ancient **whale-spotters' post** ⓫. 15 mins later, reach the **Miradouro da Pedreira da Tia Raulinha** ⓬ above Maia. Past this, the road turns again towards the island's interior. About 300m past a 180° hairpin bend that you cannot fail to notice, leave the ER 1 in Calheta, at the bus stop Calheta 1, by turning right onto a **gravel track** ⓭ (left: a power pylon with a transformer). Just after, remain on the main trail by keeping left. Descend to a bridge, cross over the Ribeira do Aveiro and continue into the forest ❹. Starting here, return along the approach route to reach the starting point in **Santo Espírito** ❶.

Santa Maria ↗ 670m | ↘ 670m | 15.1km

8 From Maia to Praia Formosa

4.50 hrs

Endurance tour from beach resort to beach resort in the remote south

Starting in the summer beach resort of Maia, this walk traverses the entire southern part of the island. It crosses several remote river valleys, passes secluded settlements as well as the fascinating basalt organ cliffs at the Ribeira do Maloás and an old whale-spotters' post. At the end, a refreshing dip at the long sandy beach at Praia Formosa will reward you for your efforts.

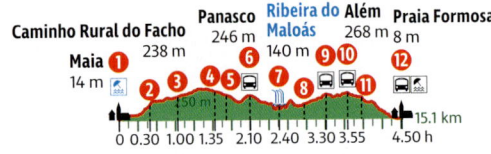

Starting point: Maia, end of the road on the Ribeira do Aveiro, 14m (next bus stop Calheta 2 at ❸).
Destination: sandy beach in Praia Formosa, 8m (bus stop Praia).
Grade: remote roads and footpaths, sometimes undefined. Some sections are on old cobblestones, which are slippery when wet.
Refreshment: bars/restaurants in Maia and Praia Formosa. Nothing en route.
Linking tip: Walks 5, 6, 7 and 9.
Bathing: seawater pool in Maia; sandy beach at Praia Formosa.

The magic organ cliffs at the hidden Ribeira do Maloás.

This long tour starts at the end of the road in **Maia** ❶ where at the bridge, a footpath leads to the waterfall at Ribeira do Aveiro. The road leads you back through the village. At the first **hairpin bend** ❷, take the shortcut and follow the stepped trail to go straight on. About 10m beyond the last house, ascend the steep stone steps on the old winegrowers' path to reach the road, where you continue to the left. After a good 5 mins, walk past the turn-off to the lighthouse Ponta do Castelo. After 150m, go straight through a wooden gate, which is in the left curve (concrete water gully). After 50m follow the old mule track left up to the road, where you go right and pass the **Miradouro da Pedreira da Tia Raulinha** (55 mins).

200m on, turn left into the **Caminho Rural do Facho de Santo Espírito** ❸. After a good 30 mins, keep left at the first **fork** ❹ (small traffic island). After about 10 mins, the small road ends at the hamlet of **Cardal** ❺. Descend the gravel trail on your right. After 200m, leave the trail. At a wooden gate, follow an old drovers' path to the right along a row of trees to reach a deep valley. From a natural stone house, the path narrows in the lower part and turns into a small grassy trail. After you have crossed the stream, follow an old cobbled path leading up again to another road in **Panasco** (2.10 hrs).

Go straight on for 50m and at the **main road** ❻ descend to your left. After a good 5 mins, you reach a sharp right bend in the road. Just below the bend, a mule track continues and merges with a country lane. Follow this lane to the left until you reach a turning spot. Go straight across and continue on the footpath. Now the path leads for a short stretch above the steep cliffs where it is quite exposed, however, the breathtaking views of the south coast and the abandoned terraced vineyards of Sul make up for it. The path finally swings back inland. On the **Ribeira do Maloás** ❼ you reach the basalt organ cliffs (2.40 hrs).

Immediately in front of the cliffs, a steep stepped trail leads down to the stream, crosses it and winds itself up the opposite slope. On top of the hill, turn left, climb over a natural stone wall after 80m, and then keep left initially staying at the same height. Here the route gets briefly confusing (pay attention to waymarkers). On the bottom of the pasture, walk along the drystone wall. After 200m, start the final ascent to the small summit with the old whale-spotters' post at **Ponta da Malbusca** (2.55 hrs).

On the western side, descend along the pasture boundary with barbed wire, pass a rocket launch site, and then continue along the pasture

The deserted whale-spotters' post at the Ponta da Malbusca.

boundary. At the western end of the pasture, pass through a cattle barrier. The path continues into the red clay mining area of **Barreiro da Piedade** ❽.
Leave the mini desert via the only roadway on the north side that leads you back to the road (Caminho Rural da Piedade). Follow the road for 15 mins going up to the left until you reach the hamlet of **Malbusca** (3.30 hrs).
In Malbusca, follow the second concrete road, the **Caminho do Pico** ❾, down to the left. Where the road turns left, go straight and follow the grassy path down to the valley. At the end of the pasture, the path turns into an old cobbled trail. After the stream crossing, the cobbles are pretty well preserved. At the housing estate Além turn right and follow the concrete trail (Caminho d'Além) until you reach the **road** ❿

Waterfall on the Ribeira do Aveiro.

(3.55 hrs, bus stop) where you turn left down the hill. After a good 10 mins, 150m beyond the village sign of Santo Espíríto, leave the road at the right bend to join a **grassy trail** ⓫ which you follow straight towards an electricity line. At the precipice, join the old mule track that leads to an old weather station. 10 mins beyond the station, walk down the old curvy path Caminho Velho da Praia. You reach the road after 15 mins. Go left here and after 20m turn right to get back onto the grassy trail. In the village, it meets the road again; go right and immediately left at an intersecting road. You have finally arrived at the long sandy beach at **Praia Formosa** ⓬.

TOP 9 — Santa Maria ↗ 330m | ↘ 370m | 8.5km **3.20 hrs**

From Vila do Porto to Praia Formosa

Geological excursion in search of old fossils

This walk gives you a good insight into the geological history of the island. It starts at the small capital of Vila do Porto and leads up to the rim of a stone quarry covered in old fossils. From here, the route continues across pasture land to an old lime kiln and the old rock caves of Figueiral with more fossils. The last adventurous stretch to the beach resort of Praia Formosa runs along the seashore.

Starting point: Vila do Porto, Forte de São Brás, 49m (bus stop Vila do Porto/Terreiro 150m towards the town centre).
Destination: Praia Formosa, sandy beach, 8m (bus stop Praia).
Grade: mix of country lanes and footpaths, sometimes undefined. The descent to the bay of Prainha requires sure-footedness. The coastal path is only safe during low tide.
Refreshment: bars and restaurants in Vila do Porto and Praia Formosa. Nothing en route.
Alternative: without bay of Prainha (825m from turn-off, 15 mins): at the turn-off ❺ continue for 100m along the stone wall. At the barbed wire fence, turn left and ascend to a group of trees and climb over the pasture gate. From here, follow the cracked dirt trail. Keep right at the fork. Finally, reach the main trail at the road.
Linking tip: Walks 5, 8 and 11.
Bathing: sandy beach in Praia Formosa.

At the trail board on the square in front of the Forte de São Brás in **Vila do Porto** ❶, follow the footpath that leads between two chapels to the wind park. At the road, turn right and immediately left again. At the bottom, cross the Ribeira de São Francisco and take the rocky mule track that leads down the valley.

On the top, follow the gravel trail for 20 mins until you reach a car park with an information board. Turn right onto the visitors' **boardwalk** ❷ which looks like a gallery to reach the viewpoint at the foot of the stone quarry (Pedreira do Campo) which is rich in fossils (35 mins).

Then walk across the meadow to the ruins of an old house of undressed stone. From here, the traces are well-trodden, however, you have to climb over several walls that separate the pastures. At the last pasture, a wooden pole marks the start of the old trail leading up the slope. From here, you quickly reach the old **cave of Figueiral** ❸ with countless fossil outcrops (1 hr). The path continues far up on the slope and meanders up and down. Then the old, partially paved mule track ascends again, meets an iron gate and broadens again. When you reach a **concrete road** ❹ continue straight past

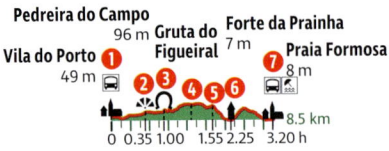

a single detached house. A good 300m beyond the house, the road descends again. At a cattle barrier, follow a mule track to the right leading down to a natural stone shed.

A tiny track continues straight towards the coast. On a footpath, pass a spring, then a rocky trail winds down in switchbacks. In a hollow climb over a barbed wire fence and take the footpath up the opposite agave slope.

At a drystone wall, you are back in pasture land. On the lower edge of the pasture, continue right for 250m to reach a small **plateau** ❺ (1.55 hrs; the alternative route continues left). This is the start of the descent on a steep scree trail, which you follow until you reach the wide sandy bay of Prainha. Turn left here. After 10 mins, reach the **Forte da Prainha** ❻ and climb left up the

Boardwalk at the Pedreira do Campo.

slope. At the top, you reach some pastureland. The path heads towards a radio mast, passes an iron cattle gate and merges with the main road. On this road, you will immediately reach the **Miradouro da Macela** on the right. About 200m further, turn right onto the first road (Caminho Velho da Praia) and continue straight until you reach the sandy beach of **Praia Formosa** ❼.

Santa Maria ↗ 580m | ↘ 580m | 13.4km

10 From Anjos to the Baía do Raposo

5.00 hrs

Across the landscape of the remote northern coast

From the seaside village of Anjos follow the shepherds' paths towards east. Stop at a whale-spotters' post (vigia) and then pass the island's former clay mining area. Finally, descend into a secluded valley with abandoned watermills. On the way back, walk through flat pastureland, and at the end, you can enjoy a refreshing dip in the natural seawater pool.

Starting point: Anjos, Columbus monument, 13m (bus stop Anjos at the swimming pool).
Grade: footpaths, walking trails and roadways. Above Anjos the trails can be a sketchy. Sure-footedness is definitely required for the descent.
Refreshment: snack bar at the pool in Anjos. Nothing en route.
Linking tip: Walk 11.
Bathing: a seawater pool in Anjos.; a pebbled beach in the Baía do Raposo.

Start at the Columbus monument at the entrance to **Anjos** ❶. Behind the monument, a concrete bridge crosses the stream and a path on the left bank leads into the valley. After 80m, keep left briefly up the slope and immediately follow the easy footpath to the right. When you reach a pastureland, walk in a straight line along the stone wall towards the hill in front of you until, after a good 5 mins, you reach an old **mule track** ❷ at level with a natural stone hut. This is where you branch off on the way back to the coast.

But for now, continue along the mule track. Before you reach a slope, turn right downhill and cross the stream below. After a short climb behind the pasture gate, continue left, cross the stream again and go through another gate. Climb up the left-hand edge of the pasture along an overgrown

On the way to the water mills at the Baía do Raposo.

natural stone wall. Shortly after the slope flattens out, an old, broken mule track starts on the right, which, after a good 150m, gets better again.
Before continuing on the dirt track to the right, follow a stony footpath straight up the hill. At the top of the stone wall, turn left to the old **whale-spotters' post** ❸ on Monte Gordo (45 mins).
Back down on the country lane, walk inland, pass a ruin with a view of the Baía da Cré and, after a short climb, reach the road in **Faneca** ❹. Where you see a small chapel on the right, continue left to reach the former clay mining area of **Barreiro de Faneca**. Circle this ochre-coloured semi-desert without a clear path mostly along the right edge of the forest. Leave the track to the left right at the start. Where you can see a **roadway** ❺ leading out of the mining area on the opposite side, continue for another 80m and follow the dirt track down into the forest. After 10 mins, you will get to the deeply cut **Ribeira do Engenho** ❻.

After crossing another stream, turn left at the fork near the creek. Once you leave the forest, continue straight for 80m until you reach the iron gate. This is where the footpath begins which soon winds down in wide switchbacks toward the **Baía do Raposo** ❼ with two ruins of old watermills (avoid taking the steep shortcut!). In the valley basin, you'll have a view back to the Salto do Raposo waterfall (2.30 hrs).

For the ascent, take the steep old fishermen's path and follow the same route back to ❷. From here, follow traces of a path crossing the meadow to the right passing a natural stone shed. The footpath ends after four stone wall openings at the cliff edge. Now walk pathless across the meadow along the boundary wall. At the lowest meadow, briefly switch to the other side of the wall. After 5 mins, you cross a **dry streambed** ❽. The now clearly visible path heads out of the valley for a short while and then veers left at the bottom, directly at the coast. After 150m across a meadow, turn inland again and follow the stream back to the starting point in **Anjos** ❶. Once you have reached your destination, it's worth taking a short detour to the bathing spot at the end of the road.

Shining red: the former clay mining area Barreiro de Faneca.

↗ 195m | ↘ 120m | 14.7km   Santa Maria

4.40 hrs

From Anjos to Vila do Porto   11

Remote walk through the west which is sun-dried in the summer

The western part of the island gets extremely dry in the summer turning into an arid steppe landscape. Nevertheless, the area around the airport is used as pastureland. From the beach resort of Anjos, first walk along the coastline before you follow the airport boundaries for a long time. In the south, you will eventually reach the Ilhéu da Vila before you get to Vila do Porto via Ponta do Malmerendo.

Starting point: Anjos, Columbus monument, 13m (bus stop Anjos 200m west).
Destination: Vila do Porto, townhall square, 88m (bus stop Vila do Porto/Farmácia).
Grade: the many pathless sections on this walk take you through fields and across pastureland. Good sense of direction required. No exit option west of the airport area. Several stone walls have to be negotiated.
Refreshment: snack bar at the swimming pool in Anjos. In Vila do Porto. Nothing en route.
Linking tip: Walk 10.
Bathing: seawater pool in Anjos.

A popular spot: seawater pool in Anjos.

From the Columbus monument in **Anjos** ❶, first follow the road until you reach its end behind the swimming pool. Beyond that, a paved trail continues. After 150m, pass the **Furna de Santana** ❷. The trail runs into a narrow footpath that crosses several stone walls and eventually ends at an iron gate. Beyond the iron gate, you will reach the wide bay of **Praia dos Lobos** with its large pebbles. A footpath continues along the coast. After 5 mins, cross a dry streambed and, after you have negotiated some scrambling, climb back up along the opposite slope by the coast ❸. There, you reach pastureland from where you continue right towards the radio masts (waymarkers). After 200m, climb over a natural stone wall, initially keeping to the right of the wall, and then cross to the left side after 120m. Continue along the right side of the pasture for another 200m until you reach the **Ribeira de Santana** ❹ (40 mins).

After the wooden bridge, turn right and follow the green fence for about a quarter of an hour. At the large gate to the NAV site, you reach a roadway. Turn right here and follow the side track to the left at an old transformer house. After 10 mins, climb up the first **dirt trail** ❺ on the right and reach

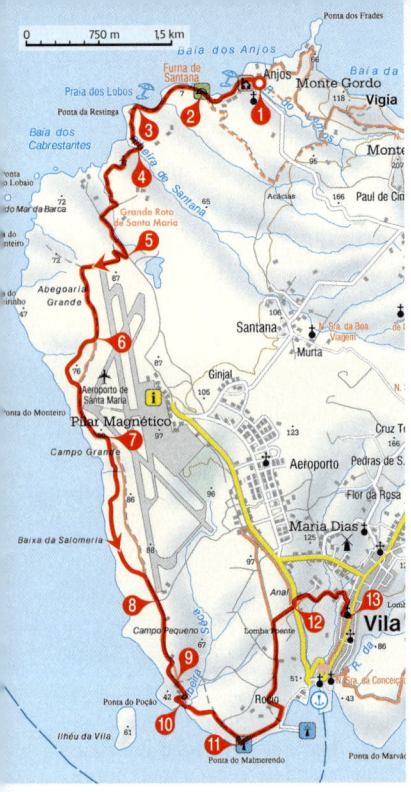

the airport grounds. The trail continues along the boundary fence and narrows behind a collapsed ruin into a footpath. Five mins later, the footpath ends at a **barbed-wire gate** ❻ (1.45 hrs).

Diagonally cross the pasture behind the gate which is pathless and head towards the natural stone ruin in front of you. Beyond the ruin, continue in a straight line (there are some waymarkers). Soon, the path continues directly along the fence. On the south side of the 'belly' ❼ of the airport grounds, the trail turns away from the fence and initially descends for a while (waymarkers), and then, about 100m away from the fence, it follows an old stone wall. After about 30 mins, you will be able to see the red airport lights. Here, walk left up again towards the fence and reach a dirt trail that veers left at the end of the airport grounds ❽ (2.50 hrs).

At this fork, continue straight on a gravel road to the right. After about 5 mins, the gravel road turns into a grassy track at an information board about the nature park. Where the grassy track turns right 100m further on, continue straight towards the iron gate in front of you. Beyond it, turn right (there is no path) and walk down across the pasture to reach the **ruins of some houses** ❾. The path continues for another 200m. Cross a stone wall and descend to the farthest end of the pasture. The white top of the lighthouse in front of you indicates your direction. At an information board, a concrete stepped trail begins, leading down into the valley of the **Ribeira Seca** ❿.

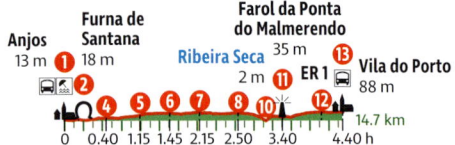

Within reach: the Ilhéu da Vila at the mouth of the Ribeira Seca.

At the bottom, turn left across the lava (there is no path), cross the mouth of the stream and climb up the slope (waymarker). Once you have reached the highest point again, there is a natural stone wall. Follow the wall for 100m to the right before you turn inland. Diagonally across, you will see the exit at a cattle gate. On the gravel road, you will reach a turning point on the right. Here, continue along the right trail for another 200m before you follow a small footpath that leads across stone walls to the lighthouse **Farol da Ponta do Malmerendo** ⑪ (3.40 hrs).

Behind the lighthouse, follow the outermost pasture boundary (there is no path) until, after 10 mins, a natural stone wall blocks the way. Here, turn left uphill and pass a barn. Beyond that, on the country lane to the right, you will reach a gravel road after 5 mins which you follow inland. At the slaughterhouse, you will reach the beginning of another road. Here, turn right (sign: 6.5 t).

At the **main road** ⑫, continue left and, after 75m, turn right onto a side road. After 150m, just before a car park, follow a mule track which, to the right, leads down into the valley of the Ribeira dos Poços. On the opposite slope, you will reach a crossroad behind the first houses at the top. Turn right here to ascend and then turn right again further up. On this road, Rua do Cotovelo, you will reach the centre at the town hall square in **Vila do Porto** ⑬ after 200m.

São Miguel – connecting to the Western World

- population: 133,400
- county seats: Ponta Delgada, 17,300 inhabitants; Lagoa, 8800; Ribeira Grande, 6400; Vila Franca do Campo, 3900; Povoação, 2200; Nordeste, 1200
- area: 745km²
- length: 64km, width: 18km
- coastline: 220km
- highest points: Pico da Vara, 1103m; Pico da Barrosa, 947m; Pico das Éguas, 873m

São Miguel is the most modern of the nine Azorean islands. At least three weeks are needed to visit all the sites worth seeing. São Miguel compresses the highlights of the Azores into the smallest microcosm: lush natural landscapes as well as tame pastures with grazing cattle are to be found here, in sharp contrast to the cosmopolitan flair of a big city. Splendid crater lakes are just waiting to be discovered. Holidaymakers can stretch out in a thermal pool in the middle of a forest. Not only the pineapple flourishes on São Miguel but also tea – Europe's only plantation.

Bathing fans can find a relaxing spot on one of the countless sandy beaches. Pass the time on a golf courses, sign up for whale-watching or any of a wide selection of activity packages ranging from jeep-safaris to rock-climbing courses. Even shop until late at night in gigantic shopping malls. On no other island is the tourism growing so quickly – a success story not without a down side: in the meantime, the island has become so popular that the infrastructure can no longer cope with the crowds in the summer months. Daily traffic has reached hectic proportions, criminality is on an upswing,

entire residential areas seem to spring up out of nowhere. Millions of Euros provided by the EU assistance programme are lavishly spent in prestige projects such as the construction of a motorway. With all their energy, the inhabitants strive to keep pace with the Western World, often at the expense of the smaller islands that would prefer a well-developed public transport system to a 5-star hotel or a cruiseship harbour. The harbour is well-frequented during the winter by big cruiseships.

The pineapple – jewel of São Miguel.

Along with Santa Maria, the island is presumed to have been discovered in 1427. Fertile soil and an optimal location quickly turned the island into a flourishing granary for Portugal. Dye plants were exported to Flanders. The first capital was Vila Franca do Campo which would be completely destroyed by an earthquake in 1522. From then on, Ponta Delgada took over the island's administration and has retained this position of power even until the present. From 1582, the island was occupied by Spanish troops and years of exploitation were to follow. Only after independence was achieved in 1640 would another page in history be turned. São Miguel developed into a centre for trade in the Atlantic and began to compete with the supremacy of the island Terceira – a period of prosperity reflected in the architecture of the time; large land-holders and the well-to-do began to build luxurious mansions. In the second half of the 18th century, the cultivation of oranges took an upswing, most of the fruit would be exported to England. But profits remained in the hands of the few. In 1831, during the power struggle between absolutists and liberals, the liberals won and, with a fleet of 3500 Azoreans helped initiate the changeover of power in Portugal. In 1860, mildew decimated the orange plantations. The motor driving the economy came to a sudden halt. Many inhabitants emigrated to America. Those who remained were forced to rethink. At the end, all bets were placed on the cultivation of pineapples and tea. São Miguel grew to become the economic centre for the Azores – political and administrative power was then transferred to the island. Meanwhile, tourism has joined in as yet another economic pillar.

Most visitors of São Miguel stay in **Ponta Delgada**, certainly the most modern city in the Azores, always striving to combine its old-fashioned flair with the demands of the present. Well worth seeing are the garden parks António Borges and José do Canto. Architecture enthusiasts should visit the churches of Matriz de São Sebastião, São José, São Pedro and Todos-os-Santos. On the major square Campo de São Francisco, the convent Nossa Senhora da Esperança boasts an effigy of Christ which attracts many Azoreans to the island for the most visited religious celebration in the entire archipelago; this takes place after Easter. Also, the ancient city gate Portas da Cidade near the city hall merits a visit. There is a much more modern venue along the seaside promenade at the cruiseship quay Portas do Mar. Take a peek into the volcanic underworld in the cave Gruta do Carvão at the city limits. Visitors with a taste for culture can while away an entire day in the Museu Carlos Machado which boasts a variety of exhibits. In the Forte and Castelo São Brás you can marvel at ancient military artwork. Those searching for local products can simply pay a visit to the municipal market. By the way, enjoy a little tour of the city by taking the Lagarta slow train.

Without seeming to cross any city boundary, urban development around the capital merges with **Lagoa**, whose history reaches back to the time of the first settlement. The churches Santa Cruz and Nossa Senhora do Rosário (16th century) merit visits as does the Franciscan monastery. Today, Lagoa is a pulsating industrial city, known for its pottery.

The county seat **Ribeira Grande**, divided by a river, proves captivating with its magnificent religious edifices. Worth seeing are the main churches Nossa Senhora da Estrela and Conceição as well as the richly embellished Igreja do Senhor dos Passos. Enjoy a restful moment in the little municipal park and on the forecourt of the elegant city hall. To gather information about the history of the Azores and its inhabitants, be sure to visit the Emigrants Museum. Marvellous beaches are an attraction for sunbathing.

The island's old capital **Vila Franca do Campo** wins attention with its simplicity. The main church, São Miguel, has been kept rather sombre. The convent São Francisco is a relic from the 16th century; the Açor Arena, just across from it, is a modern temple for public events and is architecturally unique to the Azores. A culinary speciality of the city are the little cakes *Queijadas da Vila*. The chapel of Nossa Senhora da Paz is enthroned high above the city and provides excellent views.

The thermal pool Caldeira Velha.

The history of **Povoação** reaches back to colonial times when the first settlers made their homes in this location. The old parish church at the harbour remains as relic of the past, and the chapel Santa Bárbara, counts as one of the Azores' oldest religious structures.

Ponta Delgada – the Azores' most modern city.

In the fifth county seat **Nordeste**, located in the secluded north-eastern island, daily life revolves around the central square. The city hall and the main church São Jorge (15th century) are in close proximity. The streets are quaintly decorated with flowers. The ancient vaulted bridge provides a lovely photographic motif.

From Ponta Delgada, a short excursion to the pineapple plantations in Fajã de Baixo is worthwhile. Follow the southern coastline westward to the promontory Ponta da Ferraria where hot springs can be found at the ocean. From the viewpoint on the Ponta do Escalvado, enjoy a view of the sleepy village of Mosteiros and the offshore islands. The entire western half of the island is dominated by the volcanic massif of Sete Cidades – a gigantic crater with two large and two small crater lakes. The most beautiful view of the area can be enjoyed from the overlook Vista do Rei. Continue via the northern coastline, passing little villages on the way that can be best visited by driving along the secondary road below. Further landward lies the local recreational area, Pinhal da Paz, 49ha in area. Agricultural hustle and bustle can be had at the livestock market in Santana. A fountain was buried during a volcanic eruption in Ribeira Seca in 1563 and only recently unearthed during road work. Above the county seat Ribeira Grande, the thermal bathing pool Caldeira Velha lies in the middle of a forest. On the way there, you pass environmentally-friendly geothermal power plants that supply the island with about 40% of its electricity requirements. Another thermal bathing resort is located not far away in Caldeiras da Ribeira Grande. In Porto Formoso and Gorreana, you will find the only tea plantations located in Europe, where 19th century machinery is still in use even today. A museum in Maia provides a memorial to the past success of tobacco farming. Via the natural park on the Ribeira dos Caldeirões with its lovely waterfall, pass splendid viewpoints on the way to the county seat of Nordeste. Here, a visit to the Centro do Priolo is worthwhile; the Azorean bullfinch, a 30-gram lightweight, can only be found here, around the Pico da Vara and the Ribeira do Guilherme. Continuing on, pass through Povoação to reach the thermal bathing resort of Furnas. Visiting the park, Terra Nostra, is an absolute 'must' as is taking a dip in the 38 °C thermal pools under open skies. Everywhere you go in the settlement, you will find hot springs and steaming fumaroles. On the lake at Furnas, the *cozido das Furnas* stew

SÃO MIGUEL

Getting there
During the summer there are many direct flights to São Miguel by SATA and other airlines from major European cities as well as the USA and Canada. For the rest of the year, a stopover on the mainland is required. Direct flight connections within the archipelago are available to all islands, except Corvo. The airport is located at the western city limits of Ponta Delgada. There has been no ferry service to other islands recently, and there is no ferry connection from the mainland either.

Bathing
São Miguel provides a great variety of bathing.
Sandy beaches: black sandy beach in Mosteiros; lovely sandy beaches in São Roque; Praia das Milícias and Praia do Populo in Livramento; Baixa das Areias in Caloura; Praia and Prainha in Água d'Alto; Praia da Pedreira in Rocha dos Campos; Praia Vinha da Areia in Vila Franca do Campo; Baixa de Areia in Ribeira das Tainhas; Praia da Amora at Ponta Garça; Praia do Fogo in Ribeira Quente; sandy beach in Povoação; small beach in Lombo Gordo; Praia da Viola at Lomba da Maia; small beach near the harbour in Maia; Praia dos Moinhos and Praia do Ilhéu in Porto Formoso; Praia de Monte Verde and Areal de Santa Bárbara in Ribeira Grande; Praia de Santana near Rabo de Peixe.
Swimming pools: open-air pool in Ponta Delgada; open-air pool at the harbour and enclosed pool in Lagoa; Atlântico Splash in Vila Franca do Campo; enclosed pool in Povoação; Pool Boca da Ribeira near Nordeste; open-air pool in Ribeira Grande.
Thermal bathing: thermal lake in Parque Terra Nostra and Poça da Dona Beija in Furnas; Ferraria near Ginetes; Caldeira Velha near Ribeira Grande.
Natural pools: lava pools in Mosteiros; the harbour at Caloura; a lagoon in the Ilhéu da Vila near Vila Franca do Campo; Porto dos Poços near Capelas.

Festivities
Cantar das Estrelas (Ribeira Grande), beginning of February. Pilgrim week of the Romeiros before Easter. Festa do Senhor dos Enfermos (Furnas), 1st Sunday after Easter. Festa do Senhor Santo Cristo dos Milagres (Ponta Delgada), 5th Sunday after Easter. Holy Spirit Celebrations all over the island from May until June. Festa de São João (Vila Franca), June 24. Equestrian parade Cavalhadas de São Pedro (Ribeira Seca), June 29. Semana do Chicharro (Ribeira Quente), mid-July. Festa do Pescador (Caloura), end of August. Festa do Bom Jesus da Pedra (Vila Franca), end of August. Numerous patron saint celebrations throughout the year.

is cooked in volcanic holes in the earth. Pico do Ferro provides the most beautiful view of the crater lake. Just next to it, a golf course is set in the middle of greenery. Next stop on the southern coast is the county seat Vila Franca do Campo. Via Ribeira Chã, with its potpourri of little museums, one reaches Caloura. Here is where the wealthy and well-endowed make their homes. From Lagoa, a road ascends to the crater lake Lagoa do Fogo. Before returning to the capital, pass the splendid sandy beaches of Populo and Milícias. In Livramento and Fajã de Baixo, at the end, marvel at the ancient *quintas* and mansions of 18th and 19th century upper class society.

Medical services
A hospital is located in Ponta Delgada, tel +351 296 203 000. Local health clinics in all of the county seats.

Tourist information
Turismo de São Miguel in Ponta Delgada, tel +351 296 308 610, info. turismo@azores.gov.pt; cm-pontadelgada.pt, lagoa-acores.pt, cm-ribeira-grande.pt, cmvfc.pt, cm-povoacao.pt, cmnordeste.pt. Also a limited counter at the airport. Additional regional tourist offices in Lagoa, Ribeira Grande, Maia, Furnas and Vila Franca. Free Wi-Fi at various hotspots (WIFI4EU).

Cultural activities
Museu Carlos Machado, military museum, Museum of sacred art, a lava tour at the Gruta do Carvão in Ponta Delgada; pineapple plantation and pineapple museum in Fajã de Baixo; museum of local history, Observatório Vulcanológico e Geotérmico, a blacksmith (Tenda do Ferreiro) and ceramic factory Vieira in Lagoa; local history museums in Ribeira Chã; local history museum and pottery workshop (Olaria) in Vila Franca; visitor and research centre on Furnas lake as well as the Observatório Microbiano in Furnas, Museu do Trigo near Povoação; Centro Ambiental do Priolo near Nordeste; mill museum at Ribeira dos Caldeirões; tobacco museum in Maia; tea processing plants of Gorreana and Porto Formoso; Franciscan museum, emigrants museum, local history museum and museum of modern art in Ribeira Grande; Museu das Cavalhadas in Ribeira Seca; Observatório Astronómico in Santana; local history museum in Fenais da Luz; privately-run local history and handwork museum in Capelas.

Public transport
On São Miguel, a good network of bus lines services the island in every direction with Ponta Delgada as the hub. Bus service is frequent, especially in the main towns along the southern coast as well as Ribeira Grande. There are few buses to Furnas, along the northern coast and in the peripheral areas; service may end already in the afternoon. At times, you must rely on taxis to get back again. There are no buses crossing the mountainous areas, so it is almost impossible to reach the most attractive spots on the island without a hire car. Permanent taxi ranks are located in all of the cities and larger settlements.
Taxi service centrals in Ponta Delgada, tel +351 296 382 000 and 296 101 898. APP Taxilink works in places.

Accommodation
On São Miguel, you will find all types of accommodation, from a 5-star hotel, apartments or hostels. The selection and standards are at an international level.

São Miguel ↗ 290m | ↘ 290m | 5.5km

12 Circling the Pico de Mafra

2.00 hrs

Descent to hidden, enclosed springs on a steep rock face

Vast stretches of São Miguel's north-west coast remain pristine even today and are very difficult to access. This short walk leads to the farming village of João Bom, then descends to several enclosed springs on the steep coastal cliffs. This is a route leading through a nature reserve that is very popular for bird-watchers.

Starting point: João Bom, the picnic area on the EN 1, 243m (bus stop João Bom/Cima and Centro).
Grade: at the coast, along footpaths while the rest of the walk is along gravel tracks and a road.
Refreshment: café in João Bom.

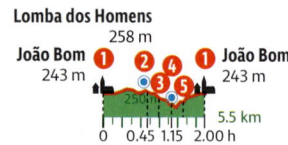

Starting at the picnic area *(Merendário)* in **João Bom** ❶ on the EN 1, follow the Rua do Argentino towards the coast and afterwards, turn left at the Minimercado Amizade to ascend. Keep steadily straight on along this road, passing a little chapel. Past the last houses, a gravel track continues that runs in constant up-and-down walking from one valley to the next. Not quite 20 mins past the settlement's limits, reach a fork and bear right. A quarter of an hour later, reach the hamlet of **Lomba dos Homens**. At the **fountain** ❷, turn right on the concrete Rua da Pedra Queimada. This leads below the Pico de Mafra and soon descends steeply. After 10 mins at about the same level of a big stable with a tin roof, keep right on the ascending **dirt trail** ❸ and continue on the grassy trail straight on. Farther down in front of you,

Precipitous walking trail.

Water collection points on the steep slope.

you can soon spot the first **water collection point** ❹ on the slope which you reach after a total time of 1.15 hrs.

Afterwards, take the left-hand trail, further below, that runs somewhat precipitously along the slope, leading to two additional water collection points. This area of coastline is also a popular haunt for bird-watchers. Past the last waterworks, wooden steps ascend up the valley to the rugged, deeply-incised Grota do Loural. After crossing over the course of a stream, a steep ascent trail leads to the left, climbing yet more wooden steps. The path passes two viewpoints and finally ends in a **country lane** ❺ which you ascend to the right all the way to **João Bom**. Here, turn left at the intersecting street to return to the **starting point** ❶.

São Miguel · ↗ 580m | ↘ 580m | 19.6km

13 Circular walk around the Caldeira das Sete Cidades
5.30 hrs

Panoramic circular walk around the Azores' biggest crater

The mighty volcanic massif of Sete Cidades reigns over the western region of São Miguel. A resource trail follows along most of the crater's rim – an easy route to follow. Time and again, enjoy a different view of the two crater lakes Lagoa Verde and Lagoa Azul. Along the last leg of the walk, cross over the summit of the Pico da Cruz and also the local recreational area at Lagoa do Canário. The island's most classic tour!

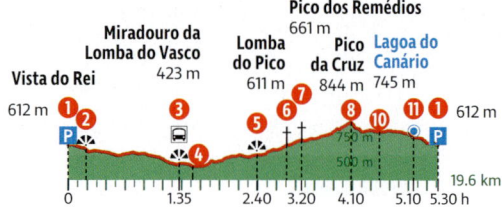

Starting point: hikers' car park at the ER 9 at the turn-off to Sete Cidades, 612m (bus stop only at the Miradouro da Lomba do Vasco on request).
Grade: along the high trail, only via dirt trails and dusty tracks. The last leg follows the road. This tour is not to be taken lightly due to its length. On clear days, be sure to be thoroughly protected from the sun.
Refreshment: nothing en route.
Alternative: short walk with descent to Sete Cidades (1.7km from the junction, 30 mins): at waypoint ❹, turn left onto the track, than follow (counting from the bend in the road) the second roadway towards the right at a long cattle water trough. The concrete road is very steep in places in the lower part and leads you directly down to Sete Cidades in a good 20 mins. At the first houses, turn right onto the first street and immediately reach the centre at the church. It is recommended to pre-book a taxi for the return trip.
Linking tip: Walk 14.

A break with a view: panorama from Pico da Cruz overlooking the vast Caldeira.

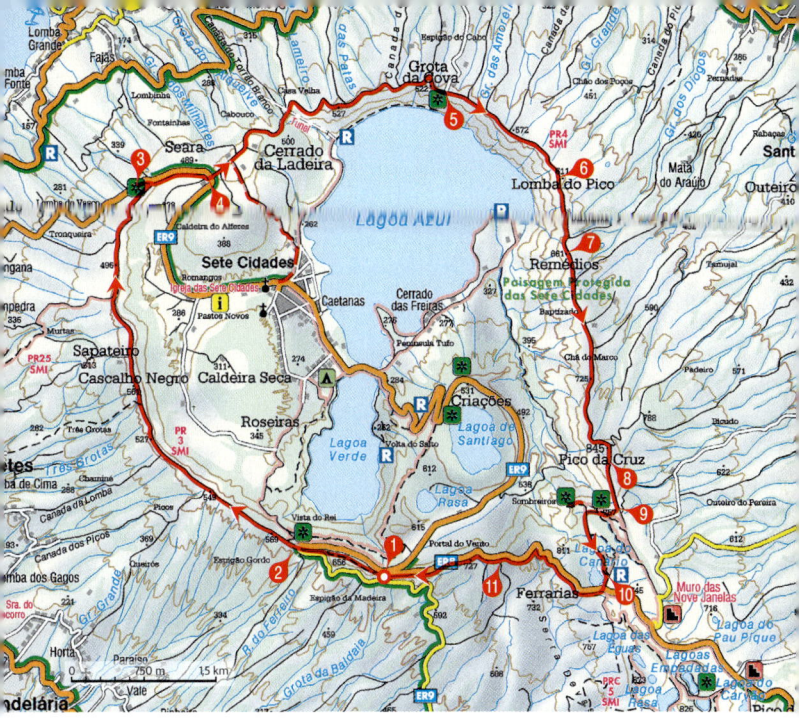

From the **hikers' car park** ❶ at the crater rim, follow the high road to the west until you reach the viewpoint **Vista do Rei** ❷. From here, bear half right on the track towards a transmission mast. Ignore all the tracks forking left and, after 1.35 hrs, reach a road and follow this to the left for a few paces to visit the viewpoint **Miradouro da Lomba do Vasco** ❸. Now return back and follow the road into the crater. 10 mins past the viewpoint and at a right-hand bend, turn left onto the first **track** ❹ you meet (after 300m on the track, the Alternative turns off to the right).

On this high trail you will soon pass an old manor house. Stay up here and walk clock-wise around the crater. Ignore all tracks forking off to your left. Circumnavigate a small wooded hillock and, at the end, the trail continues along the rim of the crater. You can see the picnic place at the water tunnel farther down ahead of you. After a total of 2.40 hrs along the track, reach the viewpoint on the northern rim of the crater, the **Miradouro das Cumeeiras** ❺, which is also accessible by road from Bretanha. Past this point, the track worsens somewhat and is normally only used for agricultural purposes. Soon the roadway begins to ascend once again.

A royal view taking in the lakes Lagoa Azul (background) and Verde (foreground).

25 mins from the last viewpoint, reach a trig point on the **Lomba do Pico** ❻ and, 15 mins later, pass the **Pico dos Remédios** ❼. The track steadily increases in steepness. Below the Pico da Cruz, reach a fork. Here, turn right to ascend and after a final steep stretch, soon reach the dual peaks of the **Pico da Cruz** ❽ which is crowned by a radiobeacon (4.10 hrs).

Now a concrete track descends again. At the **third power pylon** ❾, leave the concrete track and descend along the rim on a partially heavily eroded trace of a path. On the opposite side of the pasture, you reach a cul-de-sac. From the small viewpoint beyond it follow the track leading straight ahead. After 150m pass a picnic area. Here, an extra excursion to the right is possible by ascending the wooden steps to reach a precipitously-situated viewpoint (there and back, 15 mins).

Now go back to continue on the track and bear right at the first fork. Immediately after this, reach the **Lagoa do Canário** ❿, a number of footpaths climb down to it through the forest (4.40 hrs). Afterwards, in the recreational area, ascend to the right to reach the road ER 8.

Turn right onto this road to continue and, after passing the fountain **Fonte da Serra** ⓫, return back to the **hikers' car park** ❶ at the turn-off to Sete Cidades.

↗ 240m | ↘ 240m | 7.1km   São Miguel   **TOP 14**
2.20 hrs

Lagoas Empadadas

Gratifying walk through a hideaway lake district

Numerous little crater lakes lie idyllically set in an almost pristine natural landscape on the Serra Devassa mountain range. In the early 19th century, a water conduit was specially laid to feed the fountains of Ponta Delgada with the precious clean waters of the highlands. The views reach from Capelas all the way to and beyond Ribeira Grande on the north coast and from Ginetes all the way to Lagoa on the south coast. Crowds of tourists make their pilgrimage to the Boca do Inferno viewpoint all year round.

Starting point: recreational area Lagoa do Canário, 500m-long car park starting at the entrance, 763m.
Grade: mostly along dirt tracks and wide well-trodden footpaths. Slippery surfaces when wet.

Refreshment: nothing en route.
Linking tip: Walk 13.
Note: the Boca do Inferno viewpoint is the most popular tourist destination on the island. In summer, parking can be chaotic.

Volcanoes and crater lakes: view of the Pico das Éguas.

Across from the entrance to the **local recreational area** ❶ at **Lagoa do Canário** behind the hikers' car park, a cracked dirt trail, which is soon to be extremely eroded, leads southward over the hilly countryside of the Serra Devassa. A couple of mins later, turn left at the first fork at an iron gate. Skirt around a marshy area and, past this, the trail hooks sharp to the right. Always follow the main trail and ignore all other trails turning off. The marked footpath now climbs steeper and continues upward as a hollow way that is slippery with loose stones underfoot.

Shortly before a little wood, turn right to leave the sunken trail via some **steps** ❷. The trail is wide and well-trodden leading straight up via steps. At the top, a clear path continues to the right, offering the first beautiful view of the northern lake of the two lakes at Pico das Éguas. At the first junction after the viewpoint remain on the well-trodden main trail in the middle, which now climbs left up again along the crater rim to reach the true summit of the **Pico das Éguas** ❸ with a viewpoint (25 mins).

Here, the trail continues at first to the right along the crater's rim and, 100m on, descends to the right. A few paces in front of you is another viewpoint with a view of the next lake. After a short descent, the trail continues mostly safely across some wooden steps. The hill with antennas in front of you will point you into the right direction.

In the lower part, stay on the main trail within a very eroded, sometimes deeply cut gully, always keeping to the left. Behind an iron pipe barrier, you will reach the **Lagoa Rasa** and, at the old pumphouse, turn left onto a gravel track ❹. After circling halfway around the lake, leave the gravel track where the main trail turns away from the Lagoa Rasa ❺. Here, another 60m before you reach the vehicle track behind a stone gate, turn left onto a very washed-out trace of a path that ascends along the eastern flank of the Éguas massif. After 15 mins, you reach the outgoing trail ❷. From here, return to the **car park** ❶ (1.25 hrs).

On the opposite side of the road, follow the track and go through the gate leading into the forest park. Bear left at the first fork. At the very beginning, two footpaths on your left lead down to the hidden **Lagoa do Canário**.

Along the trail to the Miradouro da Boca do Inferno with a view of Sete Cidades.

After 15 mins, the track bends sharply right at the small picnic tables. Here, go left up the stepped trail. At first, the slippery path ascends steeply and leads to the viewpoint **Miradouro da Boca do Inferno** ❻ that offers a magnificent panorama which attracts crowds of tourists during the summer (1.55 hrs).

For the last 100m, return to the edge of the forest and take the narrow path to your right leading along the edge of the forest to the south. At the beginning, it is quite pleasant, only the last part gets increasingly steeper and is now heavily washed out.

Once you have reached the bottom of the road, turn left and return to the starting point at the entrance to the **recreational area** ❶.

São Miguel ↗ 230m | ↘ 230m | 3.6km

15 Ponta da Ferraria and Pico das Camarinhas

1.20 hrs

Geological walk across volcano hills to a hot marine spring

In 1811, a volcanic eruption about 6km off the coast created the Ilha Sabrina. However, the rough seas have long since reclaimed the small rocky island, after which the starting point of this walk is named. The volcanic cones around Ginetes still bear witness to centuries of intense activity. At Ponta da Ferraria, geothermal heat warms the natural seawater bathing area whose temperature can reach over 30 °C at low tide.

Starting point: Miradouro da Ilha Sabrina, 105m (nearest bus stop on the main road through Ginetes).
Grade: mix of rocky footpaths and wooden stepped trails. The descent to Ponta da Ferraria is on the road. Sure-footedness is helpful.
Refreshment: restaurant at the thermal baths (not always open).
Bathing: thermal baths (entry fee, often closed) and natural bathing area with hot springs at the Ponta da Ferraria.

From the Miradouro da Ilha Sabrina you can look across the Ponta da Ferraria.

A busy spot in summer: hot springs feed the natural bathing area in the bay.

Start at the **Miradouro da Ilha Sabrina** ❶ and initially head inland along the road. After 200m, take the wooden stepped trail on the left which ascends through the forest. Passing a viewpoint, you reach the summit of **Pico das Camarinhas** ❷. Beyond the peak, steep wooden steps lead back down to a track. Turn right here and at the next fork, follow the road on the right (Rua da Ilha Sabrina) to descend to the **Miradouro da Ilha Sabrina** ❶ (35 mins).

Continue down the steep winding concrete road to the thermal baths at the Ponta da Ferraria. In front of the main entrance, a dead straight footpath leads from the four tall araucaria trees down to the sea and the **natural bathing area** ❸ (55 mins) which is heated by hot springs. The temperature can exceed 30 °C at low tide. Near the changing rooms a bit higher up, a small footpath descends to a gravel path that follows the coast back toward the thermal baths. After 75m, it's worth making a short detour at info point 12 to the cliff edge, where you'll find a stunning rock arch *(arco lávico)*. Walking around the thermal baths, you will rejoin the concrete road and ascend back to the **Miradouro da Ilha Sabrina** ❶.

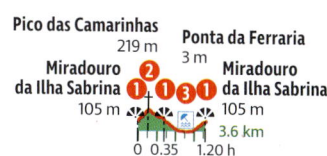

São Miguel ↗ 325m | ↘ 325m | 5.2km

16 Rocha das Feteiras

2.00 hrs

Short detour to a hidden and remote summer settlement

The summer cottages of Rocha das Feteiras with their gardens are scattered at the foot of the almost 300m-high cliffs like multi-coloured dots. A dusty track leads down to the headland of the Ponta da Fonte Grande. The ascent follows a steep donkey path which quickly takes you back to the high plateau.

Starting point: Miradouro da Vigia das Baleias das Feteiras on the EN 1, 273m (bus stop Vigia das Feteiras 650m to the west).

Grade: initially a dusty dirt track. The ascent follows a narrow, sometimes steep donkey path.
Refreshment: nothing en route.

Nestled below the towering cliffs: the fertile gardens of Rocha das Feteiras.

From the **whale-spotters' tower** ❶ near **Feteiras**, follow the EN 1 main road north for 200m before turning left onto a dusty dirt track which winds down towards the coast in numerous switchbacks. After 30 mins, when the path starts to ascend again, you reach a junction. From here, take the right-hand fork which descends steeply on an eroded roadway leading down to the sea where you get to the old harbour, **Porto de Cima** ❷, and the natural pools of Poça da Raçoula (45 mins).

From the boat ramp, return to the main trail and continue to walk to the right. 15 mins later, the roadway ends at some scattered houses in **Rocha das Feteiras** ❸.

From here, a narrow footpath, which starts with steps, goes up the slope. Continue to follow the only main path upward ignoring all side trails on the right. Small gardens are scattered across the slopes like mulit-coloured dots. After a strenuous 30-min ascent, pass a small waterhouse with a spring capture. Beyond this point, the trail gradually levels out and soon meets a dirt track. Turn left here to return to the starting point at the **whale-spotters' tower** ❶.

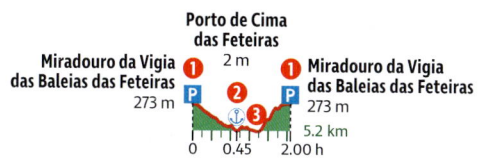

São Miguel ↗ 280m | ↘ 280m | 6.3km

17 Rocha da Relva

2.10 hrs

Easy excursion to an almost completely abandoned hamlet on the coast

The settlement Rocha da Relva is situated on one of the few cultivated coastal flats on the shores of São Miguel. Starting at a whale-spotters' lookout which is in use in the summer, first take a roadway to the grand 'Donkey Hall'. From there, continue along a descending trail that has been well-laid and leads to the shoreline. An ideal beginning for a week of walking!

Starting point: Miradouro do Caminho Novo near Relva, 147m (bus stop Relva/Padaria 200m east).
Grade: initially along a dirt road; descent along a broad, mostly reinforced donkey path. Anyone can walk this route.
Refreshment: nothing en route.

Alternative: to Rocha do Cascalho (1.3km, 35 mins): past the first zigzags at the beginning of the descent route, climb down a narrow, sign-posted footpath to the left. 5 mins later, reach a bridge. Now remain on the path until descending down to the central rest area. Take the same route back up again.

From the **Miradouro do Caminho Novo** ❶ on the EN 1, at the decorative tile for Rocha da Relva, climb down the narrow road which, past two houses, soon becomes a track. At the intersecting trail, 5 mins later, turn right to continue and pass the **Miradouro da Vigia** ❷; here you can enjoy

The secluded settlement Rocha da Relva lies right by the sea.

a first view of the steep and rugged coastline. At the end, reach a large **car park** ❸ (20 mins). The descent trail begins near a wayside shrine. If you have your own vehicle, you can make this your starting point.

After walking the first zigzags, bear right to keep to the main trail (the turn-off for the Alternative bears left). The old donkey path has been reinforced at all of the steep sections. Pass the rock face Jogo da Bola and the slope Ladeira do Tio Cardoso. Now the trail steepens and leads past a fountain at the first garden plots of Rocha da Relva.

After a total of 45 mins, reach a central square whith a **memorial** ❹. Directly at the first houses, there is a picnic area with toilets on the right. The footpath along the shoreline continues to the left of this. Pass a reinforced streambed and yet another fountain. Now the trail becomes increasingly narrow and, after a good 1 hr, finally ends at the western side of the bay near a little **cluster of houses** ❺.
Return along the same route to the starting point at the **Miradouro do Caminho Novo** ❶.

São Miguel ↗ 225m | ↘ 225m | 4.2km

18 Nascentes de Santo António

1.40 hrs

Exposed adventure walk along numerous spring water captures

At the rugged cliffs below Santo António, drinking water is sourced from numerous galleries. There used to be many watermills here in the past and this was also the place where the island's first hydroelectric power plant was developed. After passing a pleasant seawater pool and the old harbour at Ponta de Santo António, the path along the cliffs soon becomes adventurous, steep, and demanding. After a short climb back up, you reach a small picnic area where you can recharge your batteries.

Starting point: Santo António, church, 62m (bus stop Santo António/Largo da Igreja).
Grade: the old fishermen's path is often steep winding over many steps, sometimes exposed, up and down the cliffs. Sure-footedness and a head for heights are necessary.

Refreshment: cafés in Santo António.
Bathing: seawater pool at Rosário.
Note: this walk was interrupted in 2025 due to a landslide above ❸. It is not certain when it will reopen.

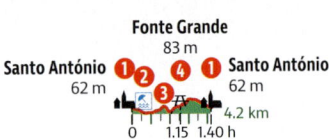

This walk starts in the centre of **Santo António** ❶ at the church. Behind the church, a concrete footpath continues across a concrete bridge and immediately meets a crossroad at the other end. Turn right here and, at the cemetery, find the Ermida do Rosário, behind which the road leads down to a large **seawater pool (Zona Balnear do Rosário)** ❷ and continues to the old harbour (15 mins).

A footpath leads back up the hill and ends at a field. Follow the edge of the field to the right, along the reed line. After 5 mins, leave the farmland. This is the point where the challenging coastal section begins. After 10 mins, you reach a crossroad and descend right down countless steep steps. At the fork, descend keeping to the left. At the mouth of the Grota da Cruz, the path becomes briefly steep and dangerous. The fishermen's path

Fountain and washing site at the Fonte Grande.

Drinking water is collected in many places along the northern coast near Santo António.

continues exposed descending to the mouth of the stream. On the slope on the opposite side, some of the sections require scrambling until the path becomes more comfortable again. Just after a wooden bridge, you reach a fork from where you initially continue straight ahead at the same level toward the former hydroelectric **power plant** ❸ built in 1908.
The re-ascent starts on a steep path. You have to cross a rushing *levada* to reach the first water galleries of the Nascentes da Rocha de Santo António as well as a waterhouse. Climbing further for 5 mins on steep concrete steps, you reach the next waterhouse. From here, a narrow concrete path continues and takes you to a pump station and the picnic area of **Fonte Grande** ❹ (1.15 hrs).
To the right, a short side path leads down to an old washing site *(lavadeiras)*. The concrete access road Rua Fonte Grande leads you to the village street at the top. Here, continue straight for another 50m past the bus stop before turning left into Rua Caminho Novo. This village street takes you back to the church of **Santo António** ❶ in 20 mins.

São Miguel ↗ 20m | ↘ 40m | 6.5km

19 From Calhetas to São Vicente Ferreira

2.10 hrs

Pleasant coastal walk with bathing opportunity

This easy introductory walk takes you to the northern coast of the island. Starting in the relatively young village of Calhetas, the walk follows the coastline through rugged eroded landscapes to the west. Along the way, you can enjoy stunning views of vast parts of the northern coast reaching beyond the Ribeira Grande. At the end, a refreshing swim awaits at the beautiful natural bathing spot below São Vicente Ferreira.

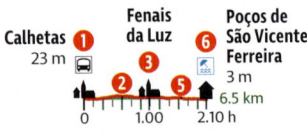

Starting point: Calhetas, church, 23m (bus stop Calhetas/Largo Gonçalo Velho on the main road).
Destination: Poços de São Vicente Ferreira, 3m (bus connection and taxi in the centre of Capelas, otherwise walk back or call a taxi).
Grade: mostly easy, flat dirt trails. In the villages, the walk follows roads.
Refreshment: cafés in Calhetas, Fenais da Luz, and at the bathing spot.
Alternative: end of the walk in Capelas (2.9km, 45 mins): from the bathing spot, continue along the coastal road. After a short distance, there are two more beautiful viewpoints on the right. At the football field, turn right onto Rua do Sertão, and after 10 mins, follow the fork to the right onto Rua de Santana, heading up to Capelas. At the end of the road, turn left into the centre of Capelas (bus connection).
Bathing: natural bathing area Poços de São Vicente Ferreira.

Starting from the church of Nossa Senhora da Boa Viagem in **Calhetas** ❶, follow the coastal road Rua da Boavista towards west passing two small viewpoints in the village. After a good 5 mins, the village road ends and continues as a footpath along a stone wall. After a hotel complex, the path becomes wider following the coastline. After 35 mins, take a right turn onto

Caution: danger of falling at the Buraco de São Pedro.

a gravel path for a detour to the **Buraco de São Pedro** ❷ (information board), which is a sinkhole-like funnel (caution: danger of falling).
Back on the main trail, continue and pass the Ermida de São Pedro. At picnic tables, you reach a street at the village edge, Rua de São Pedro. Continue straight ahead and stay on the seaward side at all junctions. At the Miradouro do Barreiro in the middle of **Fenais da Luz**, turn inland at the wayside shrine and immediately follow the **main road** ❸ to the right (1 hr). After 5 mins, turn right onto the first street (Rua 6 de Junho) and take a left at the waterfront road near the Império. After the picnic tables, follow the **gravel trail** ❹ along the coast. After another 10 mins, you will reach a short asphalt section. 250m further along, leave the track and follow a small **footpath** ❺ which is on the right continuing along the coastline.

The fishermen's path is sometimes a bit rugged and runs just below the lowest houses before it eventually leads to a street. Continue right on this street until you reach the bathing area **Poços de São Vicente Ferreira** ❻.

São Miguel — ↗ 250m | ↘ 250m | 4.1km

20 Pico Queimado

1.45 hrs

Short ascent to a small volcanic crater

The flat centre of the island between Ponta Delgada and Ribeira Grande is dotted with countless small volcanic hills. A short volcanological excursion starts at a picnic place just above Santa Bárbara and goes all the way to the summit of Pico Queimado, which was formed in 1593. On the way, pass an old volcanic vent as well as a viewpoint looking across the vast flat of Ribeira Grande.

```
              Algar do   Pico Queimado
           Pico Queimado  374 m
              282 m        ④
                         ③   ③
    EM 515    ①                 ①   EM 515
    130 m                            130 m
         0    0.50      1.45 h
                      4.1 km
```

Starting point: picnic place at Santa Bárbara at the EM 515, 130m.
Grade: ascent on a small steep footpath, which leads partially along wooden steps. Sure-footedness required. The earthy ground gets muddy in the rain.
Refreshment: nothing en route.
Note: make sure you always shut the wooden gates, even though some of them might be hard to close.

For adventurers: scrambling down into the crater.

On top: the altitude survey point on the Pico Queimado.

Start at the small **picnic place** ❶ near Santa Bárbara and at first follow the road inland. After 5 mins, keep left at the fork and stay on the main trail. After another 5 mins, you get to a **trail board** ❷.
Here, turn left onto the mule track, pass two settler houses and after 200m go through two cattle gates. Now a sunken trail marks the beginning of a steep ascent. Walk through more wooden cattle gates, and after a good 5 mins, you reach a deep crevice and the fenced-in 37-metre-deep cave **Algar do Pico Queimado** ❸ (30 mins).
Behind the cave, you leave the forest and cross a pasture. From the north side of the pasture, the views towards the plane of Ribeira Grande are magnificent. A little further along, the path leads steeply up across some steps and takes you back into the forest. Cross a small wooden bridge which leads you to the last climb of this walk.
Once at the altitude survey point, you have reached the summit of **Pico Queimado** ❹ (50 mins). From here, the path continues for a while before it drops down to the small crater across rocks. The last part requires a bit of scrambling.
Go back the same way to return to the **starting point** ❶.

São Miguel ↗ 230m | ↘ 230m | 7.8km

21 From Caldeiras to the Salto do Cabrito

2.40 hrs

From hot springs to a hidden waterfall

The Ribeira Grande is without a doubt the wildest river on São Miguel. For more than 100 years, the mighty flow has been used to produce hydro-electric power. This excursion takes you to a weir and passes two hydroelectric plants. The climax of this short walk is surely the waterfall Salto do Cabrito, hidden away in the upper reaches. Afterwards, via an exciting iron walkway, cross at a dizzying height above the gorge. At the end of the walk, a hot dip awaits you at the tiny thermal bath in Caldeiras.

Starting point: the central square by the thermal bath in Caldeiras, 261m.
Grade: mostly along good dirt trails. The climb above the waterfall is along secured iron steps that demand an excellent head for heights.
Refreshment: restaurant in Caldeiras and Ribeira Grande (see Alternative). Nothing en route.
Alternative: descent to Ribeira Grande (4.2km, 1.10 hrs): behind the iron gate, turn left on the track and then continue straight on. 35 mins later, pass the motorway. A dusty track heads towards a quarry and descends directly to the centre of Ribeira Grande.
Bathing: thermal bath with a 40 °C-outdoor pool in Caldeiras (limited access). Nature pool at the waterfall.
Note: when last walked, despite the warning sign for gas, this could still be negotiated.

From the thermal pool in **Caldeiras ❶**, descend to the main street and turn left to continue toward Lombadas, passing a rest area with a number of *cozido* cooking sites. 15 mins later, reach a gravel trail and a **green-coloured conduit ❷**. Here, bear left. 100m on, at the water collection sta-

Having fun in the pool at the Salto do Cabrito waterfall.

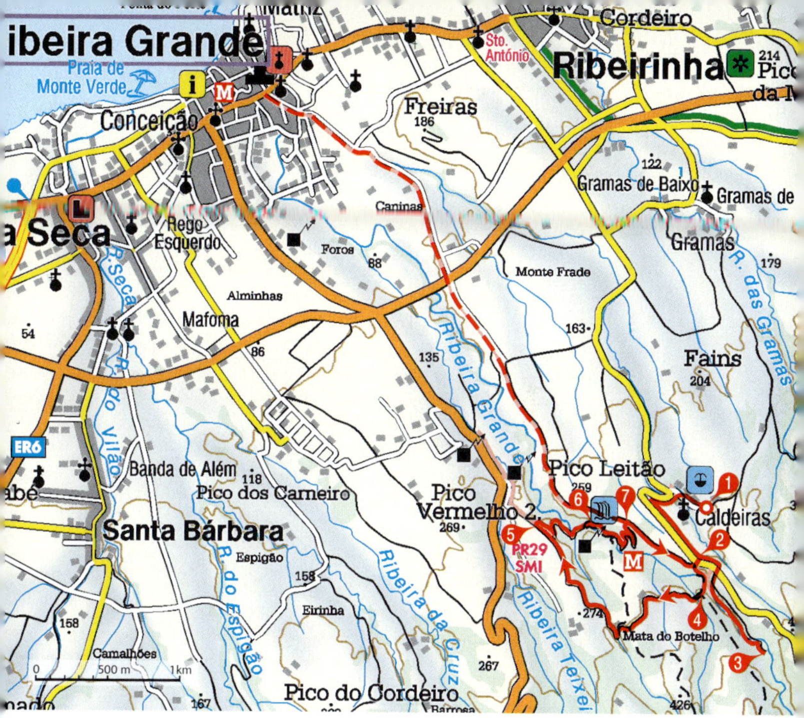

tion and past the floodgate, follow the canal to the right. This is covered most of the way by concrete slabs, leads into a valley and ends at a reservoir. At this point, you have the option to continue along a footpath to the left for a short excursion to the banks of the wild and woolly **Ribeira Grande** ❸. Afterward, head back and return to the green conduit. 10m after the track forks left away from the street, pass under the conduit and follow the track in the direction that has been crossed out and then, past a waterworks (year: 1966) climb down a precipitous slippery footpath which descends to the forest via several wooden steps.

Cross over the Ribeira Grande on an old stone bridge and, past this, continue straight on across the meadow to ascend without a distinct path to the forest's edge. Here, meet another **gravel trail** ❹ and take this to the right to pass a waterworks. Ignore all of the forks that follow.

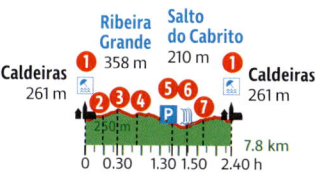

A secured walkway leads through the wild valley of the Ribeira Grande.

20 mins later, pass above a quarry. The trail climbs down again to reach a car park where you will find two large **water reservoirs** ❺. Go right and descend to the valley of the Ribeira Grande on a concrete trail. From here, you can do a short detour to the left (wooden sign) to a mineral water source. Cross a bridge and reach a hydroelectric plant. A footpath skirts around this to the left and continues to the hidden waterfall **Salto do Cabrito** ❻ (1.50 hrs).

Return to the power plant and climb up the steep steps. A pipeline walkway leads to the old power plant of **Fajã do Redondo**. Cross the Ribeira Grande on the walkway and follow the gravel trail behind the power plant all the way to the top. Before you reach the **iron gate** ❼, take the trail on the right into the forest (for the Alternative turn left). You will quickly reach the green pipeline.

Walk along the pipeline until you reach waypoint ❷ where you turn left to return back to the starting point in **Caldeiras** ❶.

↗ 240m | ↘ 240m | 7.8km São Miguel **TOP**
2.30 hrs

Janela do Inferno

22

Walk along old water canals in a wild river valley

A dense network of pipes that once fed the alcohol factory of Lagoa runs through the valley of the Ribeira Seca. Above the picnic area at Remédios, soon follow a farm road along pastures. Behind a tunnel, reach the remote wild river valley with numerous water collection points and several aqueducts. The tour ends at the 'Window of Hell', the Janela do Inferno. On the way back, the views across the Lagoa and Ponta Delgada are significant.

Starting point: Remédios, picnic area at the ER 5, 243m (bus stop Remédios/Centro, 350m away in the village).
Grade: ascent on the road. After that, good dirt trails, broad paths and secured aqueduct bridges; you have to pass through three short tunnels.
Refreshment: snack bar in Remédios, coffee stalls (snack bar) at the start.
Note: torch necessary.

Like a spider's web, a network of old pipelines runs through the river valley.

Start at the small picnic area of **Remédios** ❶ and from the car park, go down the village road on the left (sign: 6.5t). At the bus stop in the centre, turn right and go immediately right again ascending the Rua do Caminho do Mato. At a water reservoir, a footpath continues. After 5 mins, you reach a fork. Continue right on the gravel path, cross the **main road** ❷ and follow the concrete track. After another 15 mins, you reach the lowest point in the road ❸. Turn right onto a dirt trail (no parking sign) and after a good 5 mins, take the first trail descending to the right. After 200m, follow a pasture road on the left that leads to a meadow. Diagonally across at a trough, you can see the entrance to the small 50m-long tunnel **Túnel da Grota** ❹ (50 mins).

Beyond the tunnel, follow a footpath to your left leading up the valley. After 5 mins, leave the main trail at a water house and cross an **aqueduct** with two pipelines to your right. Walk up a few steps and continue up the valley. After 10 mins, continue straight at another aqueduct heading up the valley. Soon, you will reach the 'Window of Hell', the **Janela do Inferno** ❺ (1.15 hrs).

Return to the aqueduct on the same path and cross over to the left side of the valley. Crawl through a small tunnel and walk out of the valley on its eastern side. After a water house, continue straight at a fork. Soon, you cross a stream after which you go through another short tunnel. Immediately behind the tunnel, walk through an aqueduct arch. After about 10 mins, you reach the entrance of another, 70m-long, tunnel, the **Túnel do Pico da Cova** ❻, which you have to crawl through (1.40 hrs).

Ducking down through the tunnel.

Once through the tunnel, stay on the left side of the meadow and continue straight on a footpath which immediately bends to the left. 50m further on, you reach another country lane which you follow to the right. After 75m, the lane turns right. At level with a manhole cover, follow a small footpath on the left leading to a little forest. Many concrete steps and a wooden bridge lead you to a deep river basin. Behind the basin, the path continues right across the pasture and leads across a small aqueduct before it finally merges with a **gravel path** ❼.

Follow the gravel path down to your left. From here you can enjoy a marvelous view across the south coast all the way to Ponta Delgada. This path ends in a **dusty track** ❽. Take a right to get back to the starting point, the picnic area of **Remédios** ❶.

This tour's destination: 'Window of Hell', the Janela do Inferno.

São Miguel

↗ 720m | ↘ 720m | 15.3km

23 From Água d'Alto to the Lagoa do Fogo

5.15 hrs

Wonderful ascent to a picturesque crater lake

This walk is one of the island classics. Crossing a wide watercourse and the upper reaches of the Ribeira da Praia with its countless basins for spring water with very little effort, reach the southern shore of the volcano lake Lagoa do Fogo. On the way back, you pass some old, abandoned hydropower plants. At the finish, a dip is awaiting you at the sandy beach of Água d'Alto.

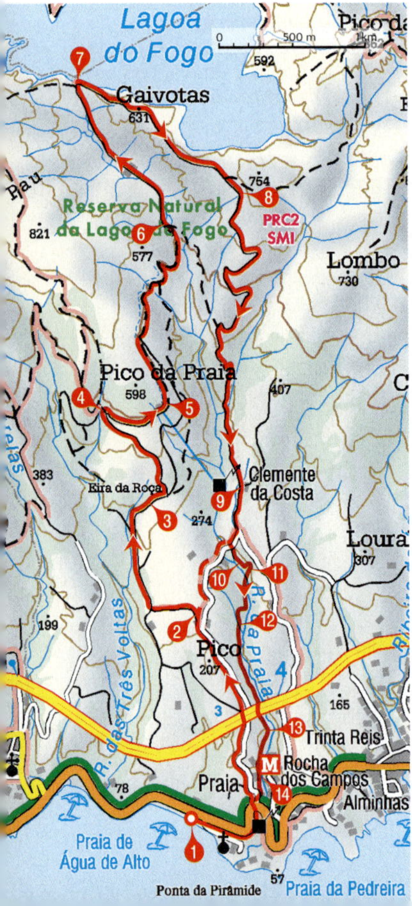

Starting point: sandy beach Praia de Água d'Alto at the hotel Bahia Praia, 15m (bus stop Água d'Alto/Bahia Praia).
Grade: the upper stretch leads only via broad dirt trails. The footpaths along the *levada* are muddy. In the lower part of the Ribeira da Praia, the footpath is slippery and exposed in places.
Refreshment: beach bar at the starting point. Nothing en route.
Notes: the Lagoa do Fogo is surrounded by a vast nature reserve. Any encroachment of the natural landscape as well as leaving your rubbish here is strictly prohibited.
In late spring, flocks of seagulls are nesting and zealously defend their territory against all intruders, including walkers.
Between ❸ and ❺ the trail might change in 2025.
Bathing: sandy beach Praia de Água d'Alto at the starting point.

From the long car park on the EN 1 above the sandy beach **Praia de Água d'Alto** ❶, at first follow the road eastward and then turn left before the broad bridge spanning the Ribeira da Praia onto the concrete-paved Caminho Ribeira da Praia to ascend. The road climbs steeply upward and crosses the motorway. After a total of 40 mins, at a trail board just past two power lines, a **dirt trail** ❷ forks off to the left. If you want, you could also reach this point by car to avoid the ascent. Along the dirt trail, pass a water reservoir on your right-hand side. Now the trail leads into a young forest area. Ignore all forks turning away. At a level area, you will notice ruins in a meadow to the right: the **Fábrica de Espadana** ❸, a remnant of the flax-processing industry, now being used as a stall (1.05 hrs).

Stay on the rough dirt trail which ascends steeply in the upper part, until 20 mins later, you reach the edge of the forest where a flat **trail** ❹ forks off to the right. This leads directly to a **waterworks** ❺ where a conduit begins which provides the means to transport water down to a power plant (1.35 hrs).

Starting here, follow a wide watercourse (*levada*) for 35 mins; some sections are leaky and cause short stretches of muddy walking. Reach the first stone bridge and, soon after, yet another. Now reach a little **water retention basin** ❻. From here, a gravel trail continues pleasantly up the valley. The waters of the upper Ribeira da Praia are collected here in countless water tunnels and then fed into channels to carry the water to hydroelectric plants.

Finally reach the southern shore of the **Lagoa do Fogo** ❼ (2.35 hrs). To the left, a path descends along the lakeshore to a monitoring station. Stay on the gravel road which ascends to the right and, 25 mins later, reach the crowning point of the walk ❽. The roadway descends again in wide hairpin bends. After 40 mins of descent, pass a bridge and, after that, pass the tumble-

Levada in the valley of the Ribeira da Praia.

The southern shore of the Lagoa do Fogo.

Derelict industrial history: the ruins of the Fábrica da Vila.

down industrial ruins of **Clemente da Costa** ❾. Pass the iron gate and reach a concrete road shortly after. Go right until you reach the concrete ford at a water basin. If you started farther up, go straight back to the car.
Follow the water canal to the left until you reach a **reservoir** ❿ (4 hrs). Go left here and after 80m descend down to the valley on a partially steep stepped trail. You will soon reach the ruin of the old hydroelectric plant **Fábrica da Cidade** ⓫. From here, the path largely continues on the right bank of the Ribeira da Praia down the valley. A short steep descent follows. You reach the ruin of the old **Fábrica da Vila** ⓬, walk underneath the flyover of the carriageway and continue to an old conduit, which you reach after a good 5 mins. It's worth taking a short detour to the left that leads to the waterfall **Cascata do Segredo** ⓭. At this point, change to the left side of the stream and continue down the valley to the hamlet of **Trinta Reis** ⓮ (5 hrs). In the centre, go right at the fountain that dates back to 1905. The last building at the end of the village houses a small museum on power plants. Follow the cobbled path down the valley. It soon crosses a stream before it turns into a concrete path and ascends again on the right side of the valley. Here, you will meet the approach trail, where you turn left down to the main road to return to the **Praia de Água d'Alto** ❶.

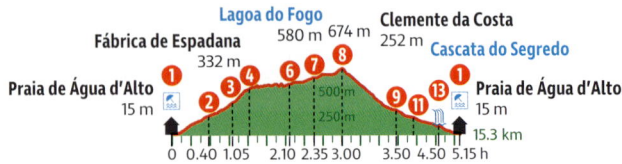

↗ 180m | ↘ 180m | 9.3km   São Miguel

2.40 hrs   **Circular walk along the**   **24**
🚌 ✕ ♨   **Lagoa das Furnas**

Circular walk around the island's most popular site

Furnas is THE thermal bath resort on São Miguel and is a must for every holidaymaker when visiting the Azores. Hot springs and steaming fumaroles give witness to primeval volcanic forces. Directly at the crater lake of Lagoa das Furnas, you will find natural hot mud cauldrons. The ground is so warm that it is used for cooking; afternoons and early evenings, you can take part in this ceremony. After the circular walk around the lake, you will return to Furnas to enjoy a meal of thermal steam-cooked cozido das Furnas in a restaurant (reservations are necessary).

Starting point: the Repsol petrol station west of Furnas, 205m (bus stop Furnas/Largo Marques da Praia 75m south).
Grade: pleasant dirt and gravel trails circle the lake. An easy walk for anyone.
Refreshment: cafés and restaurants in Furnas. Snack bar at the Caldeiras. Café en route at the CMIF.
Alternatives: 1. to the Miradouro do Pico do Ferro and back (a total of 2.3km, 1.20 hrs): at the crossroads before the Caldeiras, ascend the old footpath to the right which, at this point, follows some sort of gully. After 25 mins, you reach the high plateau. Continue left along the edge of the field. Before reaching the viewpoint at the Pico do Ferro, you have to negotiate a short ascent in the forest. Return via the same path.
2. to the waterfall on the Ribeira do Rosal (a total of 3.7km, 1 hr): on the southern side of the lake, a signed trail leads through the park Mata-Jardím José do Canto to reach the Salto do Rosal. The entrance is located opposite the orange-coloured Casa dos Barcos (tickets: € 4) near the chapel. On the way, you pass a gigantic sequoia tree. You have to allow for 1 hr to walk to the waterfall and back again; if you include a visit to the Ermida, the fern valley and the fruit garden, allow 2 hrs.
Bathing: numerous thermal pools in Furnas (Parque Terra Nostra charges a fee, Poça da Dona Beija as well – waiting times are long without pre-booking!).
Note: the Parque da Grená at the Caldeiras is worth visiting (tickets: € 10, plan 2–3 hrs for the whole visit).

Chapel Nossa Senhora das Vitórias.

At the western town limits of **Furnas** ❶ and the Repsol petrol station (decorative tile on the wall of the house), turn right onto the Canada do Ferreiro climbing up to a cluster of houses. Soon, leave the village behind. The road ascends more steeply and then leads over pastureland. 20 mins later, the road hooks sharply to the left ❷.

Here, follow a grassy trail straight ahead, climbing the slope to reach a forest and join an intersecting trail (Alternative 1 to the right). Already, get a whiff of sulphurous fumes then turn left along the steep path (slippery underfoot) to descend to the road. Turn right onto the road and follow the lakeshore to the fumaroles **Caldeiras da Lagoa das Furnas** ❸ (tickets: € 3). Here the ground is steaming throughout the year and the stone surfaces are cozy-warm. Beneath the 'molehills', cooking pots are hidden away and contain the delicious *cozido* which simmers for hours on end. Now continue counterclockwise along the lakeshore. Past the picnic grounds at the **Pinhal das Furnas**, cross over a streambed and then continue along a pleasant track. 20 mins later, reach a bamboo forest. Afterwards, reach a green iron gate, the Quinta das Carpas lies to the right, and a short dis-

Below the 'mole hills' at the Caldeiras, the cozido boils for many hours.

tance further on, the **Quinta d'Água** ❹ follows. The roadway has become cobbled. Pass the CMIF, the centre for environmental research, well worth a visit, and at the same height to the right, 70m off-route, the world's (allegedly) second tallest monkey puzzle tree. Afterwards, reach the park **Mata-Jardím José do Canto** (Alternative 2) and the neo-Gothic **Capela de Nossa Senhora das Vitórias** ❺ with the family tomb of José do Canto (1.35 hrs). On the southern side of the lake, join the EN 1 and follow it to the left until, 1km on, the first road to the Miradouro do Pico do Milho branches away. Turn right here ❻. The road soon hooks off to the left. At the fork following just afterwards, turn left again. After a short ascent, reach the **Miradouro do Pico do Milho** ❼ (2.15 hrs).

From here, an extremely steep concrete trail descends to Furnas. At the first houses, turn left and then immediately turn right onto the Rua Água Quente. A few mins later, at a fountain, a concrete trail ascends to the left to the modernized bathing area **Poça da Dona Beija** ❽, also known as Paradise Pool. On the street, continue steadily straight ahead to return to the **starting point** ❶.

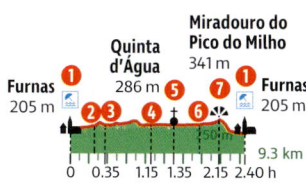

São Miguel ↗ 420m | ↘ 420m | 7.7km

25 From Ribeira Quente to Povoação

2.40 hrs

Along old connecting paths in the county of Povoação

A varied and strenuous coastal walking trail leads from Ribeira Quente towards the county seat Povoação. It used to be an important route to reach the fields for cultivation in the Agrião area, however, most of the fields are no longer cultivated and overgrown or fenced off as private land. In Lomba do Cavaleiro, you will come across settlements again. From here, the trail continues through the outskirts all the way down to Povoação.

Starting point: Ribeira Quente, harbour, 2m (bus stop Ribeira Quente/Porto 150m west).
Destination: Povoação, harbour, 4m (bus stop Povoação/Terminal along the river, 100m inland).
Grade: the ascent from Ribeira Quente follows old connecting paths that can be slippery when wet and require surefootedness.
Refreshment: cafés and restaurants in Ribeira Quente and Povoação. Nothing en route.
Alternative: circular walk back to Ribeira Quente (6.3km, 2 hrs): keep left on the gravel path ❷ above the second iron gate. After 150m, stay on the main trail to the right and continue steadily uphill. After 40 mins, walk through an iron gate to reach the main road. Follow it to the left, and then, after the bus stop in the hairpin bend, take the forest path downhill to the left. After 15 mins, the path reaches a pasture and bends to the right. Continue straight and follow the country lane. After 10 mins, before a wire-mesh gate, leave the main trail and descend left on the old footpath through the river valley. The rocky path is somewhat eroded in places, and several river crossings are necessary on this walk. After descending for 30 mins, pass under a large aqueduct bridge. From here, follow the now well-maintained trail heading out of the valley, always staying on the left side of the stream until reaching the starting point by the sea.
Bathing: sandy beach and pool in Povoação.
Linking tip: Walk 26.

Chapel Santa Rita near Ribeira Quente.

At the harbour in **Ribeira Quente** ❶, turn towards east and cross the river via the first bridge. The narrow concrete trail bends to the right behind a café and ends below two holiday homes. From here, continue on the footpath along the coast. You will soon pass the Santa Rita chapel and then, behind it, a viewpoint and a detached house on the Ponta do Garajau. Right behind the house, a track starts which is partially paved and leads steeply uphill again.

Finally, a green iron gate blocks the way ahead (30 mins).

Turn right and cross the wooden bridge. In an overgrown gully, the cracked footpath now leads uphill to another iron gate. From here, continue straight for another 15m until you reach a wide **gravel path** ❷. If you opt for the Alternative, go left.

However, your forest path continues straight ahead, ascending a little further before winding down into the deep valley of a stream whose rushing sound can be heard from far away. The final section descends in switchbacks. The **Ribeira do Agrião** ❸ can be crossed by stepping on the rocks. The ascending path on the opposite slope climbs through a landslide area and is secured with simple wooden railings. After a short but steep ascent, you will reach the first houses of **Agrião** ❹ and then a dusty track, which you now follow – somewhat arduously and steeply – straight on until you reach the **EN 1** ❺ (1.50 hrs).

Continue to the right and reach the village of **Lomba do Cavaleiro** ❻ after 10 mins. Just before you reach the viewpoint, turn right onto the first concrete road and descend through the settlement. Where the path bends left after 250m, continue straight ahead on the narrow concrete path in front of house no. 55. The path continues downhill as a small footpath before it rejoins the main road which you follow to the right. Just after the left curve, at the driveway to house no. 5e, turn right and follow a sloping small footpath through the grass. This leads directly to the sports grounds. Below them, you meet the main road again and follow it to the right until you reach **Povoação**. Just before the bridge over the Ribeira dos Pelames at the village entrance, descend steeply to the right, cross the mouth of the stream and continue left along the shore.

If the path is too steep for you, stay on the road and take the first turn to the right. Walking along the beach, reach the bathing spot and continue from there to the **harbour** ❼.

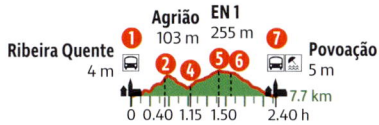

São Miguel ↗ 460m | ↘ 460m | 7.2km

26 From Faial da Terra to the Pico dos Bodes

2.50 hrs

Exhausting ascent to one of the best viewpoints in the south-east of the island

This walk mainly follows old connecting paths which earlier generations developed before roads were constructed. From Faial da Terra, the trail first ascends to the nearly 500-m-high Pico dos Bodes with its futuristic observation tower. Along the way, you pass an old whalers' lookout. Throughout the walk, there are plenty of opportunities to enjoy the magnificent views of the coastline. On the way back, you can take an alternative route through Sanguinho to visit the Salto do Prego waterfall. Those who prefer can descend directly from the summit to Povoação.

Starting point: Faial da Terra, Ponte da Praça bridge in the centre, 8m (bus stop Faial da Terra/Ponte).
Grade: mostly on old footpaths, partly through forest. Caution: the old paved sections can be slippery when wet! The ascent should not be underestimated.
Refreshment: snack bar and cafés in Faial da Terra. Nothing en route.
Alternatives: 1. end of the route in Povoação (2.7km, 1.10 hrs): at Pico dos Bodes, descend pathless westward across the meadow toward Povoação. At the bottom, you reach the start of a forest path. After 5 mins on this steep and sloping path, it joins a country lane which you follow to the right. After 50m, it turns into an old connecting path that winds gently downhill to two radio masts. Below them, you reach a road which you follow downhill to the left. This leads you directly to the lower bridge in Povoação (the final stretch is very steep!).
2. detour via Sanguinho to the Salto do Prego (4.1km, 2 hrs): at the junction ❺, turn left and follow the footpath which is steep again at the beginning. After about 10 mins, you reach an old cobbled path which you follow to the right. After a good 5 mins, it merges with a wide, newly paved path. Following it to the left, you reach Sanguinho.

Beyond the last ruins, the access road bends left at a power pylon with a transformer. Here, at the curve, take the footpath to the right. The trail continues along this only path, constantly going up and down, crossing a stream and a wooden bridge. Shortly after the bridge, the path splits into two. Taking the left path uphill, you reach a clearing and, after just under 10 mins, another fork. Here, descend to the right to the Salto do Prego waterfall. After visiting the waterfall, return to the penultimate fork above the wooden bridge and continue left down into the valley. At the bottom, you cross a stream and follow the trail leading out of the valley. Along the way, you pass an old mill canal and historic watermills before reaching a road. Continue straight ahead to the upper Ponte do Outeiro bridge. From here, follow the left side of the stream walking out of the valley and back to the starting point.
Bathing: bathing spot and pool at the Faial da Terra harbour. Sandy beach and pool in Povoação (Alternative 1). Natural pool at the waterfall (Alternative 2).
Linking tip: Walks 25 and 27.
Note: in 2024, the section between ❷ and ❺ was not in the best condition, but possible to walk on.

From the Pico dos Bodes you can look across the wide valley of Povoação.

The walk starts in **Faial da Terra** ❶ at the middle bridge, the Ponte da Praça, and on the west side heads inland past the twin fountain (1874). After 200m, you reach the village park from where you follow the narrow, paved Rua do Calço to the left of the transformer house. It soon continues as an old mule track with well-preserved cobblestones in some places. Once you reach the road, follow it uphill to the left. Just after the next right-hand bend, the old cobbled path resumes on the left, ascending via wooden steps. After 5 mins, leave the main trail and turn left at a fork,

Now just a reminder of past times: the old whaling lookout post above Faial da Terra.

crossing a concrete water channel. Continue along this footpath, cross a country lane and reach an old **whaling lookout post** ❷ (45 mins).
Beyond the lookout, the path bends inland and ascends in a wide loop along the edge of a field until it reaches the road. Follow the road to the left, and after 5 mins, turn left at a junction and, just 15m later, take the old hollow path to the right, leading uphill. In some places, the path runs through a deeply cut trench. Continue straight on this path for 20 mins until you reach a **stable** ❸. Just before the stable, the path turns right and meets the road again after another 10 mins which you follow uphill to the right. After 200m, take the road on the left that leads up to the summit of **Pico dos Bodes** ❹ (junction for Alternative 1) with its observation tower (1.40 hrs).
Then return to the lower road. Diagonally opposite, a narrow footpath leads downhill (often overgrown). At the road below, walk 80m to the left, then take the country lane to the right, which soon narrows into a footpath. It descends gently along forest and pastureland into the valley. Some sections of the old cobblestone paving are still intact. After 35 mins from the road, a **footpath** ❺ branches off to the left (Alternative 2 via Sanguinho). However, your path continues straight ahead and, after a few switchbacks, reaches the upper houses of **Faial da Terra**. At the **road** ❻, turn right. At the Ponta do Outeiro bridge, cross over to the left side of the stream. Beyond it on the east side, follow Rua Nova to go back to the starting point in the centre of **Faial da Terra** ❶.

↗ 775m | ↘ 775m | 14.8km São Miguel

From Faial da Terra to Água Retorta — 27

5.20 hrs

Untamed river landscape and two secluded waterfalls

At the start, this walk takes you far away from civilisation and through a wild natural landscape. In the valley of Faial da Terra, not easy to reach, you will follow a stream to two hidden waterfalls. Finally, passing through the local recreation area of Água Retorta, return to the southern coast. At the very end, an ancient trail through a forest returns to the starting point.

Starting point: the bridge Ponte da Praça in the centre of Faial da Terra, 8m (bus stop Faial da Terra/Ponte).
Grade: the ascent to the EN 1 and the final descent on a narrow forest footpath (slippery when wet). Return route sometimes on a secondary road. Due to the total distance and height differences, the walk is not to be underestimated.
Refreshment: snack bar and cafés in Faial da Terra. Nothing en route.
Alternative: a short walk from the waterfall back to Faial da Terra (1.1km, 30 mins from the main route): from the fork above the Salto do Prego, go back 10 mins along the approach route and then, at the next fork ❸, bear left to descend into the Ribeira do Faial da Terra valley. Sections of the ancient cobblestone trail are still preserved. Soon cross over a streambed and, some mins later, a second streambed. At the end, pass the old millstream and a few watermills before you meet up again with the approach route.
Note: the ascent crosses over numerous watercourses and dense forests; especially in the winter months from January until April, the route can become impassable after stormy weather.
Bathing: in the natural pool at the lower waterfall; bathing area east of the harbour in Faial da Terra.
Linking tip: Walk 26.

View back to Faial da Terra on the way to Sanguinho.

In **Faial da Terra** ❶, start from the middle bridge of Ponte da Praça in front of the Faialense snack bar and go inland on the Rua Nova on the eastern shore past the pavilion. At the upper bridge Ponte do Outeiro, change to the other side of the stream. From the bus stop, continue along the river on the Rua do Burguete. Just before the village border and at a fountain (house no. 55), turn left to ascend an ancient cobblestone trail that quickly gains height via zigzags and leads directly to the hamlet **Sanguinho** ❷ which was turned into a holiday village in the recent past (35 mins). Passing the restored houses, a number of ruins follow and then, at a power pylon with a transformer, an access road hooks off to the left.

In the bend, follow a footpath that leads to the right through a hedge and then passes a grove of fruit trees. Now enter a forest. From this time on, follow this only path: it leads in steady up-and-down walking, crossing over a stream and a wooden bridge. Past the bridge, soon reach a fork ❸ (later on, the Alternative descends straight on from here). Turn left to continue, reach a clearing and, not quite 10 mins later, again come to a fork. Here, turn right at first to climb down to the waterfall **Salto do Prego** ❹, lying deep below at the streambed which has formed a large basin (1.05 hrs). Along the trail climbing back up again, take a little detour to the right above the waterfall to get a peek at the basin from above.

Afterwards, ascend again to the fork in the trail (for the Alternative, turn left here to go back). At an old watering trough, a trodden path climbs up steeply for some mins but the trail will soon level out again to lead across numerous streambeds that are all easy to cross via wooden bridges. Past the third bridge, the forest thins for a short time as you walk below a pasture. However, enter a wood again immediately after and then cross over some more bridges and tributary streams.

The waterfall, Salto do Prego, lies hidden in the wood.

After a total of 2 hrs, the path leads right into a streambed and climbs down to the waterfall **Salto do Cagarrão** ❺; to reach it, you must scramble down the last few metres.

Returning to the main trail, continue the ascent and finally cross over an ancient stone bridge to reach a tumbledown **watermill** ❻ (2.25 hrs). Continue to the right of the ruins. 20m on, at the fork, bear left to follow the old mill canal further up. The trail soon becomes rougher going up and down. Small tributaries have to be crossed several times. After 2.50 hrs of walking, join the main road **EN 1** ❼. Turn right and continue for another 15 mins to reach the **Parque Florestal de Água Retorta** ❽, a local recreational area. Another 10 mins later, the EN 1 hooks to the left.

From the two gravel trails leading straight ahead, take the right-hand one to continue. At the fork 5 mins further on, bear left and descend along the road. Farther down in the **hollow** ❾, continue straight on.

Along the road, 1.15 hrs after meeting the EN 1, a view opens up into the valley of Faial da Terra and then you reach the **edge of a wood** ❿. About 100m farther along at a stone block, a descending trail which is also used by mountain bikers, leads left down into the forest. The old pavement is well preserved in places while the path is precipitous in some sections. 45 mins later, cross over the main road and descend along a flight of concrete steps. Cross the bridge, turn left and continue to the starting point in the centre of **Faial da Terra** ❶.

São Miguel

↗ 330m | ↘ 330m | 4.8km
1.45 hrs

28 Around Água Retorta

Reconnaissance walk along old mule tracks in the remote east

This circular walk takes you around one of the most remote villages on the island. Major highlights are not to be expected in the village with a population of 500 people. The entire lower valley is characterised by many wine and vegetable fields. After rainy days, you will be surprised to see a high waterfall along the way. Those who have enough energy can make a detour to Fajã do Calhau, a completely isolated weekend settlement.

Starting point: Água Retorta, church, 272m (bus stop Água Retorta/Ramal da Igreja 250m north at the junction).
Grade: old footpaths and a partly steep path down to the coast. The final stretch to the waterfall is on a very sloping trail. In the village area, the route follows the road. Sure-footedness and sturdy footwear required.
Refreshment: bar in Água Retorta.
Alternative: detour to Fajã do Calhau (5.9km, 2.15 hrs): at the concrete road above Lomba das Fagundas, continue right. After about 10 mins, the road descends along the steep slope in a rather adventurous manner and ends at the first house of Fajã do Calhau. From here, you can continue along a dirt trail for another 15 mins wandering through the remote settlement. The path ends at a pebble beach. Return on the same strenuous path.
Note: the first section to Lomba das Fagundas is not always in the best condition and is often overgrown. If needed, take the road down from the church into the hamlet, where you will rejoin the main route at the entrance.

Start at the large square of the **Nossa Senhora da Penha de França church** ❶ which is located a little on the outskirts of the village, pass the cemetery and walk up the paved Caminho Rural do Pico. After 250m, turn left onto a grassy path, partly paved with old cobblestones, which is easy to miss. After 10 mins, you reach a **gravel track** ❷ and descend left to the concrete road (Alternative to the right). Following the road downhill, you will reach the first houses of **Lomba das Fagundas** ❸. Keep to the right and continue along the village road also keeping right. The road ends at the last house and initially continues as a grassy path before it turns into a

A steep stepped trail goes down to the rocky coastline of the Ribeira do Estreito.

sloping trail with hairpin bends. After descending the trail, partially across steep steps, you will finally reach a **junction** ❹. A short but exposed detour to the right leads down to the sea via steep steps. From here, walking 100m left along the pebble beach, you will reach a 20m-high **waterfall** which is only visible on days with or after heavy rainfall (50 mins). Without proper rain, the effort isn't worthwhile!

Back at the junction, continue along the main trail. Cross the Ribeira do Estreito stream above the waterfall and, on the opposite side, climb up the many steep steps which are quite strenuous. After 15 mins, you reach a country lane, which a little higher up turns into a concrete path and then, as you approach the first houses of **Água Retorta** ❺, it becomes an asphalt road. Go straight through the village. After the hairpin bend in the valley, the road splits. Here, at the bus stop, turn right uphill and walk back to the starting point at the church, **Nossa Senhora da Penha de França** ❶.

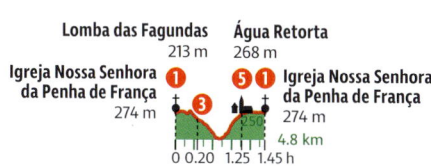

29 Fajã do Araújo

São Miguel — ↗ 230m | ↘ 230m | 4.0km — 1.40 hrs

One of the most remote summer settlements on the island

If you are looking for peace and quiet, the summer settlement of Fajã do Araújo is definitely the right place. Before the new road down to the sea was built, it was one of the most isolated settlements on the island. From Pedreira, you can reach the sea quickly on a comfortable footpath. The lower section runs along the cliff and is secured by a railing. If you want to go for a swim, you can continue along the shore to the Praia do Lombo Godo, a sandy beach which varies in size depending on nature's whims.

Starting point: Pedreira, church, 205m (bus stop Lomba da Pedreira 500m away on the EN 1).
Grade: pleasant descent on a comfortable footpath. The final section is secured with railings. The Alternative runs mostly along the sea over large stones. This section requires a high level of sure-footedness.
Refreshment: café in Pedreira. Nothing en route.
Bathing: sandy beach Praia do Lombo Gordo (Alternative).

Alternative: detour to Praia do Lombo Gordo (1.7km, 1 hr): in Fajã do Araújo, cross the bridge over the Ribeira da Tosquiada. After the bridge, traces of a path continue below the cliffside (risk of falling rocks). The path soon becomes rough with conditions changing after every winter storm. The walk continues over coarse rocks directly along the sea. After a somewhat strenuous 30 mins, you reach the sandy beach of Praia do Lombo Gordo. Return via the same route.

The summer cottages of Fajã do Araújo are nestled at the foot of the cliff.

An adventurous path along the rocky cliff leads down to Fajã do Araújo.

Start at the Nossa Senhora da Luz church in **Pedreira** ❶ and from the car park next to it, follow the Rua das Machadas southwards. After 150m, a concrete footpath continues straight ahead at a fountain. After just 5 mins, the view opens up already revealing your destination. The concrete path starts off descending steeply in switchbacks before it continues down in a wide curve along the valley. After 15 mins of descent, cross a **stream** ❷ in a deeply cut gorge. Beyond the stream, the path narrows and runs mostly along the hillside, secured with railings.

After a total of 35 mins, you reach the first houses. Continue on the main trail until you get to a car park at the end of the access road. Just beyond, the old footpath continues to the left. More houses follow, stretching down all the way to the mouth of the Ribeira da Tosquiada (the Alternative continues along the sea). Here, in **Fajã do Araújo** ❸, you have also reached the end of the descent.

Return the same way, heading back up to the church in **Pedreira** ❶.

São Miguel ↗ 260m | ↘ 260m | 5.7km

30 From Lomba da Fazenda to the Ribeira do Guilherme

2.00 hrs

A short circular walk in the secluded north-east of the island

Daily life in São Miguel's remote north-east is still quiet and unhurried. Many excursionists like to stop over here in the county of Nordeste only to stay for the day. This trail passes the botanical gardens of Lomba da Fazenda which features many endemic species, and continues to the delta of Ribeira do Guilherme, where many old watermills can be found when climbing up the valley. The final stage of the return route leads past an idyllically-situated campsite.

Starting point: the church in Lomba da Fazenda, 145m (bus stop Lomba da Fazenda/Restaurante Cardoso 50m to the west).
Grade: a mishmash of dirt trails and footpaths.
Refreshment: cafés and a restaurant in Lomba da Fazenda. Nothing en route.
Bathing: seawater pool Piscina da Boca da Ribeira.

Along the coastal trail to the Parque de Endémicas do Pelado.

Opposite the Igreja de Nossa Senhora da Conceição in **Lomba da Fazenda** ❶, walk down the stairs past the pavilion. At the small chapel, immediately go right and turn left again at the next intersecting path. Now pass the cemetery and continue over pastureland. A good 10 mins later, where the street hooks sharply to the right at an old cul-de-sac, continue straight ahead along a footpath at the upper edge of the meadow towards the coast and reach a fork. Here on the left, a stepped trail leads down to the former, now-abandoned harbour. Back at the junction, follow a cobbled path to the right to reach the viewpoint with a sheltered picnic spot in the **Parque de Endémicas do Pelado** ❷ (30 mins). All of the flora here is provided with carefully written explanatory stone plaques. A second viewpoint follows immediately after; to the right of the overlook, a footpath leads into a valley notch. At the end, reach a meadow. At the right-hand edge of the meadow, continue by ascending until meeting up with a country lane. Now follow the lane for some mins until reaching a junction located at a white watering trough. Turn left here but after only another 10m, turn right onto a footpath which continues along the edge of the field. Now an extremely zigzagged descent begins to the mouth of the Ribeira do Guilherme. Once below, reach the swimming pool **Piscina da Boca da Ribeira** ❸ (1.05 hrs). To the right, cross over the bridge to reach the access road and ascend steeply along this road to reach the top again. Pass a viewpoint to get to a cul-de-sac. Continue straight ahead to climb down again (sign: Moinhos de Água). Before the car park at the **campsite** ❹ of Nordeste, by some tumbledown watermills, turn right onto a footpath and cross over the long bridge spanning the Ribeira do Guilherme (1.30 hrs). On the other side, a street to the right ascends. The street climbs up steadily straight ahead until reaching the main road EN 1. Turn right onto the EN 1 to return to the starting point in **Lomba da Fazenda** ❶.

Piscina da Boca da Ribeira.

São Miguel · ↗ 640m | ↘ 640m | 7.7km | 3.00 hrs

31 Pico da Vara

A demanding ascent to the island's highest mountain

During this walk, you reach the island's highest summit at 1103m and pass through a truly unique nature reserve. Above Santo António, an old trade route takes you directly to the Tronqueira mountain range, which is rarely without cloud cover. This ascent route currently is the only officially approved walking trail to Pico da Vara. You need a permit to walk this route!

Starting point: Casa da Guarda Florestal above Santo António, 465m. Access via Santo António de Nordestinho: at the westernmost end of Santo António (Eira Velha district), take the village road uphill opposite the Miradouro da Borda da Ladeira (sign: Pico da Vara). After 50m, keep right, then immediately turn right again, and as soon as you reach the car park, turn left. The road soon becomes a rough gravel track. After crossing the highway bridge, stay on the middle track at the fork. Follow this track uphill for another 1.8km to the new visitor centre (was not open in 2024).

Grade: the ascent to Pico da Vara follows a slippery trail which can also be boggy when wet. The upper section is often damp. Walking boots with ankle support are recommended. This walk requires good physical fitness and sure-footedness. Do not attempt this walk in fog!

Refreshment: nothing en route.

Note: the area around Pico da Vara is a protected nature reserve. For this walk, you need a permit from the environmental agency. Apply online at: servicos-sraa.azores.gov.pt/doit/mdls/fill.asp?id_modelo=1451.

From Pico da Vara, the view extends across the Planalto dos Graminhais to the Fogo massif.

From the new visitor centre, the **Casa da Guarda Florestal** ❶, follow the gravel track uphill past the hikers' information board. After 150m, at a water reservoir, ascend the steep right-hand path. Passing through a cleared area, continue along the main trail. After 15 mins, you reach another clearing. Just after a forest path branches off to the right, leave the main trail and follow an old **footpath** ❷ which ascends to the right.

For a long time, the trail, which is sometimes steep, climbs up along a densely forested ridge lined with tall Japanese cedars. The ground is often very damp requiring sturdy footwear. After a total of 1.25 hrs, the forest starts to thin. The path narrows into a well-trodden trail, which now largely follows wooden walkways.

Eventually, you reach a high mountain path which you initially follow to the left. As quickly as after the next right-hand bend, you will finally reach the grassy summit of **Pico da Vara** ❸ from where you can enjoy a wide view in all directions.

Return along the same route to the **visitor centre** ❶.

At the time of writing, all other walking trails in the highlands were officially closed.

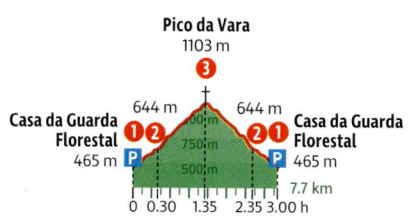

32 From Achadinha to the Ribeira dos Caldeirões

São Miguel ↗ 225m | ↘ 225m | 4.5km
1.45 hrs

Walking across hills and valleys and through a romantic stream

An old pilgrimage path leads from the church in Achadinha into the valley of the Ribeira dos Caldeirões. Keeping your feet dry when crossing the stream without a bridge is the greatest challenge of this walk. After the crossing, you pass some old, dilapidated water mills. Through dense forest, the trail climbs back up to the Lomba d'El Rei ridge and, past a spring with a washhouse, returns to the village.

Starting point: Achadinha, church, 148m (bus stop Achadinha 600m south, above on the EN 1).
Grade: along the coast and through the forested valley on a comfortable footpath, which leads partly across some wooden steps.
Refreshment: bars and restaurants in Achadinha. Nothing en route.
Bathing: refreshing dip in the Ribeira dos Caldeirões.
Linking tip: Walk 33.
Note: the trail was not well-maintained in 2024, however, it was passable.

A pleasant refreshment: old fountain in the Ribeira dos Caldeirões valley.

Pass the Igreja de Nossa Senhora do Rósario in **Achadinha** ❶ to the left and then follow the steep, concrete Caminho do Concelho leading into a steep valley notch. Just after the stream crossing, turn left onto the wide grassy path leading down the valley. After 5 mins, wooden steps lead steeply up the slope to the right for a short stretch. The path flattens and crosses a field. Once the path curves inland again, leave the main trail and, at a point which is easy to miss, follow the wooden steps to the left leading down to the valley. Here, cross the wild **Ribeira dos Caldeirões** ❷, barefoot if necessary (40 mins).

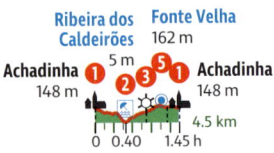

On the paved road, pass a picnic area and then head uphill again. Where the road turns left, continue straight ahead on the dirt trail, heading further into the valley. Below the high bridge of the highway, you reach the ruins of the old

Moinhos do Januário ❸ at the Ribeira dos Caldeirões. Here, go half right passing underneath the two bridge pillars and climb up the concrete steps. In the forest, a footpath continues under the cypress trees. The path first leads through the mill canal, and after 75m, it crosses the stream via a wooden bridge. From here, the path ascends again, and you reach the ridge of Lomba d'El Rei via countless wooden steps. At the edge of the forest, continue along a grassy trail to a road. Continue on the road to the right and cross the bridge over the **highway** ❹ (1.25 hrs).

After 5 mins (large eucalyptus tree on the left), leave the road to the left onto a grassy trail. It leads down to a concrete bridge and a washhouse at the **Fonte Velha** ❺. The footpath continues back towards Achadinha. After 5 mins, you reach a junction. Turn right here and continue straight down through **Achadinha** until you reach the **starting point** ❶. Below the car park, you will find a pretty picnic area.

Difficult to cross without getting your feet wet: the Ribeira dos Caldeirões.

São Miguel ↗ 350m | ↘ 350m | 7.3km

33 Alminhas de Achadinha

2.40 hrs

Historical monuments and abandoned traditions

This walk starts in one of the oldest communities in the north. It follows the old connection path along the northern coast, leads through two picturesque valleys and passes old memorials (alminhas), a blue lagoon as well as derelict water mills. A side trip takes you to the bottom of a waterfall. On the way back, pass the spot where the liberal troops of Terceira – under the command of Conde de Vila Flor – rushed to the island to support it in its resistance in 1831.

Starting point: Achadinha, church, 148m (bus stop Achadinha 600m south, up at the EN 1).
Grade: steep wooden steps at the Riberia do Cachaço, otherwise easy and safe footpaths, in the village on roads.
Refreshment: bars and restaurant in Achadinha. Nothing en route.
Bathing: blue lagoon (Poço Azul) and a small sandy beach (Zona Balnear da Foz das Coelhas).
Linking tip: Walk 32.

Rarely quiet: the Poço Azul is a popular bathing spot in the summer.

From the Igreja Nossa Senhora do Rosário in **Achadinha** ❶, pass the pavilion on the right and follow the Rua Direita through Achadinha to the west. After 15 mins, you reach the small Jardim Público (public garden) at the EN 1. In front of the **memorial stone** ❷ (Padrão Histórico 1956/1957), turn right. The road immediately turns into a gravel track which leads into the deep valley of the Ribeira do Cachaço which you cross via a wooden bridge.

After 5 mins, you leave the main trail at a **fork** ❸ and ascend to the left. On top, you meet a country lane. Go left and once you reach a road, turn right. After 70m, turn left and follow the second grassy trail uphill. Cross the road again

Salto da Farinha.

and walk down the narrow concrete path until you reach an **iron gate** ❹. Immediately after the gate just before the bridge, take the footpath on your right down the valley. After 15 mins, you reach a white building in a picnic area. From here, you can take a short trip to the 40m-high waterfall Salto da Farinha. Back at the picnic area, from the building follow the path leading down to the **sea** ❺ to the bathing spot Zona Balnear da Salga which also has a pool (1.20 hrs).

From here, go back to the **fork** ❸ in the Ribeira do Cachaço valley and follow the trail down the valley towards the coast. After 50m, a short path on the right leads down to the hidden blue lagoon, the **Poço Azul** ❻ (2 hrs). Afterwards, return the short distance and continue walking out of the valley. At the first fork, after a few mins, keep right and descend again in a zigzag pattern following the steps down to the stream. Behind the wooden bridge, continue left along a water canal with numerous rocky springs flowing into it. The canal ends at a concrete road. Follow the concrete road which ascends steeply to the **Miradouro do Pesqueiro** ❼ and continue up to the village. Turn left at the transverse road to get back to the starting point in **Achadinha** ❶.

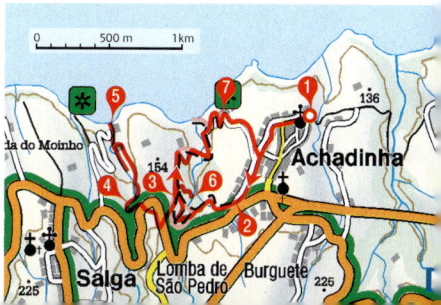

TOP 34 — São Miguel
From Fenais da Ajuda to the Ribeira da Salga

↗ 350m | ↘ 350m | 8.5km
2.45 hrs

Detour to an imposing headland and many waterfalls

A few ruins remain as a sole reminder of the old, tiny harbour from Fenais da Ajuda, where only a few divers are on the hunt for fish these days. A pleasant ramble descends to a remote rest area and to the seaside. You return along a fishermen's path and through two wild river valleys with mill ruins and natural pools in a wide loop.

Starting point: the church in Fenais da Ajuda, 150m (bus stop Fenais da Ajuda/Junta de Freguesia, 300m up towards the EN 1).
Grade: a hodge-podge of dirt trails and footpaths. At the harbour, a short stretch is steep and slippery underfoot.
Refreshment: café in Lomba de Baixo.
Bathing: nature pools at the Ribeira da Salga.

From the square at the Igreja de Nossa Senhora da Ajuda in **Fenais da Ajuda** ❶, follow the road downhill eastwards and, after 150m, turn left at the fork with a watering trough. This side road leads to a **picnic area** ❷ (15 mins) from where you initially continue left. The road soon turns into a dirt trail which slowly winds its way down to the headland where you reach the two magnificent viewpoints **Miradouro do José Furtado** and **Miradouro da Vera Cruz** ❸ more or less next to each other. After you've enjoyed the views, return to the **picnic area** ❷ (40 mins).
Turn left here and follow a steep concrete road down to the old **harbour** ❹. Above the eroded rock with the hole at the dam, climb up the slope via wooden steps and continue on an easy grassy path inland which eventually takes you up to a field. Keep to the right edge along the reeds until you meet a gravel path at the top. Follow it left to continue to the **Miradouro da Rocha** ❺ (1.10 hrs). The final stretch is paved again.
A steep concrete path continues down to the bay. 40m after the concrete ford at the first hairpin bend, a path that can be easily missed disappears into the undergrowth on the right (if you follow the concrete path down, you will reach the Cascata do Homem waterfall at the Ribeira da Salga).

Lighthouse at the Miradouro da Vera Cruz.   *Cascata do Teófilo.*

The old fishermen's path climbs steeply at first, with some stone steps along the ridge, then levels out before descending as a serpentine path lined with wooden railings and numerous steps to the ruins of the **Moinho do Félix** ❻. Wooden stairs on the left lead further down to the Cascata do Teófilo waterfall.

From the ruins, the trail continues uphill along the right side of the stream underneath Japanese cedars. After 5 mins, a side path leads down to the Cascata da Gruta waterfall. Back on the main trail, you soon reach the turn-off to the Poço da Truta natural pool with its cascade. From the turn-off, a stepped trail leads uphill and eventually meets the main road above a rock spring. Continue right here and, after 150m, at the junction at the village entrance to **Lomba de Baixo** ❼, turn right again (2.05 hrs).

Continue on the main trail straight through the village. At the end of the village, the road ascends behind the church and merges with a **cross-road** ❽. Turn left here (Rua Forno da Telha) and then right just before you reach a picnic area. Follow the dirt trail downhill into the Ribeira do Mato da Cruz valley, crossing it via a wooden bridge, the **Ponte das Ladeiras** ❾. The trail which used to be the main connecting route now ascends back to **Fenais da Ajuda** in 5 mins. After you reach the stop sign, turn right twice before you head straight downhill back to the **starting point** ❶.

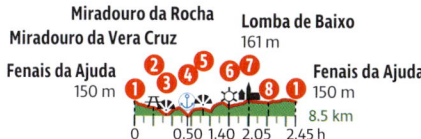

São Miguel ↗ 260m | ↘ 260m | 3.8km

35 Moinhos da Ribeira Funda

1.40 hrs

Visiting the dilapidated mills at the north coast

The highlights of this short circular route on the north coast are the two dilapidated old mill ensembles and the deep river valley with several cascades. The way back follows a steep fishermen's path with countless wooden steps.

Starting point: Ribeira Funda, bus stop and turn-off on the EN 1, 245m. Car park further down at the chapel.
Grade: mainly on good dirt trails and footpaths. The ascent along wooden steps is steep and slightly exposed.
Refreshment: café in Ribeira Funda. Nothing en route.
Bathing: small blue lagoon at the Moinhos do Crim.
Linking tip: Walk 36.

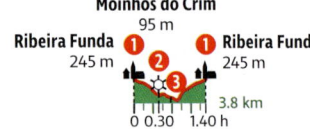

From the bus stop in **Ribeira Funda** ❶ next to a café at the EN 1, walk down the Rua Direita past the Império and the Igreja de Nossa Senhora da Aflição (hikers' car park) to reach the village. At a cul-de-sac, the road turns into a dirt track. 75m behind the power line, turn left at a watering trough and follow traces of a path below a row of reed. Finally, the path turns right and zigzags down the valley to some old water mills, the **Moinhos do Crim** ❷ which you can explore by walking

Moinhos do Crim at the Ribeira Funda.

Hiking trail along old water mills in the Ribeira Funda valley.

on a small circular path going clockwise. At the picturesque stream **Ribeira Funda**, the detour ends in a blue lagoon (30 mins).
Above the uppermost of the three ruins, walk half way up to the left down the valley until you reach another **group of mills** after about 15 mins. Shortly after, you reach a fork ❸. Keep on the right side of the stream. If you go left, you will see a connecting path towards Maia. At the coast, the path climbs steeply up the hill over countless wooden and rock steps at the Rocha do Padre do Norte (1.10 hrs). The view reaches from the north coast all the way to the Ponta do Cintrão.
After the arduous 20-min climb, you reach a **double trough** ❹. Behind the trough, follow a dirt track up to the village and return to the starting point in **Ribeira Funda** ❶.

36 From Lomba da Maia to Maia

↗ 280m | ↘ 500m | 6.5km
2.30 hrs

Follow old fishermen's paths to the hidden beaches on the north coast

A remote sandy beach on the north coast, rows of old decaying water mills and a delightful coastal path await you on this walk. From Lomba da Maia, follow the fishermen's path to the sandy beach of Praia da Viola. Pass abandoned water mills and walk along the coast to finish the walk in the fishing village of Maia.

Starting point: Lomba da Maia, church, 251m (bus stop Lomba da Maia/Igreja).
Destination: Maia, church, 28m (bus stop Maia/Canto de Santo António on the main road 200m south-west).
Grade: the main part of this walk is on good dirt trails and footpaths.
Refreshment: cafés and restaurants in Lomba da Maia and Maia. Nothing en route.
Alternative: circular walk with return route to Lomba da Maia (2.5km, 50 mins from the turn-off from the main trail): at the intersecting path above the water mills, turn left and pass a stream. About 70m beyond the stream, leave the main trail and follow a grassy trail to the right that ascends in between stone walls.

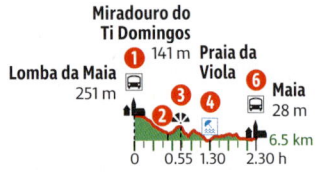

The trail soon widens and quickly ascends on hairpin bends. Walk past a few gardens until you reach the first house. From here, follow the steadily ascending country lane. At the main road EN 1 continue left and return to the starting point
Bathing: sandy beach Praia da Viola and in Maia.
Linking tip: Walks 35 and 37.

The sandy beach of Praia da Viola is hardly ever crowded.

From the Igreja de Nossa Senhora do Rosário in **Lomba da Maia** ❶, walk along the main road for 10 mins to the north-east. At the end of the village, leave the road at the beginning of a stone wall (grey iron gate) to your left and continue on a footpath. Via steps, follow the path to the left into the forest, which continues down and out of the valley. After 10 mins, continue straight on the main trail (if you are sure-footed, you can take the very steep parallel path on the right that leads down to the Três Bicas waterfall). 30 mins later, the descending path ends at the coast at a **crossroads** ❷ (the right path leads towards Ribeira Funda). On this coastal path ascend left up the hill, pass the Miradouro da Eira and reach a roadway after 15 mins. Turn right for the **Miradouro do Ti Domingos** ❸ (55 mins).

At the toilets of the picnic area, a grassy trail leads down to the right into the deep valley of Ribeira do Preto. Once at the bottom, bear left at the fork and cross a wooden bridge. Beyond the bridge, climb up the stepped trail to reach a concrete road. Turn right and continue into the next valley until you reach the cul-de-sac at the car park. From here, a footpath continues across the Ribeira do Salto that goes down to the sandy beach of **Praia da Viola** ❹ along a row of restored water mills (1.30 hrs). In the middle of the sandy beach, there is another row of old mills leading up the hill. At a prominent rock, where a second stream disappears in the sand, an old stepped trail zigzags up the hill past the ruins where it meets a crossroads (for Alternative, go left).

Follow the footpath to the right and immediately pass another group of mills. You will soon reach a concrete bridge. 150m after an old stone arch bridge, turn right at a **picnic hut** ❺ and follow a steep, secured stepped trail that leads past the rocky spring of Fonte Santa down to the coast. Walking directly along the coast, you pass another spring pool. Then you have already reached the harbour. From here, walk up to the road and take the second intersecting road on your left until you reach the church in **Maia** ❻.

São Miguel ↗ 320m | ↘ 320m | 6.5km

37 Around Maia

2.15 hrs

Remote pastures and a wild coast – a walk with colourful impressions

This circular walk takes you almost on a figure-of-eight route around Maia and is split into two sections. Above Maia, the trail goes mainly along farmland and vegetable fields. The second part is largely flat and follows long stretches along the coast. On the way, you pass several different bathing spots. And if you have some time to spare, there's also a chance to learn about regional tobacco cultivation at a local museum.

Starting point: Maia, Largo de Santo António in the centre, 38m (bus stop Maia/Canto de Santo António).
Grade: strenuous ascent along an old connecting path. Easy walking along the coast. Roads within the village.
Refreshment: cafés and restaurants in Maia.
Bathing: beach Calhau da Areia and Zona Balnear do Frade in Maia.
Linking tip: Walk 36.

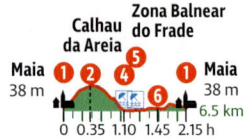

Start at the Largo de Santo António on the main road in the centre of **Maia** ❶ and walk up the narrow concrete alleyway between house no. 2 and no. 4, which soon becomes an old cart track. At the water house (1959), turn right and cross the stone arch bridge, continuing uphill along the footpath (Caminho de Lajinha). After passing two ancient stone arch bridges, you will reach a fork after about 30 mins. Just before a wide wooden bridge, turn left and follow the footpath which is separated by wooden slats. At the top, you reach a **road** ❷ where you turn left. After 5 mins, a country lane crosses your path. 50m further on, turn left again and walk down a set of steps leading towards the coast.

Here you pass through pastureland again, some of which is fenced in by a dilapidated wooden fence. After 10 mins, the actual descent to Maia begins which leads past a num-

Descent to Maia.

Along the coast, the layered lava formations are clearly visible.

ber of gardens. At the **Fonte Velha** drinking fountain ❸, you will meet the road again and turn left downhill at the bridge (1.05 hrs).
Turn right once you reach the first street which leads above the harbour and the bathing bay of **Calhau da Areia** ❹. Here, turn left into the 3a Travessa da Rua Santa Catarina. After 200m, take the third street on the right (Rua Almirante Gago Coutinho). Once you are at the coast, reach the Melo Nunes viewpoint and continue left to the natural bathing area of **Zona Balnear do Frade** ❺.
From here, follow the promenade to the right until it ends at a picnic spot with a hut. Just beyond it, a well-maintained coastal path continues across the Ribeira da Cruz. After 10 mins, a **wooden staircase trail** ❻ branches off to the right (1.45 hrs). This short detour leads to another quiet, secluded natural bathing area and crosses the layered rock formations of an old lava flow.
Afterwards, continue along the main trail which now heads inland and eventually rejoins the road. Turn left and cross the bridge. Just ahead on the left is the Tobacco Museum. Follow the road straight ahead to return to the starting point in the centre of **Maia** ❶.

São Miguel ↗ 180 m | ↘ 180m | 3.3km

38 Chá Gorreana

1.15 hrs

An excursion through Europe's only tea-growing area

The only tea-growing area in Europe is found on São Miguel and the tea factory that belongs to it is the starting point for this short excursion through the sprawling plantations. After you had a chance to look at the organic farming, you also have the opportunity to taste some tea and visit the little operation – tea shopping included.

Starting point: tea factory Chá Gorreana, 212m (bus stop Gorreana on the main road).
Grade: an easy walk along good dirt trails and grassy ones.
Refreshment: café/bar in the tea factory. Nothing en route.
Alternative: detour to the waterfall Salto da Cidreira (1.7km there and back, 35 mins): halfway between the tea factory and the main road at the trail board, go left up through the tea plantations to a painted building. Go left past a water reservoir. After 50m, turn right and follow the narrow water canal. Once you are under the big stone arch bridge, walk through the riverbed and cross underneath the main road. On the land side, walk up the steps and follow the footpath through an opening in the wall at the road. Pass an old water mill and turn right and walk along the old mill canal. You reach the waterfall after 175m.

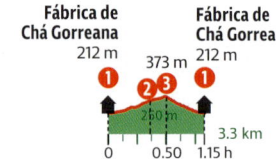

The tea factory Chá Gorreana has become a tourist hotspot on the island.

The sprawling tea plantations above Gorreana.

From the tea factory **Chá Gorreana** ❶, walk to the main road. On the other side of the road behind the barbed wire fence at the edge of the tea plantation, follow traces of a path to the left. After 150m, the path turns into a gravel trail which you follow to the right. At the next fork after 5 mins, stay on the left main trail and walk gradually uphill. After a good 15 mins, the roadway bends sharply to the right just ahead of an iron gate ❷. After a total of 50 mins, you pass a small cedar **forest** ❸.

Immediately after the forest, walk downhill along a slatted wooden fence at the edge of the forest. The fence ends after 150m at a pasture, which you cross in a straight line for about 50m. Beyond the pasture, walk along the path that leads you back down through more tea plantations.

From here, stay always on the marked main trail and return to the **starting point** ❶.

São Miguel ↗ 360m | ↘ 360m | 5.4km

39 Porto Formoso – Ladeira da Velha

2.00 hrs

Detour to secluded dilapidated mineral baths

A dream beach and an old dilapidated mineral bath at the wide Baía de Santa Iría are the highlights of this short walk. At the very beginning, pass a small waterfall at the Ribeira do Limbo. Footpaths and farm roads finally lead to the old, hot mineral springs of Ladeira da Velha which are situated directly at the coast. On the way back, pass several beautiful scenic viewpoints.

Starting point: Porto Formoso, lowest bridge in the quarter of Moinhos, 20m.
Grade: mostly good footpaths and dirt trails. Descent down to the bay partly very steep and slippery. Sure-footedness required. Partly earthy ground, slippery when wet.
Refreshment: snack bar and restaurant in Moinhos. Nothing en route.
Bathing: sandy beach Praia dos Moinhos.
Alternative: adventurous shortcut to the Miradouro do Furado (1km, 30 mins): on the way back up from ❹, turn left at the ruins of the bathhouse. Just behind it, somewhat hidden, a footpath continues. Pass through the bamboo grove, Garden of Soul. The path continues beneath a tall rock wall into a cove, then up countless wooden steps to pasture land and the wooden viewpoint, Miradouro do Furado. From here, continue straight ahead on the main route.
Note: this alternative was closed in 2024 due to rock fall and is only passable at your own risk. It is still uncertain when it will reopen.

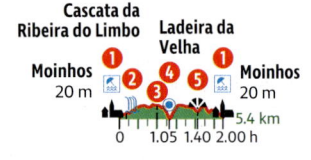

This circular walk starts at the lowest point of the road in the quarter of **Moinhos** ❶. From here, follow a small concrete path opposite a trail board next to house no. 35. The concrete path immediately turns into a footpath and leads up the valley along an old mill canal. At the first picnic table, stay on the middle main path. It leads through a deep valley to a hidden waterfall, the **Cascata da Ribeira do Limbo** ❷.
On the other side of the water basin, continue down the valley. At the same height as a well (Água Férrea das Pachecas), the trail immediately climbs steeply upwards across steps. Once you leave the forest, continue to walk along the wooden railings at the edge of the pasture.

The old thermal pool of Ladeira de Velha is directly by the sea.

At a stable, follow a dirt track to your left (25 mins). After 5 mins, go down to the right at the intersecting path. Beyond a concrete ford, the trail soon narrows into a footpath. From here, cross two more streams and several cattle barriers before you reach a **road** ❸.

On the other side, a footpath continues up the hill. It is very steep in parts and partially leads along countless wooden steps down to the coast. In the lower part, you come past the ruins of an old bathing hut. The path ends at the coast at the tiny thermal pool of **Ladeira da Velha** ❹ (1.05 hrs).

Return to the **road** ❸, go down a good 100m to the left and then take the left of the two dirt trails leading to the coast. The trail ends at the lower end of a meadow at a wooden gate. At first, a short detour on the left to the **Miradouro do Furado** ❺ with its wooden observation tower is well worth the effort of walking the extra distance.

Afterwards, go back and continue to follow the footpath along the wooden railings to the Miradouro dos Ilhéus. Descend across wooden steps to the **Miradouro da Ladeira da Velha** ❻ above the bathing bay. The footpath finally meets a road. Go left and walk back down to the starting point in **Moinhos** ❶.

Pico – the whalers' island

- population: 13,900
- county seats: Madalena, 2900 inhabitants; Lajes, 1700; São Roque, 1300
- area: 445km²
- length: 46km, width: 16km
- coastline: 147km
- highest points: Pico, 2351m; Topo, 1007m

Pico is the Ilha Montanha, the 'mountainous island'. There is hardly another island on the Azores that is as rough and, with over 100 volcanoes, as high in volcanic activity as this one. Portugal's highest mountain, also called Pico, reigns over the island. The mountain's flanks plunge steeply down to the seashore. The second largest island of the archipelago, Pico offers incomparable contrast. The deep-blue of the ocean waters butt up against the raven-black volcanic rock at the shoreline. Above the coastal road, there is a dense belt of greenery and in the highlands, crater lakes seem to pop up out of nowhere. Pico even wears a white cap in winter and thereby bestows upon the Azores snow, most unusual to the islands. For a very long time, Pico was the whalers' island; today, the gigantic mammals have become friends to the men who once hunted them and tourists ride the waves for whale-watching – an adventure that you should not miss!

Jácome de Bruges discovered Pico in 1450 but the island would not be settled until a decade later. When Father Pedro Gigante landed here, he brought viniculture to the island. A century later, São Roque was established on the northern shore and Madalena on the western. In the mid-16th century and many more times in the 18th century, Pico became volcanically active. Lava flowed right down to the ocean and many inhabitants emigrated. Viniculture boomed in the 18th century; barrels of wine were

When Pico 'wears a cap', bad weather is almost sure to come.

shipped to Horta and exported from there to America and Russia. In the mid-19th century, vineyards were decimated, at first by mildew and later by the phylloxera vine pest – the economy collapsed. A wave of emigration began. Other islanders tried their luck in the flourishing whaling trade which soon became the most important economic pillar and remained so until 1984, when the last whale-processing plant closed. Since 2004, vineyards in the north and west island have enjoyed protected status under the UNESCO World Heritage programme.

The county seat **Madalena** lies far to the west. The village centre is small and simple for orientation. Year-round, ferries from the neighbouring Horta dock frequently in the new harbour every day. Tuna fishing boats have their ports here. The way to the centre leads past the tiny old fishing harbour and the central church Matriz de Santa Maria Madalena. Somewhat outside of the centre, in the district of Carmo, an ancient Carmelite monastery houses the viniculture museum – another attraction. The winegrower's cooperative is to the south in Areia Larga.

Just about as modest is the second county seat **São Roque**. The settlement is better known for its harbour district Cais do Pico since this is more important locally; all of the large supply ships anchor here and, until 1984, whales were brought here to be processed. In the meantime, the old whale-processing plant has been converted to an industrial museum and definitely merits a visit. Aside from the ancient Franciscan monastery São Pedro de Alcântara, the church Matriz de São Roque counts as one of the few sites worth seeing.

PICO

Getting there
From Lisbon, SATA operates several flights to Pico per week. Within the Azores, there are daily flights from Pico to Terceira and São Miguel. The airport is located on the northern coast between Madalena and São Roque. The two ferry harbours for the island are in Madalena and in São Roque (Cais do Pico). Ferry service to Faial is provided year-round, many times every day. There are year-round connections to São Jorge, but limited during the winter. In the summer months, a ferry service to Graciosa and Terceira also operates several times a week.

Bathing
Natural bathing areas in Pocinho, São Mateus, São João, Calheta de Nesquim, Ponta da Ilha, Ribeirinha, Prainha do Norte and Santo António. Pools in Madalena, São Roque and Santa Cruz das Ribeiras. Other bathing areas in the countless little harbours. Small sandy beach at Prainha do Norte.

Festivities
Holy Spirit Celebrations from Whitsun until summer. Festa de Santa Maria Madalena (Madalena), end of July. Cais de Agosto in São Roque, end of July. Festa do Senhor Bom Jesus Milagroso (São Mateus), August 6. Semana dos Baleeiros (Lajes), end of August. Festa das Vindimas in Madalena, mid of September.

Medical services
Clinic in Lajes, tel +351 292 679 400, Madalena, tel +351 292 628 800, and São Roque, tel +351 292 648 070.

Tourist information
Turismo do Pico in Madalena in the centre, tel +351 292 623 524, pt.pic@azores.gov.pt; also in Lajes and São Roque; cm-madalena.pt, cm-lajesdopico.pt, cm-saoroquedopico.pt.

Cultural activities
Museu dos Baleeiros and Centro de Artes e de Ciências do Mar in the old whale-processing plant in Lajes. Museu da Indústria Baleeira in São Roque. Casa de Artesanato from the school for arts and crafts as well as a private oceanographic museum in Santo Amaro. Museu do Vinho in Carmo near Madalena. Grape-growers cooperative in Areia Larga. Moinho do Frade windmill near Criação Velha. Lava tunnel Gruta das Torres above Criação Velha (in the summer, it is necessary to book several days in advance)! Visitor centre about wine cultivation and Casa dos Vulcões in Lajido.

Public transport
Two bus connections during the week along the north and south coast from Piedade to Madalena. Other busses from Lajes and São Roque to Madalena. As the distances are great, it is best to hire a car. Taxis are available in Lajes, Madalena and São Roque.

Accommodation
There are hotels near Lajes and in and around Madalena. There are also some apartment complexes and many holiday homes, mostly built of natural stone and scattered throughout the island. A youth hostel in São Roque. Lovely campsite in Santo António, two others Lajes and Madalena.

The third county seat is **Lajes** in the south – an old whalers' village and the island's centre for whaling backed by decades of tradition. Times have changed but the whale still takes the spotlight. Today, you can ride over the ocean waves on a fibreglass motorboat from Lajes; harpoons have been traded for cameras. The church Matriz da Santíssima Trindade towers over the roofs of the fishing village. Also worth seeing are the whaling museum and the information centre in the former whale-processing plant located somewhat outside of the village borders. Just next to it is the restored bastion Santa Catarina. On the main street, the monastery São Francisco reigns over the village. Somewhat eastward of Lajes and below the coast road is the whale-spotters' lookout Vigía da Queimada which is still manned during the day.

Pico art: Sorrisos de Pedra.

Pico is only settled on the coast despite the fact that in many places the shoreline drops steeply to the ocean. All of the settlements lie along the coast road and the highlands are still unspoiled. The western island around Criação Velha and the northern coast between Bandeiras and São Roque are old grape-growing areas which have been declared UNESCO World Heritage Sites since 2004. The majority of the grapes is now cmmercially used to produce pricey wines. The little hamlets on the northern coast with houses builft of raven-black natural stone, typical for the island, are only inhabited in summer and autumn for the coming grape harvest. The airport is also located here; it was expanded in 2005 and can now provide landing for larger aircraft as well.

A good hour of driving time separates Madalena in the west from Piedade and the prominently-perched lighthouse in Manhenha on the eastern tip of the island. At the halfway point, pass the harbour town São Roque and the coastal town Santo Amaro, known for its handicrafts. Perched on the eastern island, the dizzying viewpoint, Terra Alta. Returning along the southern coast, at the halfway point, pass the old whaling village Lajes with its new harbour breakwater. Enjoy a picnic in the local recreational areas São João, Quinta das Rosas, Prainha and Santa Luzia. Pico Mountain dominates the western highlands. The eastern island ridge with the high plateau Planalto da Achada is marked by a long chain of volcanic cones. From the west to the east, pass by the crater lakes Capitão, Caiado, Paul and Peixinho to name a few. These are, however, often hidden by dense cloudcover and fog. Above Criação Velha, another attraction lies hidden away from the light of day: the lava tunnel Gruta das Torres belongs to the list of the world's twenty longest and is also the longest on the Azores. The tunnel is open for a limited stretch to tourists on foot.

TOP 40 — Zona do Verdelho

Pico ↗ 140m | ↘ 190m | 10.4km
3.00 hrs

Walk through the vineyards of the delicious Pico wine

Vineyards can be found all around the Pico, however, nowhere else does the cultivation seem to be as rewarding as on the west coast, where the yellow-golden Verdelho grows – a jewel of the island, which is definitely worth its steep price. The people of many generations have arduously built stonewalls to protect the vine, which was – very rightly so – classified as a UNESCO World Heritage Site in 2004. This walk will give you a good idea of how difficult it is to grow vine on the island.

Starting point: Candelária, church, 73m (bus stop Candelária/Igreja).
Destination: Criação Velha, church square Largo 20 de Novembro, 25m (bus stop Criação Velha/Casa do Povo 75m south).
Grade: leisurely walk on gravel trails, partially on side roads. In windy conditions, it can get rather uncomfortable due to the sand that whirls up from the ground and the salty sea spray.
Refreshment: cafés in Candelária and Criação Velha. Nothing en route.
Bathing: at Calhau harbour at the small sandy bay in Pocinho or in the natural pools of Laja das Rosas.

Opposite the church in **Candelária** ❶, follow the Caminho do Poço down to the sea to the few *adegas* of **Ana Clara** ❷. The path bends to the right after a tide well (beyond the tide well, the first trail on the left leads to the picnic area Zona de Lazer dos Fogos).

Now go straight on and stay on the main path (Caminho dos Fogos) which soon turns into a gravel trail that leads through numerous vineyards. After 5 mins, keep left on the main trail, which soon veers off toward the coast. From here follow the **track** ❸ on your right (35 mins). After just under 20 mins, you reach several natural stone steps going down on your left (watch out, they are easy to miss). Take these steps and follow the path to the deserted ruin village of **Mingato** ❹ (1 hr). 10 mins later, the track merges with

The restored windmill Moinho do Frade lies in the heart of the wine-growing area.

a road. Go left down to the **Porto do Calhau** ❺. Now follow the coastal road to the right and after 15 mins, you reach **Pocinho** ❻ (1.30 hrs) with a small bathing bay and a picnic area.

The Caminho do Pocinho leads you back up the hill where you go left at the first road (stop sign). Once on top, you meet a crossroad, where you descend to the left. On the north side of the Monte hill, the road forks after 5 mins ❼. Here, ascend to the right and follow the dirt trail. After 10 mins, you get to a junction with a road coming from your right. Take the dirt trail on your left and follow it all the way to the coast (2.15 hrs).

At an **adega** ❽, return to the coastal road and keep right (if you went left, you would reach the natural pool Laja das Rosas after 5 mins). After 250m, go right to join the second gravel trail. After 5 mins, follow the first dirt trail on your left for about 70m, then turn right into a narrow access trail that meanders through the vineyards.

Take a left at the **track** ❾ on top of the hill. Once you reach the first houses, the track turns into a tarmac road. After about 100m, you may want to take a detour on the left to the windmill **Moinho do Frade** ❿. Afterwards, go back to the road and first turn left and then right again at the main road. After 200m, you have reached the church and the centre of **Criação Velha** ⓫.

41 From the Furna de Frei Matias to Madalena

Pico — ↗ 0m | ↘ 660m | 10.1km — 3.00 hrs

Descent through lush vegetation from the foot of Pico to the capital

After a short excursion in the lava tunnel Furna de Frei Matias, walk towards Madalena while enjoying a view of the neighbouring island of Faial. On the way, take a break in the delightfully-landscaped local recreational area of Quinta das Rosas.

Starting point: ER 3 at km9.5, the country lane to the Furna de Frei Matias, 667m.
Destination: Madalena, church, 10m (bus stop at the ferry terminal).
Grade: easy descent along pleasant dirt trails; tarmac at the end.
Refreshment: cafés, bars and restaurants in Madalena. Nothing en route.
Note: remember to bring a torch!
Bathing: a seawater swimming pool and a natural bathing area in Madalena offer a great opportunity for a swim.

At km9.5 on the **ER 3** ❶ coming from Madalena and at a left-hand bend in the road, turn right onto a country lane (a power line crosses the route). The lane heads toward two hills and passes an iron gate 100m on. Opposite a cattle trough and to the right below the right-hand hill, look for a couple of steps. Here, at a stone wall, you can find the upper entrance to the cave **Furna de Frei Matias** ❷. A second entrance, much easier to use, can be found 40m further on toward Madalena.

The Furna de Frei Matias is an old, dried-up lava tunnel.

Return again to the road, turn left and at a junction a good 10 mins later, turn right onto a **dirt track** ❸. 15 mins later, cross over the **ER 3** ❹ and continue on a gravel trail for another 15 mins to reach a **crossroad** ❺. Turn right for a few metres to find the continuation of the track on the other side of the road. You reach a forest area and pass some old orchards before you finally pass two small houses that are next to each other after just under half an hour. Shortly afterwards, you will see a newish house of undressed stone to your left. 50m further on, go right at the **crossing** ❻ and continue to the road junction. Go left and follow the wide **ER 3** ❼ down, only to leave it again 100m further on by turning right onto a dirt trail at the cattle-loading area. Along the western side of the Cabeço Grande, the trail now follows stone walls. 10 mins later, at the next turn-off but one, turn right on the north side of a small hill. The trail soon starts to descend steeply before it ends at the **Quinta das Rosas** ❽, a pretty little local recreational area with many exotic plants (2 hrs).

Take the road to the left to continue until, not quite 10 mins later, a **gravel trail** ❾ turns off to the left following stone walls. The trail hooks immediately off to the right and leads past a heap of volcanic stones that have been stacked a few metres high. After 15 mins of walking, the trail ends at a stop sign for a **road** ❿.

Turn right on the road to continue to the next stop sign 400m further on. Turn right again here and then 50m on, turn left onto the Rua Sec. Teles Bettencourt. Now continue straight ahead to reach the centre of **Madalena** ⓫.

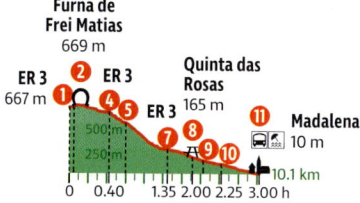

TOP 42 Pico ↗ 1140m | ↘ 1140m | 7.8km
6.00 hrs

Montanha do Pico, 2351m

The Azores' royal route

No other walk on the Azores is as strenuous as the ascent to Pico – Portugal's highest mountain. As a reward and an incentive, a breathtaking 360° view is awaiting you here. Indeed, the route is by no means a real rock-climbing adventure, however, the mountain has claimed several victims in recent years due to overconfidence and carelessness.

Starting point: the trail head for the Pico ascent is at the Casa da Montanha, at level with the Cabeço das Cabras, 1225m.
Grade: very demanding high mountain hike over bare rock without a distinct trail. The final ascent to Piquinho requires easy scrambling and the use of your hands. A good sense of direction and absolute sure-footedness are definitely required as well as the proper hiking gear. Only to be undertaken when the weather is good and stable!
Refreshment: café/bar at the start.
Note: for the ascent, you must register at the Casa da Montanha and sign out again when you return. The ascent is only permitted after you are given a GPS rescue device and after you have paid a fee (€ 15–25)! In summer, the office is open 24 hrs while from October to the end of April, it is only open during daytime hours. The number of people allowed to be on the mountain at the same time is limited to 160. Reservations possible on montanhapico.azores.gov.pt (long waiting times possible in summer – sometimes you need to book more than 14 days in advance!).

Directly at the **Casa da Montanha** ❶, the base camp of the Mountain Rescue Station at the foot of Pico, and after registering, begin the ascent route. The trail starts off through an eroded gully with a stony underground and low-growing scrub. After 25 mins reach the old **volcanic cone** ❷ that has been enclosed by a wall of loosely stacked stones. The ascent continues to the right and leads, at first clearly, towards a rocky ridge. The increasingly more difficult path is lost in the multitude of tread marks which, starting at **post no. 7** ❸, begin to lead in chaotic zigzags winding up the mountain. Time and again, you must climb up knee-high steps or continue directly

Above the clouds: the crater peak with the Piquinho.

over bare rock. At post no. 17, reach a little flat area to catch a breath. At about 1900m above sea level, the vegetation thins out noticeably and at about 2100m, only simple flora can be seen (2.05 hrs). Starting at **post no. 35** ❹, the trail, which is initially flatter and straight, continues to the right. At post no. 36, turn left at the fork. The final ascent begins at the **crater's rim** ❺, which drops inward and vertically down. At post no. 46, you have reached the top (2.45 hrs).

If you are absolutely sure-footed and feel drawn to a bit of scrambling, from here, descend into the crater. The ascent of Pico's little cone, Piquinho, situated in the main crater of Pico, is negotiated from the southern side. Above post no. 47, continue by climbing up a steep furrow, scrambling with the active use of hands to finally reach the summit of **Piquinho** ❻ (3.05 hrs). The easiest descent is to return along the approach route. Two alternative routes climb down along the northern side. A path keeps to the right over the northern slope heading straight toward Sao Roque. The second path runs directly to the left heading for the monitoring station on the crater floor. Both paths are extremely dangerous since scree and loose stones are continuously slipping underfoot! If you wish to explore the floor of the crater, you should especially watch out for the northern side. The rock wall is a sheer drop.

Return to the crater's rim and, in any case, the descent to **Casa da Montanha** ❶ follows the approach route.

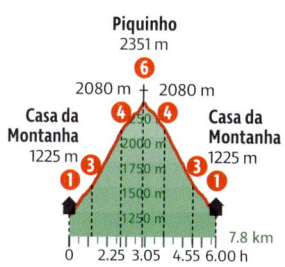

Pico ↗ 350m | ↘ 350m | 16.3km

43 Circling Santa Luzia

5.00 hrs

Circular walk in the vineyards on the rugged northern coast

During this walk, you will learn more about the conditions for cultivating the Pico grape on the northern coast as well as in the interior. Especially in autumn, the hustle and bustle of wine production reigns here. On this tour, much blessed with diversity, you will pass a number of hamlets with bathing spots as well as a viniculture museum with an adega and a distillery.

Starting point: Santa Luzia, church, 124m (bus stop Santa Luzia/Igreja).
Grade: pleasant walk, usually along gravel or tarmac trails. Some stretches follow ancient cart tracks. On the coast, slippery scree underfoot.
Refreshment: café Montanha in Santa Luzia. Summer bars in Arcos and Lajido.
Alternative: shorter walk leaving out of Lajido (partial stretch 975m, 15 mins; time saved compared to the main route 80 mins): at the wayside shrine above Arcos, follow the gravel trail straight on to continue ascending, heading directly for the Pico. 15 mins later, turn left onto the ER 1 to return to the starting point.
Bathing: seawater swimming pools in Cabrito, Arcos and Lajido.

Behind the church in **Santa Luzia** ❶, turn right onto the Rua da Outeiro. At the cemetery, the street becomes a gravel trail and forks 200m further on. If you prefer a shorter walk, pass to the left of the **stone built house, no. 7** ❷, following the gravel trail to the right. However, follow the main

Around Lajido, the walk follows an old ox cart path.

route by continuing the climb up, heading directly toward Pico. At the fork not quite 10 mins later, bear left and 200m past this point, at the end of the vehicle tracks, turn left onto an ancient cobblestone trail which ascends. A good 5 mins later, a narrow **mule track** ❸, leading on the level, turns off to the left. This soon narrows even more to become an overgrown footpath, following ancient stone walls and finally ends at a cart track (40 mins).

This leads left to continue and descends to **tumbledown houses** ❹. On the right-hand side, reach a tarmac road and turn right onto this to ascend. In the next right-hand bend, a good 5 mins later, turn left onto the **dirt trail** ❺. The trail forks again immediately; bear left at this point. Finally, reach the first houses of **Santana** and a street which you follow straight on. After 10 mins along the **village street** ❻, shortly after passing a transformer station, descend to the left and return to the ER 1 (1.35 hrs).

Natural arches at Cabrito.

On the other side of the road, continue to descend toward the sea. Where the road hooks left, continue straight ahead onto a **cart track** ❼, hardly discernible at the outset, which shortly after also hooks left above the coast and then ends at a cul-de-sac and some *adegas*. Passing to the right of a house with a red door and stone table, the old coastal path continues along the edge of the cliff (do not follow the roadway). You will soon reach an impassable **broken-away section** ❽. Skirt around this through a breach in the natural stone wall to the left along a trodden path. 120m on, take the cart track along the coast to reach **Cabrito** ❾ (2.10 hrs).

From the wayside shrine, a concrete trail leads to a little seawater swimming pool. From this point, continue without a distinct trail along the coast, crossing over the rugged lava flows (signposts), always keeping a safe distance from the overhanging edge of the cliffs. After you have passed two stone arches, follow the old wall, marking the borderline (traces of wheel tracks) until reaching the **Ermida de São Mateus** ❿.

Turn right onto the road to continue, passing a radio beacon for the airport. Now reach the next settlement of **Arcos**; across from the chapel, you could turn right to descend to the natural swimming area (2.55 hrs).

Past the tide-powered well, in the village centre, follow the **Rua dos Arcos** ⓫ landwards and when it ends at a roadside shrine, turn right onto the **Rua do Lajido de Baixo** ⓬ (the Alternative continues straight on). After 100m, continue half left on the gravel trail. Where it bends left, go straight and continue on the cart track. Follow the deep oxcart ruts on the old track that runs parallel to the road for about 20 mins until it ends at the village entrance. Continue left here and after 50m go immediately right again to join the continuation of the old cart track. 50m further along the road, there is an old **kiln** ⓭.

At the end of the cart track, turn left at the coastal road to reach the village centre of **Lajido** ⓮ boasting an information centre on viticulture with distillery as well as the museum of volcanology (3.50 hrs). After your visit, at first take the street back 200m towards Arcos and then turn right onto the Rua do Lajido de Baixo. 150m on, a tarmac trail forks off to the right (sign: dead end). This heads straight as an arrow toward Pico and soon becomes a gravel trail which narrows into an ancient cart track just a little later, ascending along tumbledown stone walls. Back on a road (Rua da Eira), turn left to climb up to the **ER 1** ⓯ and turn left to return to the starting point in **Santa Luzia** ❶.

↗ 160m | ↘ 160m | 3.6km   Pico

1.15 hrs
Loop around São Roque do Pico — 44

Along the old watermills of São Roque

This circular walk above São Roque follows centuries-old farm tracks, some of which are still remarkably well-preserved. It passes numerous historic watermills and winds through open pastureland. Along the way, there are splendid views of the town and to the island of São Jorge. In some places, the path leads directly through rocky gullies carved by mostly dry streambeds.

Starting point: São Roque, church, 16m (next bus stop São Roque/Rotunda 700m west at the roundabout).
Grade: much of the route follows ancient farm tracks. The ascent is partly along the rocky streambed, where sure-footedness is required in places.
Refreshment: nothing en route.
Linking tip: Walk 45.

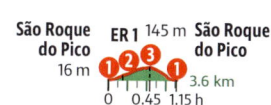

High above São Roque, the view extends across the canal to São Jorge.

The return route to São Roque follows centuries-old cobblestone paths.

From the church in **São Roque** ❶, follow the Rua das Dores eastward and, after about 100m, turn right onto a country lane just before the bridge. The track crosses a ford and turns into a footpath, now leading inland along the mostly dry Ribeira do Dentro. After 5 mins, you cross a country lane where you turn left for 50m, then immediately right onto the old mule track which continues uphill. Soon, after you cross the **ER 1** ❷, continue along the footpath which follows the gully uphill. After 5 mins, you will reach a road again. Here, turn left for 25m and then immediately after the bridge go right onto a dirt trail which continues uphill. Passing a watermill, the path finally merges with a road (35 mins).

Continue left on the road which runs high above São Roque along the pastureland. After 10 mins, a **stream** ❸ crosses the road near a small Cryptomeria forest. Just beyond the forest, turn left and descend, initially along an old hollow way.

After another 10 mins, you cross the road. Continuing straight ahead on the grassy path, you will eventually reach the Rua da Palha. At a large water reservoir, cross the **ER 1** ❹ and follow a well-preserved cobblestone path downhill, passing the ruins of old watermills. Finally, you will reach the Rua da Calçada which you follow downhill for another 75m.

At the lowest crossroad, turn left and cross the bridge over the Ribeira Nova, returning to the starting point in **São Roque** ❶.

↗ 150m | ↘ 910m | 14.7km

Pico

4.30 hrs

From the Lagoa do Capitão to the Baía de Canas

45

Descent from the high plateau to an adega settlement

A heavenly-situated lake with a panorama of Pico, an endless chain of volcanic cones, the wooded eruption zone, Mistério da Prainha, an idyllic woodland park and a hidden adega settlement – these are the sites awaiting you on this walking route. During the ascent from the high plateau, follow the ancient Caminho dos Burros (Donkey Trail) to the northern coastline below, accompanied by a view of São Jorge.

Starting point: Lagoa do Capitão, car park, 780m.
Destination: end of the road at the Baía de Canas, 9m (next bus stop Prainha/Parque Florestal above ❽ on the ER 1).
Grade: a mish-mash of dirt and asphalt trails. The descents through the Mistério and to the bay follow scree-slippery paths.
Refreshment: nothing en route.
Alternative: destination in Cais do Pico (7.5km, 2.10 hrs from the main route): at the fork ❼, turn left onto the lower gravel trail to continue. This soon leads towards São Roque and meets up with the ER 1 in São Miguel Arcanjo, 50 mins later. Keep left on the main road and after 20 mins turn left onto the Rua Eng. José Maria de Medeiros. 7 mins more, past house no. 12, turn right, in front of a bridge, onto a grassy trail to descend. Cross over the ER 1 and follow the cobblestone trail, heading towards the church from São Roque. Way down at the bottom, on the road, turn left until reaching the striking, main church (90 mins). Diagonally opposite at the Chapel of the Holy Spirit, turn right. At the seashore, follow the Avenida do Mar to the left to continue to Cais do Pico's centre.
Linking tip: Walks 44 and 46.

The Caminho dos Burros with a view of São Jorge.

Starting from the **Lagoa do Capitão** ❶, head for the ER 3 and turn left there. 30 mins later, join the ER 2 and turn right toward Lajes. 10 mins later, just opposite of two forestry buildings, a **road** ❷ forks off to the left (sign: Lagoas/Piedade). The tarmac surface soon runs out and is taken over by ancient cobblestones. Another 25 mins later, about 200m after passing under power lines, reach a trail board (1.35 hrs). Here, past an iron gate, a **dirt trail** ❸ sets off to the left and 8 mins later, bends slightly to the left. Exactly at this point, a footpath begins on the right-hand side, the **Caminho dos Burros** ❹ (trail marking), which is very modest at first and easy to miss although it is an ancient connecting trail leading over the Mistério da Prainha.

The trail ascends to the volcanic cones **Cabeços do Mistério** ❺, created during the eruption of 1562–64. Some stretches still reveal the ancient cobblestones. Soon enjoy a sweeping panoramic view, taking in the entire island of São Jorge and then the 30-min descent begins. At the end, reach a **road** ❻ and turn right to continue (2.25 hrs). At the next red-coloured track, turn sharp left, reversing. The track ends 15 mins later, further down at a drivable track. Take this to the right and, at the following **fork** ❼ a good 150m further on, take the right-hand, main trail (the Alternative turns left). 25 mins

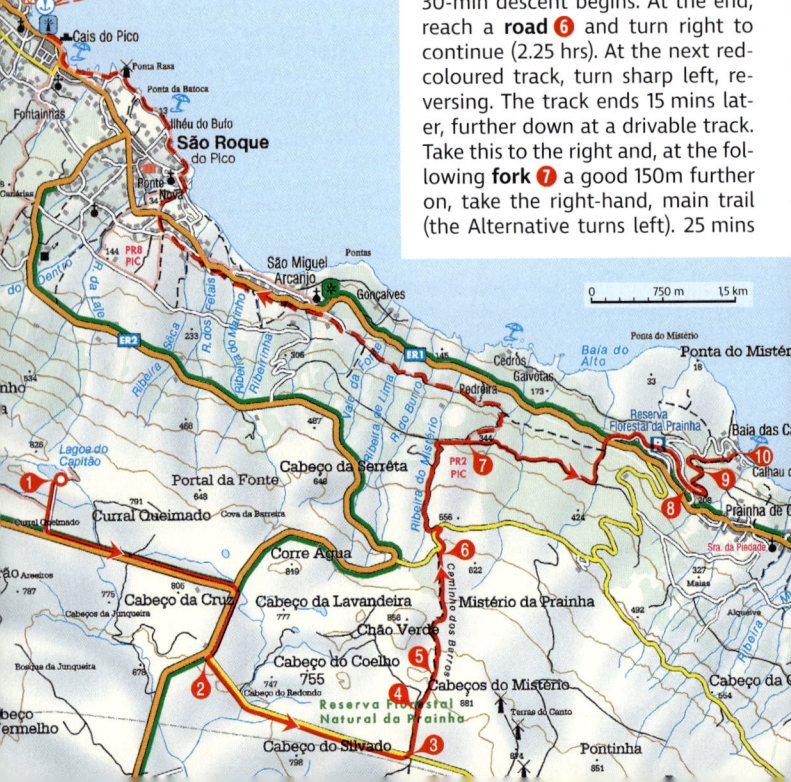

Early morning ambience at the Lagoa do Capitão.

later, a footpath turns left into the wood (waymarker) and descends to the ER 1. 50m further to the right, on the opposite side, a secondary road leads through the **local recreation area** for **Prainha**. After passing a viewpoint, you reach the **picnic area** ❽ (3.50 hrs).
Here, cross over the road and descend through the rose-bush flanked two-lane avenue and continue past the football grounds. Afterwards, at the fork, turn left. The trail peters out on the meadow. At the lower end of the meadow at a wooden bench, a **footpath** ❾ enters the wood by turning left and immediately hooks to the left. At first leading on the level, the path veers to the right, down towards the bay, **Baía de Canas** and ends at the first houses. Now continue straight ahead along a cobblestone trail through the *adega* settlement all the way down to the sea, to reach the end of the **roadway** ❿.

Pico ↗ 80 m | ↘ 840 m | 9.2 km

46 From the Lagoa do Capitão to Cais do Pico

3.15 hrs

Along ancient connecting trails from the highlands to the north coast

Starting at a highland lake, located in a picturesque setting, descend from the plateau along a strenuous connecting trail that has lapsed into oblivion for some time now, down to São Roque. En route, stop off at a remote reservoir and pass a lava tube.

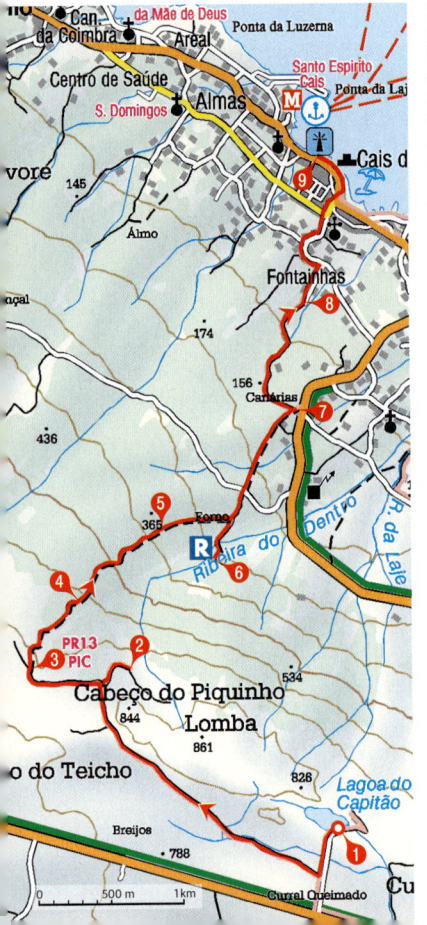

Starting point: Lagoa do Capitão, car park, 780m.
Destination: Cais do Pico, seaside promenade, 8m (bus stop São Roque/Centro do Cais).
Grade: mostly along good dirt trails; descent via a footpath (slippery underfoot). Absolute sure-footedness is required. Walking poles would be useful for the descent.
Refreshment: cafés, bars and restaurants in Cais do Pico. Nothing en route.
Bathing: natural bathing area in São Roque.
Linking tip: Walks 45 and 49.

From the **Lagoa do Capitão** ❶, follow the access road towards the main road and, at the second cattle grid, turn right along a gravel trail. This leads through remote pastureland, always presenting a marvellous view of Pico. 30 mins later, the trail descends. Where it hooks to the left, continue straight ahead, along a grasy trail at the beginning, skirting around the hillock. At the old **water reservoir** ❷, enjoy a view of São Roque and the northern coast, which stretches all the way to São Jorge. Now return to the trail and turn right to continue. Just after you have walked underneath two power lines, the roadway ends (1 hr). Here, turn right to pass through an **iron gate** ❸ and then immediately

An ancient, partially collapsed mule track leads down to Cais do Pico.

turn left, passing a watering trough. Now continue cross-country, descending along the trodden-down pasture, keeping to the left-hand side of the pasture and following along the hedge. For orientation, keep heading towards Velas on São Jorge. 10 mins later, at the lower end of the pasture, reach a massive wooden gate. Past this, in the primeval laurisilva forest, a narrow, wet descent trail begins – a truly adventurous path that demands your constant attention. 15 mins later, at a stone wall, join the ancient **mule track** ❹, now flanked by moss-covered stone walls. After another 40 mins of descending, you reach the **edge of the forest** ❺ from where you continue to descend on a wide grassy trail. Afterwards, reach a narrow road and turn right onto it to ascend at first. Past the cul-de-sac, a footpath continues which leads to the ancient water reservoir **Tanque Velho** ❻ (2.15 hrs). Behind the reservoir, you will find a hidden fresh water source.
Now, go back along the road, cross an intersecting road and join a cart track that descends through the wood. Meeting up with a stable building, continue straight ahead along the main trail, heading steadily towards São Jorge. Before reaching the main road, turn left along a red-coloured **gravel trail** ❼.
A short stretch of tarmac follows. When reaching the first houses, pass by the **Gruta das Canárias** ❽. Once you are down, turn left on the main road and then immediately turn right to reach the centre of **Cais do Pico** ❾.

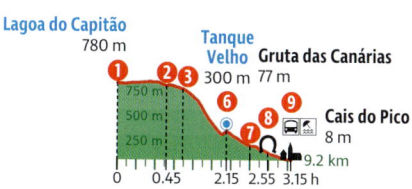

Pico ↗ 90m | ↘ 490m | 6.3km

47 From the Miradouro da Terra Alta to Santo Amaro

2.00 hrs

Traditional shipbuilding and a panoramic view

From the viewpoint Terra Alta with a panoramic view of São Jorge, the well-preserved, ancient cobbled trail along the northern coast descends through the forest down to the seaside. Via the Baía do Canto, you will reach the port town of Santo Amaro with an arts and crafts school and a traditional shipbuilder's dock. There is a bus back to the starting point.

Starting point: Miradouro da Terra Alta on the ER 1, 405m (bus stop Terra Alta/Miradouro 75m east).
Destination: Santo Amaro, harbour, 4m (bus stop Santo Amaro/Porto).
Grade: a pleasant descent along a forest trail. The outset is slippery when wet. The end stretch is along a road.
Refreshment: restaurant Magma in Terra Alta. Cafés in Santo Amaro.
Linking tip: Walks 48 and 49.

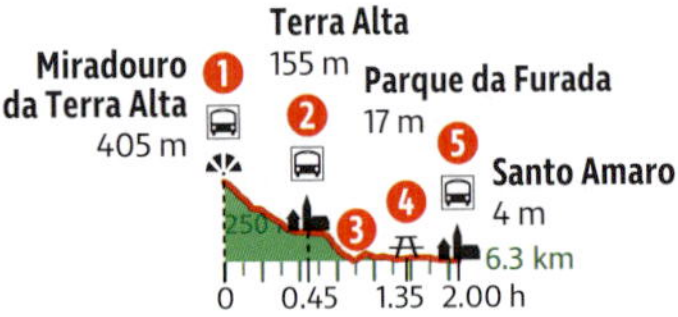

Bathing: natural bathing area at the Caisinho and a harbour basin in Santo Amaro.

Just before Santo Amaro, a quick dip at the natural bathing area Caisinho is well worth it.

The walk starts at the **Miradouro da Terra Alta** ❶ which offers a marvelous panoramic view of the neighbouring island of São Jorge. 70m westwards, an ancient, stony trail turns right into a dense forest. The old cobblestones of the former main connecting trail for the northern island are well-preserved in some places. 20 mins later, the wood soon thins out and you will get a clear view of São Roque and the neighbouring island. Afterwards, at the first houses, reach the village limits of **Terra Alta** and follow the roadway further to reach the **main road** ❷ with a stop sign (45 mins).
Along this road, the Rua Amaro Justino de Azevedo Gomes, go straight ahead to descend. A good 5 mins later, 150m past the second bus stop and opposite a power pylon, turn right onto the secondary road. After 30m and just before you reach the restaurant, go immediately right again and follow an old mule track that is overgrown with grass and takes you through a holiday complex. Just below, traverse a country lane diagonally to the right and after a few steep zigzags, reach the little village square down below and yet another roadway. Turn right along this roadway until it ends at the pebble beach bay, **Baía do Canto** ❸ sporting a tide-powered well (1.10 hrs). Afterwards, return again through the little *adega* settlement and then continue towards Santo Amaro. 20 mins from the bay, the Rua do Caisinho (dead end) turns off to the right and leads to the natural bathing area Zona Balnear do Caisinho. At the last lamp post, ascend again to the left along a trodden path climbing up the embankment. Continuing along the coast, thus reach the picnic area, **Parque da Furada** ❹.
Climb up the access road and, once at the top, turn right onto the main village street Rua do Canto. At the following intersecting street, turn right to descend to **Santo Amaro**. At the first houses, an arts and crafts school with a small museum can be seen to the left. Along the street, passing the church, now continue until reaching the **harbour** ❺ and a little dock. If you would like to learn more about the traditional local handicrafts, you have the opportunity to visit the Museu Marítimo, diagonally opposite – that is, if it's open.

Pico ↗ 330m | ↘ 580m | 11.6km

48 From the Miradouro da Terra Alta to Piedade

3.50 hrs

A panoramic view, a romantic village and a refreshing dip in the Atlantic

From the viewpoint Terra Alta which opens a lovely view of São Jorge, this walk descends via an ancient cart and drover's track, circling Ribeirinha, to the sea. Here, you have two bathing areas where you could take a refreshing swim in the Atlantic. At the end, in Piedade, a bus connection is available.

Starting point: Miradouro da Terra Alta on the ER 1, 405m (bus stop Terra Alta/Miradouro 75m east).
Destination: Piedade's centre, 151m (bus stop Piedade/Curral da Pedra).
Grade: ancient cart and farm tracks. Numerous ascents some of which are steep. In Ribeirinha and Piedade along the village roads.
Refreshment: café in Ribeirinha, at the Porto de Calhau and in Piedade.
Linking tip: Walks 47, 49 and 50.
Bathing: natural bathing area Baixa da Ribeirinha and seawater pool in Calhau.

Along the Canada da Ladeira near Ribeirinha.

Start off at the **Miradouro da Terra Alta** ❶ with a panoramic view of the neighbouring island of São Jorge. From here, continue eastwards along the main road ER 1. 5 mins later, turn left after a trail board onto a **country lane** ❷ and descend; immediately after, turn right along the ancient mule track (Caminho da Atalhada). This is often overgrown as it leads below the ER 1 and, 20 mins later, crosses over a **road** ❸. Just a few steps to the left, you will find a viewpoint. Straight ahead, continue a descent towards Ribeirinha. At the first building, leave the main trail and head left to the **road** ❹. On the opposite side, a mule track continues towards the coast (Canada da Rocha). This ends, 10 mins later, at the viewpoint **Alto dos Cedros** ❺ (45 mins).

Now return to the **village street** ❹ and turn left to enter the village. 10 mins later, in front of the house no. 158 turn left to descend along a grassy trail, the **Caminho da Quebrada** ❻. After 10 mins, a roadway continues towards the right. It immediately turns into a concrete trail and ascends again. After 120m at the first fork, go down to the left and follow the dirt trail beyond it, staying at the same level. 3 mins later, meet an intersecting trail and turn right. This grassy trail (Canada dos Vais) now ascends steeply. At the football pitch, reach the road once again, turn left to the village centre of **Ribeirinha** ❼ and then continue straight on (1.35 hrs).

161

The natural bathing area Baixa da Ribeirinha with a view of São Jorge.

A quarter of an hour later, at a fountain (1955) turn left to descend along the **Canada da Ladeira** ❽ which immediately becomes a mule track. At the fork, 10 mins later, bear left. Then, at the road, turn left to continue and, in the **depression** ❾ go right into the dead end road (Canada do Mar). The mule track bends sharply right at the bottom-most vineyards. Follow the footpath straight ahead that, as an old stepped trail, climbs down to the bathing area **Baixa da Ribeirinha** ❿ at the old harbour (2.20 hrs).

Along the access road to the harbour, the path continues uphill. 5 mins later, at the first possibility, turn left. The secondary road finally ends down at the seaside; afterwards, a footpath continues. This ancient coastal connection path leads over rough and smooth terrain along the lowest boundary wall. It is mainly very pleasant to walk on. After passing the Ponta das Trombetas, the path eventually ends at the bathing area of **Calhau** ⓫ (3.10 hrs).

Head left to walk along the seaside and continue to reach the **Porto do Calhau** ⓬. Here, ascend along the village main street and, 150m further on, turn left (Caminho de Cima da Rocha). Five mins later, follow the first small road, the **Canada do Morgado** ⓭, ascending to the right. Up above, on the road, turn left to continue to Piedade's centre ⓮.

↗ 380m | ↘ 750m | 25.7km   Pico
7.00 hrs
Pico's highland lakes — 49

Relaxed ramble along the highland lakes

Volcanic cones line up like the pearls on a necklace in Pico's highlands. Many of these have created natural crater lakes. Follow the 'transversale' through the highlands which is being used as open pastureland. Almost the entire route leads through a natural reserve. When the weather is clear, you can spot the neighbouring islands of São Jorge and Terceira.

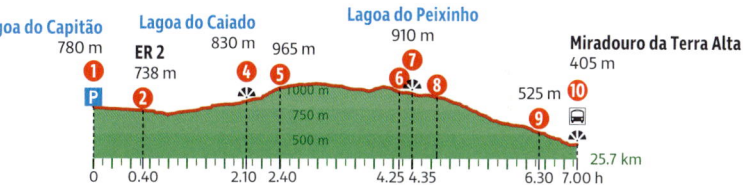

Starting point: car park on the Lagoa do Capitão, 780m.
Destination: Miradouro da Terra Alta on the ER 1, 405m (bus stop Terra Alta/Miradouro 75m east).
Grade: a pleasant but very prolonged ramble along a little-used road. This is not really a walking trail in the normal sense. The starting point can be further along the way. Walk this route only when the weather is clear!
Refreshment: there is nothing available en route.
Linking tip: Walks 45–48.

Idyllic: the highland lake Lagoa o Peixinho in the midst of the lava hills.

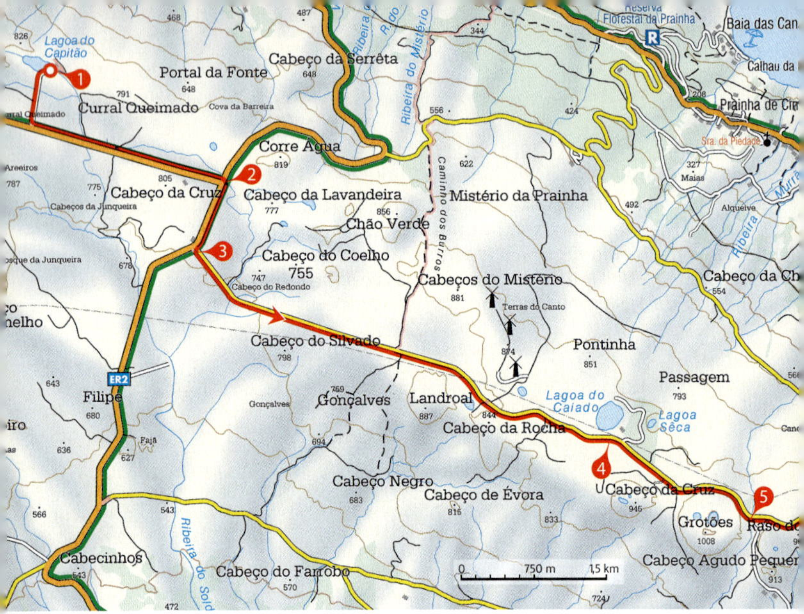

Start at the **Lagoa do Capitão** ❶ and head in the direction of the ER 3; turn left to continue. 30 mins later, reach the **ER 2** ❷ and turn right towards Lajes. 10 mins on, opposite two forestry houses, the **transversale** ❸ forks off to the left (sign: Lagoas/Piedade, 50 mins). 50 mins more along the mountain trail, you will reach open pastureland separated by numerous cattle grids. To the left, the island's wind farm can be seen.

Reach the next lake, the **Lagoa do Caiado** ❹ (2.10 hrs). 30 mins later, at the **turn-off** ❺ to the Lagoa do Paúl, keep straight on along the high mountain road which, afterwards, veers off to the southern side of the mountain ridge. To the right and below, the smaller **Lagoa da Rosada** (4.10 hrs) follows, and then you reach another **fork** ❻. Here, too, keep heading straight on along the high mountain road. Afterwards, the **Lagoa do Peixinho** ❼ follows (4.35 hrs).

The chain of hills now gently levels out and then you reach a **trail junction** ❽; continue by heading straight on. The road now descends

164

The little crater lake Lagoa do Caiado – with São Jorge in the background.

gently. To your left, you can spot the sprawling neighbouring island of São Jorge. At first, ignore all of the trails that fork away, especially at the cattle loading stations.

After a total of 6.30 hrs, from a level stretch of the trail, you can spot a large livestock pen. 100m before reaching this, turn sharp to the left ❾. Along this narrow road, descend in 25 mins to the ER 1. Turn left onto it and, 5 mins later, arrive at the **Miradouro da Terra Alta** ❿ with a bus connection.

50 Ponta da Ilha

↗ 210m | ↘ 210m | 11.7km
4.00 hrs

Coastline walk along the rugged eastern tip with bathing opportunity

Today, only a few footpaths lead directly along the rugged coast. On this walk you can get a good impression of the jagged, broken coastline of the island. The ancient fishermen's path through the lava-blanketed terrain is very demanding and only suitable for the absolutely sure-footed walker. All others are advised to use the alternative route leading somewhat away from the coastline. In any case, be sure to bring your bathing gear!

Starting point: Manhenha, fishing harbour, 8m.
Grade: the ancient fishermen's path along the coastline leads through untamed, jagged basalt cliffs with razor-sharp edges and numerous rock crevices. Absolute sure-footedness, a well-developed sense of direction and the best footgear are required. Aside from this, broad gravel trails lead the way.
Refreshment: cafés in Manhenha and at the harbour of Calhau.
Alternative: avoiding the coastline route via the Pico de Castelete to Manhenha (3.3km, 1.20 hrs from the main route): if you are not absolutely sure-footed, at the outset of the fishermen's path, follow the dirt trail ❾ for 10 mins and ascend to the main road. Turn left and, 5 mins later, bear diagonally left. 150m on, a mule track (tile sign) turns off left to the Pico de Castelete. The last metres to the distinctive hill are across steep wooden steps. Then head back to the road and descend in 15 mins to Engrade. Continue straight ahead and stay on the road all the way to Manhenha.
Bathing: seawater pool in Calhau, bathing area at Cais do Galego, natural bathing area at the Baía de Engrade, seawater pool in Manhenha.
Linking tip: Walk 48.

Delightful: the coastal walk leading below Engrade.

Begin the walk at the fishing harbour in **Manhenha** ❶ and follow the street between the café and the chapel, heading south-westwards directly along the seaside. At the last house, the street becomes a gravel track. Past this, at the first **fork** ❷ ascend to the right, then cross over the road and at the top turn diagonally left to continue along the broad **gravel track** ❸. Past the quarry, at the **fork** ❹ follow the road going down on your right. From now on, continue straight ahead towards Piedade. A good 15 mins along the road, opposite from house no. 16 at a garage, turn right along a **dirt trail** ❺ heading towards the coast and, at the following junction, a good 5 mins later, turn left. The trail soon veers again to the right to reach the coast. Afterwards, at another junction, turn left to continue and then, at the next intersecting trail, below a house built from undressed stone,

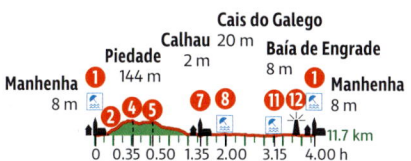

167

turn right and continue all the way to the seaside. Here, at the **intersecting trail** ❻, at first turn left and, when the road ends, descend directly to the harbour at **Calhau** ❼ (1.35 hrs).

Afterwards, return back along the coastal trail, but then keep straight ahead along the Caminho de Cima da Rocha to reach the Largo do Cais do Galego with an area for barbecuing. 50m further on, bear left at a **fork** ❽ to climb down to the sea. The narrow road hooks off to the right and becomes a footpath that leads along the coastline just below a stone wall. 250m on, at the natural stone-built house, **Adega do Avô**, turn left onto a footpath.

Rugged lava at the Ponta da Ilha.

Along the rim of the cliff, reach another house built of natural stone and bear left here to continue along the sometimes cobbled coastal footpath until a **dirt trail** ❾ merges from the right, 200m on (turn right here for the Alternative). Here, past an opening in the drystone wall, continue to the left to follow the traces of a path across the meadow.

Now the challenging ancient **fishermen's path** begins, leading along the coast over the mostly rugged and sharp-edged rocky terrain. It is best to pick out your own way over the lava surface, keeping always keeping a safe distance from the cliff edge. From time to time, trail markings help point the way. 50 mins later, a trail descends from the right. 150m past this point along the coastline, you can spot the red roof of a solitary house perched above the coast (3.05 hrs). Just before reaching this point, turn away from the coast and climb up a short slope on some stone steps before you reach a **road** ❿. Here, pass the house to the left and follow the old coastal path along the bottom-most drystone wall until you reach the **Baía de Engrade** ⓫ with a picnic table. Continue your descent on the concrete steps. The trail continues along the lowest natural stone wall and leads for a short time along a beaten-down path through low scrub. Following the drystone wall, reach the still-inhabited **Farol da Ponta da Ilha** ⓬. At the wastewater pipe, take a few steps to the left and, just as if you were on a paper chase, follow the waymarkers to circumvent the lighthouse, which takes you through the rugged lava landscape. Beyond it, you reach the Caminho do Farol. Go left and return to the starting point in **Manhenha** ❶.

Rough coastal section at the Ponta do Castelete at the foot of the uncovered lava dome.

Pico | ↗ 410m | ↘ 410m | 10.1km

51 Around Calheta de Nesquim

3.10 hrs

Stroll around a former whaling village in the south-east

Calheta de Nesquim is a traditional whaling village where the charm of past days can still be felt. From the small fishing harbour, there is a short detour to the summer settlement of Feteira. Narrow farm tracks lead you uphill to Fetais. On the descent, you pass an old whale-spotters' post. On the way back through a cluster of adegas, it's worth stopping at a lovely natural bathing area.

Starting point: Calheta de Nesquim, church, 6m (bus stop Calheta/Igreja).
Grade: large parts of this walk follow old farm and cart tracks. The descent is stony in parts and requires absolute sure-footedness.
Refreshment: cafés and restaurant in Calheta de Nesquim. Nothing en route.
Bathing: natural bathing area at Poça das Mujas and Portinho.

Start at the Igreja de São Sebastião in **Calheta de Nesquim** ❶ and head uphill along the steep village road to the north-east. After a 10-min climb, turn right into **Rua da Feteira de Baixo** ❷ which leads down into the lower part of Feteira. In the dip, take the first road on the right. The road soon turns into a gravel track by the sea, curving down to the natural bathing area of **Zona Balnear do Portinho** ❸ by the old harbour.

A steep access road takes you uphill again. About 50m above the picnic area, turn left and then immediately turn right to ascend by the Adega Vieira (sign: dead end). At the last house, the road turns into an old mule track which joins a dirt trail after 5 mins. Follow the dirt trail uphill to the left. In the upper part of Feteira, cross the village road and continue uphill along the mule track through the forest. At the old school building, you reach the **ER 1** ❹ (50 mins).

Turn left here. After 250m, just past kilometre marker 49, take a footpath to the right that leads into the forest. After 5 mins, the path joins a crossroad in **Fetais**. Turn left here and 5 mins later, after passing house no. 27, follow a dirt trail inland. After a 15-min climb, you will reach a **junction** ❺ where you turn left. The trail now descends again and crosses a road after 10 mins. Continue straight on the country lane, which eventually joins the **village road** ❻ in the district of **Cascalheira**. Here, first turn right and then continue straight ahead. After 10 mins, the road becomes an old cart track at the last building. After 200m, the cart track joins a cross trail where you first go left and, after 25m, take the old footpath left down to the **ER 1** ❼ (2 hrs).

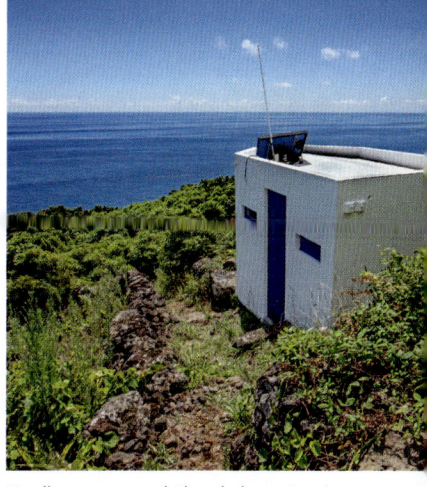

Hardly ever manned: the whale-spotters' post of Calheta de Nesquim.

Keep to the left here. 25m after kilometre marker 51, turn right and, just 10m later, but before the garage, take another right to join an old footpath. After 10 mins, you will reach a country lane where you continue to the left. After another 5 mins, leave the lane to the right (sign: Vigia) and follow the stony path to a former **whale-spotters' post** ❽. Beyond it, the trail descends steeply for a short distance through vineyards. At the road at the bottom, turn right (2.30 hrs).

Skirting around the cemetery, the path curves back and now follows the coastline. After 15 mins, turn right at a radio mast and descend to the windmill **Moinho do Mourricão** ❾. From here, it's worth making a detour to the natural bathing area **Poça das Mujas**.

At the picnic area, below the windmill and the old playground, exit the grounds through a small wooden gate. The final stretch back to the harbour follows the rocky shoreline (follow the trail markers). This takes you back to the starting point in **Calheta de Nesquim** ❶.

Pico ↗ 150m | ↘ 180m | 9.3km

52 From the Parque Florestal de São João to Silveira
3.00 hrs

Pleasant coastal walk with a possible swim in the sea

Along this pleasant ramble on Pico's southern coast, you will pass numerous, little, solitary spots for bathing. If you take the bus to return to the starting point, you can also take the opportunity to enjoy a picnic in the lovely local recreational area serving São João.

Starting point: Parque Florestal de São João, 81m (bus stop São João/Canada do Arrasto 300m to the east).

Destination: Silveira, church, 51m (bus stop Silveira/Caminho da Fonte 150m to the west).

Grade: mostly via pleasant gravel tracks. In São João, along a road.

Refreshment: restaurant in São João, café in Silveira.

Bathing: natural bathing area at Ponta do Admoiro, Verdoso, Arrinhas and Silveira.

Twilight at the Moinho da Ponta Rasa just past São João.

From the Largo São João Batista in the **Parque Florestal de São João** ❶, follow the trail between the wild animal pens and the children's playground whilst heading towards the coast. At the restroom, veer to the left and, below a football pitch, reach a narrow road. Turn right here to continue then immediately left to follow the gravel trail. Not quite 10 mins later, pass a tide-powered well on the **Baía da Arruda** ❷ with picnic tables. 10 mins later, reach an intersecting street. Here, you could descend at first, over stone steps, to the natural bathing area at the **Ponta do Admoiro** ❸, also provided with a picnic area and a tide-powered well (35 mins).

At the street (Rua do Verdoso) turn right. A good 10 mins later, stone steps climb down to the **tide-powered well** of **Verdoso** ❹. A small natural bathing area is situated on the seaside. Afterwards, turn right along the street to continue. 70m further on, an excursion along the passageway branching off and ascending to the museum **Casa do Pico** is worthwhile (often closed). Now join the village street and turn right. The second house to the left is a cheese-makers' museum (also often closed). Soon, reach the church from **São João** ❺ (1.05 hrs).

10 mins past the church and the harbour, a cobbled trail climbs down to the bathing area of **Arrinhas** ❻ with a picnic site. 30m before reaching the main street, turn off onto the secondary trail to the right. This becomes a dirt trail afterwards and then ends at the windmill on the **Ponta Rasa** ❼.

On the main road ER 1 turn right to continue and, immediately past the football pitch, turn right onto the gravel track. 30 mins later, waymarkers point to the right for a **footpath** ❽. The stony path leads for 10 mins along the coast and rejoins the gravel track. If you aren't wearing proper footgear, it's better to continue along the track. Shortly after the track becomes tarmac-paved, reach the **Fonte da Silveira** ❾ with a picnic area and a natural swimming pool (2.30 hrs). Once you reach the junction, stay on the seaside. The road ascends towards **Silveira** up above. Here, on the main street, turn right and continue to the **church** ❿.

Faial – a sailors' paradise

- population: 14,400
- capital: Horta, 5600 inhabitants
- area: 173km²
- length: 21km, width: 14km
- coastline: 80km
- highest point: Cabeço Gordo, 1043m

Faial is an island replete in history and is well worth a trip there. Violent volcanic eruptions and frequent earthquakes have often tested the islanders' perseverance, right up to the 20th century. From a plane, the imposing gigantic crater Caldeira in the heart of the island's interior with its sweeping green flanks can be seen from far off. Those arriving by ferry have a panoramic view of the capital city of Horta to savour; here, not only cultural variety but also architectural treasures are waiting. In July, the bright blue of hydrangea hedges, which can grow up to two metres high and are ubiquitous on the island, bestow upon Faial the epithet Ilha Azul (blue island).
Officially, the discovery of Faial is attributed to Jácome de Bruges in 1450. Settlement of the island began a decade later and soon over 1500 people were living here. Large areas were cleared for cultivation and at the beginning, the pastel plant, used in dyeing, proved to be a good source of income. Pirates caught wind of the city's wealth and the newly-founded city would be frequently raided. In 1672, the Cabeço do Fogo erupted and buried the island under a thick layer of ash; the first wave of emigration began. In 1765, American whalers dropped anchor off the island shores and soon ushered in a new era. In 1808, the American consul John Bass Dabney arrived on the island; 50 years later, he and the equally well-to-do Bensaúde family founded the first Azorean whaling enterprise. When in 1893, Telcon laid its first underwater telecommunications cable between Lisbon and the Azores, yet another important period of the island's history began. More underwater cables were to follow and Horta would become the most important communications post in the Atlantic between the Old and the New Worlds. An economic boom began which was to last until the last line was discontinued in 1969. The first seaplane landed in the harbour basin in 1919. Later, even Lufthansa frequently used the island as a stopover on the way to and from America.
In 1957/58, a momentous volcanic eruption took place near Capelo. This spectacular event went on for 13 months and, at the end, gave birth to a new promontory 2.4km² in area. In the following year, 5000 inhabitants emigrated. A violent earthquake destroyed large areas of the eastern island in 1998. Some buildings lie in ruins even now, giving testimony to the past.
Right from the beginning, life on Faial revolved around the capital **Horta**. The city centre is fairly easy to absorb but nevertheless, a certain flair can

be found in the narrow passageways here. This also exudes from the yacht harbour where over 1000 yachts per year make it a port of call, with world travellers providing a colourful international mixture. The prettiest view of the city can be enjoyed offshore, from the ocean. The various churches tower splendidly above the white sea of houses. Most of the buildings go back to the 18th and 19th centuries, some in the old colonial style. The little balconies are artfully embellished; the oriels ornate and many gables still show the style of the classic whaling era. Later edifices contain elements of art deco. The best way to explore the city is to get a city map at the *turismo* and then take a full day's tour. A multitude of interesting buildings are scattered about, starting from the barbecue and bathing area on the northeastern side, all the way to the Monte de Guia on the south-western side of the bay. Definitely worth visiting are: the Jardim de Florêncio Terra with the Torre do Relógio, the Praca da República, the Palácio do Colégio with the island museum, the huge and marvelous parish churches of Matriz de São Salvador, Nossa Senhora do Carmo and Nossa Senhora das Angústias; also visit the marina, the Peter Café Sport with a Scrimshaw Museum (engraved whalebone) and the town quarter with the old telegraph company buildings. Be sure to climb the Monte da Guia and another scenic overview of the city can be enjoyed from the heights of Espalamaca. Lovingly restored windmills are also found here. Somewhat outside of the city, toward Flamengos, marvel at the only official botanic gardens on the Azores.

FAIAL

Getting there
From Lisbon with SATA. Within the Azores, there are daily flights from Faial to Terceira and São Miguel as well as to Flores and Corvo numerous times during the week. The airport is located in Castelo Branco, 8km from Horta. The ferry harbour is situated in Horta. Year round, numerous daily ferry connections are scheduled to Pico. São Jorge is also serviced the whole year through. During the winter months, however, service is limited. From June to September, a ferry operates to Graciosa and Terceira several times per week.

Bathing
Lovely sandy beaches at the Porto Pim in Horta, in Fajã da Praia do Norte as well as in Almoxarife. Natural bathing areas in Castelo Branco, Cedros, Salão and Varadouro. An enclosed pool in Horta.

Festivities
Holy Spirit Celebrations in late spring until end of August. Festa de Nossa Senhora das Angústias (Horta), 6th Sunday after Easter. Triatlo Peter Café Sport (Horta), end of May. Festa de São João (near Flamengos), June 24. Festa de Nossa Senhora da Guia (Horta), beginning of August. Semana do Mar (Horta), beginning of August. Festa de Nossa Senhora de Lurdes (Feteira), end of August. Festa de Nossa Senhora da Saúde (Varadouro), beginning of September.

Medical services
Hospital in Horta, tel +351 292 201 000.

Tourist information
Turismo do Faial with a service desk at the airport and an office in Horta, tel +351 292 237, pt.fai@azores.gov.pt, cmhorta.pt. Free Wi-Fi at numerous hotspots on the island.

Cultural activities
Museu da Horta island museum, Museu de Arte Sacra, Museu de Scrimshaw, Fábrica da Baleia, Centro do Mar, Casa dos Dabney and Aquarium at the Porto Pim in Horta. Information centre at the lighthouse on Capelinhos, focusing on the 1957/58 eruption and Casa dos Botes at the port. Botanical garden in Flamengos.

Public transport
The bus network is only partially suitable for tourism since the only service is along the coastal road (only twice a day). There is no bus service on Sundays. Without a hire car, you can use taxis to get to your destination. Taxi central in Horta, tel +351 292 101 631 (also via APP Taxilink).

Accommodation
There are some hotels as well as sufficient *residenciais* and private rooms in Horta. In the island's west and north, many holiday homes are available, usually built of natural stone. A large, well-kept campsite can be found at the Praia do Almoxarife. Two more basic sites are located outside of Salão and below the airport at the harbour of Castelo Branco.

Harbour artwork in Horta.

Horta's churches gleaming in the light of daybreak.

Faial has a pentagonal form; all the attractions found on the island can be visited by car in a single day. The island is dominated by the grand crater of the Caldeira; the entire area is a protected nature reserve. On a clear day, you can see the neighbouring islands of Pico, São Jorge and Graciosa from the rim of the Caldeira. To the west, smaller volcanic cones are lined up like the links on a chain. These end at the Ponta dos Capelinhos, a piece of land that was formed only 50 years ago during a volcanic eruption. Today, the lighthouse there, outfitted with a documentation centre, no longer perches on the sealine, but instead lies somewhat landward toward the interior. In this microclimate, it is even possible to grow expensive island wine. The southern coast is rugged and hardly accessible. Caves and rock arches can usually only be seen from out to sea. Even more interesting is the Morro de Castelo Branco, a rock massif that towers directly out of the sea. Varadouro is a small, protected seaside resort. A thermal bath was located here until 1998 but since the last violent earthquake, the water pumps have been laid to rest. At the oceanside below the Praia do Norte, you can find a lovely sandy beach. Somewhat further along the main road, the most beautiful viewpoint is situated at the Ribeira das Cabras. The northern coast is generally rural in nature; the little villages seem to flow one into the other. Even today, the east coast is marked by the consequences of the last major earthquake. Some churches that were damaged are still being reconstructed, and also the lighthouse at Ribeirinha is dilapidated. Some of the islanders still live in portable cabins. In Praia do Almoxarife you will find Horta's second most popular beach, only a 10-min drive from the city centre. Three local recreational areas at Capelo, Cabouco Velho and Falca also merit visits. Holidaymakers expecting a long sojourn on Faial should be sure to make at least a daytrip by ferry to the neighbouring island of Pico.

Faial ↗ 180m | ↘ 180m | 3.6km

53 Monte da Guia and Monte Queimado

1.30 hrs

Panoramic walk on the outskirts of the city

This circular walk leads across the peninsular that lies in front of the town of Horta with its 'hell crater'. It also leads you past the spot where the first telegraphic submarine cable was laid in 1893. You pass three museums and several old fortresses from the 16th and 17th centuries. During the second part of this walk, the views across Horta are fantastic.

Views from Monte Queimado back to Monte da Guia.

Starting point: Horta, Fábrica da Baleia, car park, 7m.
Grade: mostly pleasant footpaths, ascents and descents steep and slippery along many steps, a high degree of sure-footedness required.
Refreshment: cafés and snack bars at Porto Pim.

Bathing: sandy beach at Porto Pim.

Starting point is the car park at the **Fábrica da Baleia** ❶, the old whale-processing plant. Passing the museum on the left, follow the cobbled path. Shortly after you have passed the Casa dos Dabney museum, you reach the aquarium. From here, follow a footpath above the coast. It ends at the **Miradouro do Neptuno** ❷ (Beware: risk of falling off the cliff).

Now climb up the steep slope to your left. The wooden steps on the lower part are pretty good while the stone steps further up require some scrambling. At the top, the high trail bends to the left. Pass a radio installation before you reach the **Ermida Nossa Senhora da Guia** ❸ (35 mins) on **Monte da Guia**. You will see the wide sunken crater on your right.

Below the chapel, there is a viewpoint across the bay of Porto Pim. From here, first concrete steps and then carved rock steps lead back down the hill. At the edge of the forest above the aquarium, turn right and pass the **Miradouro da Lira**. The footpath finally ends behind the Casa dos Dabney. Turn right back to the **starting point** ❶ (55 mins).

The ascent of **Monte Queimado** starts from the three former cable head stations in the dunes opposite the car park. Numerous wooden steps lead uphill to a viewpoint above the bay of Porto Pim. Walk past old military positions to soon reach another **viewpoint** ❹ above the wide harbour bay. Take the path which leads down to the bay again and once you have passed an iron gate, you get to a small road. From here, go left to the bay of **Porto Pim** ❺ and continue across the wide sandy beach back to the **starting point** ❶.

Beautiful beach at Porto Pim.

Faial ↗ 480m | ↘ 480m | 10.6km

54 Circling Ribeirinha

3.40 hrs

🚌 ✕ 🏊

Pleasant circular walk through the scattered settlements in the east

Most buildings on the eastern side of Faial were destroyed during a violent earthquake in 1998. Along the way, pass the ruins of a church and the collapsed lighthouse in Ribeirinha which are both reminders of this quake. At the edge of the forest, ascend to the pastureland. The walk continues along a ridge before it leads you back to the coast. At the end of the circular walk, you can take a break for bathing if you wish.

Starting point: Ribeirinha, bus stop Ribeirinha/Igreja in front of the ruins of the church, 113m.
Grade: mostly pleasant footpaths and gravel trails. The dirt trail goes up and down. Boggy and slippery when wet.
Refreshment: bar in Ribeirinha. Nothing en route.
Alternative: extension via Espalhafatos (5.3 km, 1.30 hrs): continue on the high path at junction ❺. After 20 mins, the high path leads to a crossroad. Turn right here onto the road (sign: Ribeirinha) and descend to the main road in Espalhafatos. Turn right and walk past the Fonte do Parol as well as a transformer. Directly opposite, follow the road past a fountain and continue left uphill. The road soon bends right, heading across the Lomba dos Espalhafatos towards the east coast. At a junction, meet a crossroad. Continue straight on and soon reach the Miradouro da Ribeirinha.
Linking tip: Walk 55.
Bathing: the secluded harbour Porto da Boca da Ribeira with a picnic area.

The old lighthouse of Ribeirinha.

The walk starts at the **church ruins** ❶ in **Ribeirinha** and follows the village street towards Horta for 15 mins passing two Holy Spirit chapels on the way. Where the road starts to ascend again, take the left trail at the fork. At the main road EN 1, turn left onto the concrete trail behind the crash barrier. Pass the rather unremarkable **Miradouro do Ribeiro Seco** ❷.

Another 150m ahead, just behind the curve, leave the main road and climb up wooden steps on the right which start off very steep. At the top, you reach a grassy trail which you follow to the left. Along the edge of the forest, continue uphill on a footpath for 20 mins until you reach another **road** ❸ in a bend.

Continue on the road to the left. At the fork, after 200m, keep left and reach the **Miradouro do Cabeço das Pedras Negras** ❹ 5 mins later. After you enjoyed the view, return to the fork and follow the high path which is rather flat (sign: Espalhafatos). The high path turns into a track after 300m which gradually descends after almost nearly 15 mins. Here, a **forest trail** ❺ branches off to the right via wooden steps. The ancient connecting trail leads down to the main road EN 1. The footpath continues diagonally across the road. Eventually, the now crumbling cart track reaches another **road** ❻.

Turn right here and, after 75m, take the paved path to the left by two benches passing the Fonte do Valado. Beyond the spring, cross a roadway and follow the narrow old footpath diagonally opposite, which climbs steeply up. Once at the top, continue right along the road to the

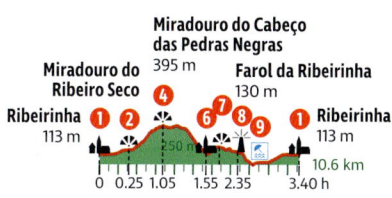

From the Miradouro do Cabeço das Pedras Negras the view extends across the canal towards Pico.

Miradouro da Ribeirinha ❼ (2.15 hrs). After another 200m, leave the road and, behind a wooden gate, follow the footpath to the right that leads into the forest. Once again on the road, turn right and continue to the ruins of the **Farol da Ribeirinha** ❽ which was destroyed in the 1998 earthquake (2.35 hrs). Caution: Do not climb over the barriers!
Back from the lighthouse, follow the wooden fence to your left in the first curve. Here, an extremely steep stepped trail leads you through the forest. (If you have problems with steep descents, follow the gravel road to the left immediately after the bend; after 10 mins take the country lane that leads sharply left back towards the coast). Once you reach the dirt trail at the bottom, turn left to soon reach the **Porto da Boca da Ribeira** ❾ (2.55 hrs) with bathing area, barbecue spot and toilets. On the other side of the stream, ascend on the road. After the first two switchbacks, follow the wooden steps to the left at the first field, then continue along the barbed wire fence at the edge of the pasture. The small footpath winds in a wide arc above the coastline around the pasture and rejoins the road after 20 mins. Turn left here to head up to **Ribeirinha**. At the **village street** ❿, turn right to return to the starting point at the **church ruins** ❶.

↗ 150m | ↘ 960m | 13.9km   Faial

From the Caldeira to Ribeirinha 55
4.15 hrs

Descent from idyllic nature to the island's eastern tip

The contrasts on the island of Faial could not be greater: up at the Caldeira, you get some of the best views across the island. Here, you are alone with hundreds of birds and just a few tourists. On the descent via the old connecting trails through the long ditch of Pedro Miguel, cows are your only companions while down in the village, you see the damage of the frequent earthquakes.

Starting point: cul-de-sac at the rim of the Caldeira, 904m.
Destination: Ribeirinha, bus stop Ribeirinha/Igreja, in front of the ruins of the church, 113m.
Grade: at the start, good but dusty track. Later, pleasant footpaths and farm roads. The paths are partially earthy and slippery when wet.
Refreshment: there is nothing available en route.
Linking tip: Walks 54, 56 and 57.

This walk starts at the cul-de-sac at the **viewpoint** of the **Caldeira** ❶ from where you follow the the road down for a good 5 mins. Take the first road on the left, cross the cattle grid and soon pass a **viewpoint** ❷. After the next cattle grid, the road turns into a dusty track and leads you down the Caldeira slope in countless serpentines until it finally merges with the ER 2. Turn left here and reach the **Parque Florestal do Cabouco Velho** ❸ with picnic areas (1.20 hrs).

After 200m, take the red track to your right (sign: Ribeirinha) and initially pass five wind turbines. A good 5 mins after the last turbine, the road is tarmaced again. At an old **water house** ❹, take the footpath to your right and follow it down through the forest. At the bottom, you get to a road, where you continue to the left. Follow the road for a quarter of an hour. Where the road bends to the right, continue straight on the dirt trail. You pass a bird observation hut at the **Charcos de Pedro Miguel** ❺ wetland (2.30 hrs).

After 10 mins, keep right at the fork at the quarry (Caminho das Fraldas). After 175m you get to another fork, where you turn left up the hill. The dirt trail turns into a road after a quarter of an hour. Here, go right. Directly

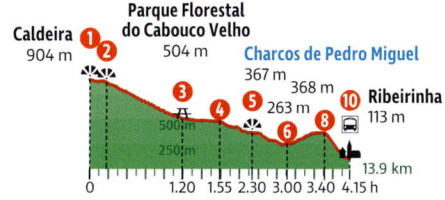

Shady ascent on the old Caminho da Vila.

behind a **stable** ❻, follow a country lane to the left. The lane immediately turns into a footpath, crosses two pastures and, partially along steps, winds itself up through the forest (Caminho da Vila).
After a total of 3.25 hrs, you reach another **road** ❼ in a curve, continue left and turn right after a good 200m (sign: Espalhafatos). After 15 mins, the track goes slightly downhill again. Walk to the right down to the forest along **wooden steps** ❽ and follow the old connecting path all the way to the main road **EN 1** ❾. Diagonally opposite, the footpath continues downhill. Finally, the now-collapsed cart track reaches a road again. Go right here. After 250m, you reach the ruins of the church in **Ribeirinha** ❿ and the bus stop.

↗ 230m | ↘ 230m | 6.9km   Faial

2.30 hrs

Circular walk around the Caldeira — 56

Panoramic trail running along the crater's rim

No other walk presents a better overlook of the island of Faial than the one described here. From the marvellous viewpoint at the rim of the gigantic crater, you will climb up to the island's highest peak. The view reaches below to the little settlements on the coast and also takes in the neighbouring islands of Pico, São Jorge and Graciosa – unfortunately, only during clear weather.

Starting point: the cul-de-sac at the rim of the Caldeira, 904m.
Grade: mostly along unpaved paths. At the beginning, a steep, well-trodden ascent route at the Cabeço Gordo.
Refreshment: nothing en route.
Linking tip: Walks 55 and 57.
Note: the entire area around the crater belongs to the Reserva Natural da Caldeira do Faial. Because of this, you must always keep to the designated trails and refrain from collecting or damaging any of the flora. The descent to the bottom of the crater is only permitted in the company of an official park guide (fee charged).

The grand crater in Faial's heart is a protected nature reserve.

The starting point is the cul-de-sac at the upper rim of the **Caldeira** ❶. At first, begin walking a few paces through a short tunnel to the marvellous viewpoint. The walking route begins at the trail board. Here, a short, stepped trail ascends to the ridgeline and then a footpath flanked by hydrangea hedges turns left toward the Cabeço Gordo, crowned by a thicket of aerials. Past the first altitude survey point at the Canto dos Saquinhos, the ancient trail becomes quite steep and overtrodden for some mins. Once you have reached the same level as some old concrete posts, the path veers to the right half way below the **Cabeço Gordo**. Where the path forks, keep to the right and beyond it right again ❷ and continue on the most obvious trail at the upper and inner edge of the Caldeira, just below the crater rim that runs parallel to the road leading to the summit. Once you have circumvented about a quater of the crater, climb up to the crater rim.

Where the road to the Cabeço Gordo bends sharply (45 mins), the trail ❸ continues towards the right on the high ridge of the Caldeira (do not take the gravel trail beyond it). Pass the trig points of the **Alto do Guarda-Sol** ❹ and **Alto do Brejo** ❺. This single ridgeline trail now continues steadily clockwise around the rim. On the eastern side, the view reaches all the way to the islands of Graciosa, São Jorge and Pico. Here, the trail narrows along some stretches due to the encroachment of the hydrangea hedges. After a total of 2.05 hrs, past the **Alto do Cabouco** ❻, reach a barbed wire fence and follow it by turning right to carry on to reach the **starting point** ❶.

↗ 240m | ↘ 1000m | 17km   Faial

5.15 hrs

From the Caldeira to Cedros   57

Descent through green forests along a levada towards the north

Enjoy nature and walk leisurely – this is what this walk is all about. It leads across the highest peak of the island, takes you along the rim of the Caldeira and ends up in a beautifully located levada. After a longish descent, this walk finishes in the rural north of the island.

Starting point: the cul-de-sac at the rim of the Caldeira, 904m.
Destination: Cascalho de Cima, district of Cedros, snack bar Aldina, 145m (bus stop Cascalho/Império 100m west).
Grade: mainly good dirt trails. At the start, steep and well-trodden ascent to Cabeço Gordo. Along the *levada*, it can be muddy after rain. Long descent on a tarmaced road.
Refreshment: cafés and snack bars in Cascalho de Cima. Nothing en route.
Alternative: circular walk back to the starting point (3.3km, 1 hr from the *levada*): after the first *levada* section ❺, follow the track right up to the rim of the Caldeira. 5 mins after the only cattle grid, leave the track and follow traces of a path uphill. Once up on the hill, turn right and continue to the road ❸. From there, walk on the same trail you used on the way out back to the starting point.
Linking tip: Walk 55 and 56.
Note: the entire area around the crater belongs to the Reserva Natural da Caldeira do Faial. Because of this, you must always keep to the designated trails and refrain from collecting or damaging any of the flora. The descent to the bottom of the crater is only permitted in the company of an official park guide (fee charged).

The rim of the Caldeira rises from the clouds high above the Triângulo.

The starting point is the cul-de-sac at the upper rim of the **Caldeira** ❶. At first, begin walking a few paces through a short tunnel to the marvellous viewpoint. The walking route begins at the trail board. Here, a short, stepped trail ascends to the ridgeline and then a footpath flanked by hydrangea hedges turns left toward the Cabeço Gordo, crowned by a thicket of aerials. Past the first altitude survey point at the Canto dos Saquinhos, the ancient trail becomes quite steep and overtrodden for some mins. Once you have reached the same level as some old concrete posts, the path veers to the right half way below the Cabeço Gordo. Where the path forks, keep to the right and beyond it right again ❷ and continue on the most obvious trail at the upper and inner edge of the Caldeira, just below the crater rim that runs parallel to the road leading to the summit.

Once you have circumvented about a quater of the crater, climb up to the crater rim where the road bends sharply to the left ❸. From here, the walk continues on the road zigzagging its way down the slope of the Caldeira towards west and passes the turn-off to Serra da Feteira. After a total of 1.40 hrs, turn right at the **trail board** ❹ and follow the red gravel trail (sign: Levadas).

The trail first goes uphill and splits after 100m. Keep left and go down to the water basin. From here, a path leads along a small *levada*. After rain, this section of the trail can be pretty muddy. After 40 mins, you reach a 10-metre-long, secured *levada* bridge high above the streambed. Go straight where the *levada* meets the gravel trail again ❺ to reach the next *levada* section (for the Alternative turn right). Some bridges are safely secured by wooden railings. After 45 mins, circumvent a short section where the rock has broken off. Five mins later, the collapsed canal suddenly ends at a **break-off point** ❻ where you can still see the remains of a landslide (3.20 hrs).

Follow the grassy, partially steep trail that leads along wooden steps left down the hill. Cross a small bridge over the washed-out stream. The path leads down the valley on

Leisurely walk along the levada.

the right bank of the stream and immediately bends right. At the following fork, keep right and climb up the extremely steep scree slope. After this rather arduous ascent, continue left along the water canal. 10 mins later, you reach a short **tunnel** ❼. After another 25 mins, a heavily eroded dirt trail crosses the *levada* where you leave the canal to the left. The trail quickly leads to a **cul-de-sac** ❽ which is also a possible pick-up spot (4.10 hrs).
From here, continue straight on the road downhill. After 40 mins, the Canada Larga crosses the **ER 2** ❾ at a water reservoir. Continue straight down towards **Cedros (Cascalho de Cima)**. After another 25 mins of descent, turn right at the transverse trail and continue to the main road **EN 1** ❿ where you see a bus stop and a little further the Aldina snack bar.

Faial ↗ 400m | ↘ 330m | 7.5km

58 From Capelo to Praia do Norte

2.40 hrs

Varied linear walk along the western slope of the Caldeira

Lush forests, a marvellous view of the western island and splendid walking trails await you during this walk between Capelo and Praia do Norte. You also climb several lava domes, which line up along the western flank of the Caldeira. At the end of this walk, a donkey path leads down to the coast to a lovely wave-lapped sandy beach. If this is not enough and you would like to see and walk more, you can take a detour along a former water canal on the way.

Starting point: Capelo, café O Vulcão in the centre, 190m (bus stop Capelo/Cruzeiro).
Destination: Praia do Norte, church, 265m (bus stop Ramal da Praia 200m south-west).
Grade: trail across the Cabeços partially steep and exposed. Last stretch on the road.
Refreshment: café O Vulcão in Capelo, snack bar Rumar in Praia do Norte.
Alternative: longer walk with *levada*

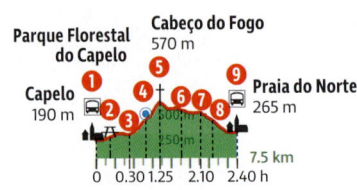

hike (section 6.3km, 2 hrs): on the road ❻, continue to the right until you get to the junction. Here, go diagonally left through the wooden gate in the hydrangea hedge, walk uphill along stone steps and turn left at the edge of the pasture from where you walk along a fence until you reach the road. Go right here. After 100m, a country lane branches off to the left. Here, a footpath disappears in the forest. It gets increasingly steep along high wooden steps which allows you to gain altitude quickly. Pass two rock caves. At a water pipe, the trail finally flattens out. Here, continue left to the water basin. From here, a path leads along a small *levada*. After 40 mins, reach a 10-metre long, but secured, *levada* bridge high above a stream. Shortly after, a gravel trail crosses the canal. Follow it down to the left until you get to a track. Continue left and after 15 mins, go right down the road ❼.
Linking tip: Walk 59.

Steep ascent to the Cabeço do Fogo.

From the junction in the centre of **Capelo** ❶ with a small supermarket and a café, follow the main road towards Horta and pass the Centro de Artesanato. Immediately after, go left at the end of the village and reach the **Parque Florestal do Capelo** ❷. Turn right at the small museum (Casa Rural Típica). At the end of the forest park, the road turns into a forest trail which ends at a **crossroad** ❸ after 15 mins. Go left here. After another 15 mins, turn left at the next crossroad and continue until you get to a road. Diagonally opposite, there is a washing site at the **Fonte das Areias** ❹ (50 mins).

Above the water reservoir, a footpath disappears in the undergrowth. It starts off as a trail covered in loose stones and later climbs up the hill along wooden steps. There are wooden railings along the last and very steep section of the ascent. Once you reach the altitude survey point on top of the **Cabeço do Fogo** ❺, go right and walk down along the eastern flank. At the bottom, you reach a pasture with a trough. Walk right up the hill on a pasture trail. After a short section in the forest, the hiking trail bends left at a cattle trough and leads steeply along wooden steps up to another volcanic hill. Behind it, the footpath rejoins a **road** ❻ (1.40 hrs; for Alternative, go right).

Turn left and after 15 mins, you meet the **turn-off** ❼ (Alternative from the right) that leads down to Praia do Norte (sign: Ramal da Praia do Norte). 10 mins later and a good 50m past the first left-hand bend, leave the road and turn right. Alongside the edge of a pasture, walk downhill on a **grassy trail** ❽ seamed by hortensias. After another 10 mins, you reach the first houses from where a road starts. Continuing straight ahead, reach the EN 1. Here, turn left towards the church in **Praia do Norte** ❾.

Faial ↗ 590m | ↘ 590m | 16.1km

59 From Praia do Norte to Norte Pequeno

4.50 hrs

Walk through the area created by an eruption in 1672 in the west

This walk takes you through Faial's geologically youngest area, which was only formed 10,000 years ago. The landscape as we see it today was last shaped in 1672. A donkey path first takes you down to the coast with a beautiful sandy beach which is often swept by waves. There are quite a few summer houses scattered across the area. After reaching Norte Pequeno, an ancient connecting trail takes you through the undergrowth back to Norte Pequeno. The return route leads past one of the island's finest springs.

Starting point: Praia do Norte, Rumar snack bar, 260m (bus stop Ramal da Praia 200m south-west).
Grade: descent and ascent to and from Fajã on a donkey path. Coastal section on rocky ground; some stretches on dusty sandy tracks.
Refreshment: Rumar snack bar in Praia do Norte, Fajã snack bar in Fajã.
Alternative: shorter walk without the coastal section (660m, 10 mins): in Fajã, just above the chapel, turn left, then after 150m at a fountain turn right onto the Caminho da Quinta. Leave Fajã and continue to a water reservoir. 100m beyond, join the main route and turn left onto the forest path ⓬ to follow it uphill.
Bathing: sandy beach in Fajã.
Linking tip: Walk 58.

From the Rumar snack bar in **Praia do Norte** ❶, follow the main road towards the church and turn left downhill after 50m. At the bottom, turn right onto the crossroad and continue straight ahead keeping the same elevation. After 5 mins, leave the road as it turns inland again, and turn left at a fountain, crossing a ford onto a narrow side path. After 150m, a path branches off to the left – this is your descent route ❷ to Fajã. But for now, continue straight ahead and, after you have passed the cemetery, turn left at the next crossroad. This leads you to the EN 1, and just on the left, you reach the enchanting **Miradouro da Ribeira das Cabras** ❸.
Return the same way past the cemetery to the junction with the country lane ❷. From here, follow the country lane downhill to the right

View from the Miradouro da Ribeira das Cabras to Fajã.

towards the coast where it ends at a cattle trough. A faint trail continues straight ahead across the meadow toward the reeds, from where you start the pleasant but slightly hidden descent to Fajã. In the second left-hand bend, you can make a short detour to a viewpoint. After 15 mins, you reach **Fajã** ❹ (1.05 hrs). Follow the road to the right all the way to the coast. Here, a path on the right leads down to the sandy swimming bay of Baía da Ribeira das Cabras.

From here, continue along the coastal road to the left before you turn right onto the Caminho do Porto at the next barbecue spot. Just past the old tidal well, turn left just before the port and, after 100m, follow an old cart track uphill to a small chapel. Behind the chapel, continue going uphill until you reach the **main road** ❺ (for the Alternative, turn left). Turn right here, and after 25m, take the footpath downhill to the right. It continues as a gravel track, bends to the right after 80m, and eventually joins a road which you follow downhill to the right for 100m. Just before the quarry, a dirt path begins on the left which, after 10 mins, ends again at another quarry which is being refilled. The trail gets a little confusing here. Walk through the quarry in a straight line. Directly at the coast, the old **coastal walking trail** ❻ begins (1.45 hrs). The unmarked entry point is the lowest north-western spot of the quarry.

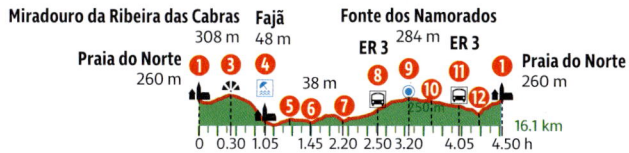

Old coastal path to Norte Pequeno. *Cheers – Fonte dos Namorados.*

After 35 mins, the adventure trail ends at a **gravel trail** ❼ which you follow uphill to the left. It merges with a road which you follow to the right. The houses of **Norte Pequeno** are widely scattered and remind of a hidden world. The road soon turns into a dirt trail which merges with the **ER 3** ❽ after 20 mins. Follow the road straight uphill (sign: Cabeço Verde). The road turns into a red dirt track and bends sharply to the left after 5 mins. 20m before the bend, turn left and follow a grassy path which soon becomes a red dirt track again. Follow it uphill to the left. After 10 mins, you pass the **Fonte dos Namorados** ❾ with picnic tables and some of the best spring water on the island (3.20 hrs).

About 10 mins later, leave the main trail and descend on a road to the left (if you want to finish the walk in Capelo, continue straight on and after 10 mins turn right onto the main road which leads directly to the centre of Capelo). At the next fork, keep right and at the next junction go right again until you reach the **EN 1** ❿. Go left here and follow the dusty Caminho do Goulart. The wide red dirt track veers back towards the north and merges with the ER 3 after 20 mins. Ascend the ER 3 for 200m to the right, then follow the red **dirt trail** ⓫ downhill through the forest. After 15 mins, a **forest trail** ⓬ branches off to the right (sign: Praia do Norte). It soon turns into a path that climbs steeply up the slope and then traverses it. Once at the top, keep slightly left at the first fork, pass under the telephone line, and then continue climbing right until you reach the road.

Here, rejoin the outward route and follow it to the right, back into the centre of **Praia do Norte** ❶.

↗ 620m | ↘ 620m | 12.9km Faial **TOP**

4.20 hrs

Ponta dos Capelinhos

60

Green volcanic cones and a barren lunar landscape

Hardly any other walk could offer such contrast as this excursion on the western tip of Faial. Starting at the densely wooded volcanic peaks of Cabeço Verde and Cabeço do Canto, walk along the former island coast line where in 1957/58, after a volcanic eruption that went on for months, new land was formed. Even today, this area looks like a lunar landscape.

Starting point: Capelo, church, 187m (bus stop Capelo/Igreja).
Grade: mostly broad gravel tracks; the descent from Caldeirão leads along a steep, narrow footpath; sure-footedness is required for this walk.
Refreshment: nothing en route.
Bathing: when the sea is calm, in the natural bathing area at the old harbour in Comprido.

Near the buried village of Comprido, the coast is very rugged – Capelinhos in the background.

View of Capelinhos during the descent of Caldeirão.

Begin the walk at the car park at the church in **Capelo** ❶ and follow the street for 130m toward the western peak. At the point past the kindergarten where the street hooks slightly to the right, ascend along the first grassy trail. 5 mins later, cross over a meadow and then continue along the right-hand edge following a row of Japanese cedars and wild ginger plants. Finally get to a red **dirt trail** ❷ and turn left onto it. 300m on, turn left on the track to continue. The track forks again soon; take the right-hand **road** ❸ to ascend toward the Cabeço Verde crowned by aerials. Past a wide, right-hand bend, the return route that you will follow later on forks off to the left (sign: Furna Ruim/ Caldeirão). However, you continue ascending along the road to reach the **Cabeço Verde** ❹ which you reach after a climb totalling 1 hour. Follow the circular trail clockwise around the rim of the crater. The view reaches from the caldeira down to the western tip of the island.

Afterward, turn back again to the trail below the crater. Follow the sign for a few paces to the right to leave the track and cross over a meadow. Here, steps climb down to the **Furna Ruim** ❺, only a few metres away; this is a caved-in lava tunnel that lies at the trail's edge, unfortunately buried under a thick blanket of vegetation. 30m past this, follow the trail markings to the left through a short stretch of dense woodland and then reach a viewpoint, taking in the western tip of the island and the **Caldeirão** (1.30 hrs). From here, a steep, stony trail begins to descend continuing the route downward, sometimes over steps. Soon another viewpoint appears at the rim of the Caldeirão. 250m from this point, your trail forks to the left and descends (the right-hand trail is the northern route to circle the rim of the crater). After some steeper stretches, finally reach a **track** ❻.

On the opposite side of this road, pick up a trodden path which ascends to the **Cabeço do Canto** ❼ and, at the top, turn left. After circling round half-way, at the western side, leave the crater trail behind by

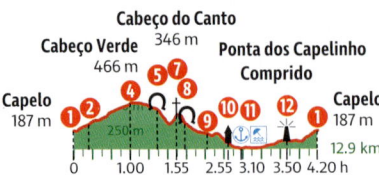

turning left again and, past a gate, descend steeply again towards Capelinhos. Once you are down, meet the dirt trail again, however, turn right at first to reach the entrance to the cave **Gruta do Cabeço do Canto** ❽ (you'll need a torch).

Return to the dirt trail and a good 5 mins of walking brings you to an open area. Now the landscape begins to change. At first, follow traces of a path on the left along the forest edge. After 200m, the trail bends sharply, after which a path leads through the undergrowth to reach an old *vigia* and, past this, descend further to get to the **ER 3** ❾.

On the other side behind the crash barrier, a well-trodden path cuts through the barren landscape and leads up the hill, where you turn left along the old cliff edge. The dusty, rocky path over loose ground leads down to the visitor centre at the old lighthouse at the **Ponta dos Capelinhos** ❿ (2.55 hrs). The entire protruding terrain was created by the eruption of the Vulcão dos Capelinhos in 1957/58. Pathless, descend through the ash landscape in a southerly direction to a car park and continue to the old harbour of **Comprido** ⓫. When the sea is calm, you can bathe in the lava pools. But be careful: there are dangerous currents! Just before reaching the almost completely buried ruins of Comprido, immediately beyond the car park at the small museum Casa dos Botes, a broad, dusty track forks off to follow the seaside south-eastward. Take this track for a good 40 mins to reach the new **Farol do Vale Formoso** ⓬. Continue along the track and, a good 10 mins later, turn left onto the first red dirt trail ⓭. Follow the transversal path halfway up the slope to the left and take this back to the ER 3 in **Capelo**. Turn right to return to the **starting point** ❶.

Faial ↗ 190m | ↘ 190m | 3.7km

61 Morro de Castelo Branco

1.10 hrs

Easy circular walk through a nature reserve area for seabirds

The area around the volcanic rock Morro de Castelo Branco is a nature reserve and protected habitat for many seabirds. On the descent, you can already enjoy views stretching as far as the Capelo peninsula on the western tip of the island. Passing through cattle pastures, you will soon reach the roughly 30,000-year-old rock formation. The ascent on the return leads you along an easier side road.

Starting point: Lombega, Pastelaria Bico Doce, 200m (bus stop Lombega/Bico Doce).
Grade: descent via country lanes and a grassy path (sometimes a bit overgrown); ascent to Lombega on a road.
Refreshment: Pastelaria in Lombega.

The approx. 30,000-year-old Morro de Castelo Branco is a protected nature reserve.

The Cabeço Verde rises proudly above the villages of Capelo and Varadouro.

From the Pastelaria Bico Doce in **Lombega** ❶, follow the main road north for 50m and turn left at the bus stop onto a narrow side street, which soon turns into a gravel track. Continue along the main trail which leads towards the coast. The trail gradually narrows into a grassy country lane and bends left across a pasture ❷.

Leave the country lane here and follow a faint path in the grass to the right. It turns left again along the coastline, runs between two rows of reeds, and is not always in the best condition. You can already see the Morro from here rising into view. After 15 mins on the grassy path, you reach a **parking area** ❸ at the end of a paved road.

Here, first walk down the trail to the right. At the bottom, a visitor centre with an exhibition on seabirds (Centro de Interpretaçao das Aves Marinhas) was being developed in 2025. The trail continues a few more metres before it joins the ascent ridge to **Morro de Castelo Branco** ❹. The rock itself can no longer be climbed (35 mins).

Return to the **parking area** ❸, follow the road for 50m, and immediately turn left uphill. After 20 mins, you reach the main road again. Turning left there, you will soon be back at the starting point in **Lombega** ❶.

São Jorge – a paradise for the cheese gourmet

- population: 8400
- county seats: Velas, 1800 inhabitants; Calheta, 1300 inhabitants
- area: 244km²
- length: 55km, width: 7km
- coastline: 140km
- highest points: Pico da Esperança, 1053m; Morro Pelado, 1019m

After Flores, São Jorge is another walkers' dream on the Azores. No other island can compare when it comes to the sheer number of coastal walks and descent routes. The island stretches its central spine into the Atlantic as if it might never end; one volcanic crater runs into another, all in a row. The coastline drops steeply on all sides. Through the centuries, even the smallest patches of level ground below the sheer cliffs have been settled and cleared for cultivation. Today, most of these *fajãs* (small coastal plains), about 75 in all, have been abandoned because often the only access is a descent along a stepped path. Since the earthquake of 1980, living at the foot of constantly slipping cliffs is deemed too dangerous by many islanders; numerous access trails have been destroyed anyway. Most *fajãs* are now only used for vegetable gardens and summer residences; very few are inhabited year-round. São Jorge attracts not only the holidaymaker but is also a Mecca for gourmets since the Azores' finest cheeses are produced here – by hand!

Like the other central islands, São Jorge was discovered around 1430 but active settlement began years later when Jácome de Bruges landed near Velas around 1450. In 1470, the Flemish Wilhelm van der Hagen settled

A picture postcard view from the northern coast above Fajã dos Cubres (Walk 69).

in Topo after an unsuccessful attempt on Flores. Velas received a town charter in 1500; by 1534, Topo and Calheta, too. The administrative seat of the island often changed. Plants used in dyeing and viniculture provided an economic boom in the 16th century. A violent volcanic eruption in 1580 caused the first serious setback. Frequent pirate attacks brought fear and uncertainty. In the late 18th century, the export of oranges revived prosperity. In 1808, another violent volcanic eruption destroyed Urzelina. In 1850, phylloxera put a sudden end to viniculture and in 1860, mildew decimated orange plantations. Each new misfortune set off another wave of emigration. In the last 100 years alone, the population has decreased by 50% and this trend continues. Lack of a large commercial harbour sets São Jorge apart economically even today. In 1980, the most destructive earthquake since many years occurred (7.0 on the Richter scale). Afterwards, most of the *fajãs* were abandoned and became ghost towns. Inadequate public transport, an airport at the mercy of fickle winds and poor prospects for the future block the way of economic improvement. The island's only gold mine today is a delicately sharp cheese, produced in 10kg rounds, ripened for many months until ready for export.

São Jorge is made up of two counties. **Velas** on the west coast, the main town, although small, shows flair and has spilled out onto the peninsula. The harbour with the marina lies protected in a small bay. The culture centre is housed in the old fortress. One enters the town through the old harbour

SÃO JORGE

Getting there
Scheduled flights within the Azores are only provided by SATA to São Miguel and Terceira. The airport is located 6km east of Velas in Fajã de Santo Amaro. There is also a year-round connection with the passenger ferry from Faial and Pico to Velas. In the summer, it also runs four times a week to Terceira, twice via Graciosa. In the winter months, connections are limited.

Bathing
Lovely pool in Urzelina. Natural bathing areas in Velas, Urzelina, Manadas, Fajã Grande, on the Ponta do Topo and in Fajã do Ouvidor. Protected lagoon at Fajã da Caldeira de Santo Cristo. Pebble beach in Fajã dos Vimes. Bathing area in the harbour at Calheta and in smaller harbours at Fajãs de Santo Amaro, Almas, Vimes and São João.

Festivities
Festa de São Jorge (Velas), April 23. Holy Spirit Celebrations from Easter until after Whitsun. Semana Cultural (Velas), beginning of July. In the summer, bullfighting in the streets with a tethered bull. Romaria a Nossa Senhora do Carmo (Fajã dos Vimes), beginning of September. Festa de Santa Catarina (Calheta), November 25.

Medical services
Hospital in Velas, tel +351 295 412 122. Clinic in Calheta, tel +351 295 460 120.

Tourist information
Turismo de São Jorge with a head office in Velas, tel +351 295 412 440, pt.sjo@azores.gov.pt, cmvelas.pt, cm-calheta.pt. Free Wi-Fi at the harbour in Velas, as well as at the airport and the harbour at Calheta.

Cultural activities
Island museum Casa Museu Cunha da Silveira and museum of sacred art in Velas. Ethnographical museum in Urzelina and Rosais (often closed). Museu Francisco de Lacerda in Calheta. Cheese-making cooperatives in Beira, Ribeira Seca (Lourais) and Santo Antão (Topo). Carpet weaving on a hand loom in Fajã dos Vimes. Handicrafts in the cooperative at Ribeira do Nabo. A visitor centre is located in Fajã da Caldeira de Santo Cristo.

Public transport
There are only a few bus connections. On weekdays, there are two buses from Calheta via the north coast to Velas and back, as well as one from Topo to Calheta and back, and two buses to Rosais. There are no buses on Sundays. A bus schedule is available at the *turismo*. Taxi ranks in Velas and Calheta, otherwise only by telephone. Due to the distances involved, best to hire a car. Prebook taxis for walks with a different starting and end point.

Accommodation
Very limited accommodation. Hotel and hostels in Velas. Some private rooms and small holiday homes are scattered throughout the island. A lovely campsite in Fajã Grande. Other campsites in Urzelina and Velas. A youth hostel is located near Calheta.

gate. Some of the buildings in the town centre still reflect the architecture of the 18th and 19th centuries and a few old mansions have remained. From the centrally-located Jardim da República with a little municipal garden, you can head off in any direction. The triple-naved church, Matriz de São Jorge, with an integrated museum of sacred art, merits a visit. From the tuff cone Morro Grande, you can enjoy a sweeping view taking in the entire town. Pleasant bathing spots complete the offer. The second county seat, **Calheta** has much less to offer. The harbour has just recently been enlarged. The tuna-processing factory at the town limits provides employment. Santa Catarina, the main church, is rather lacking in splendour. For an insight into daily life, visit the little museum of local history. Perched high above

Art deco in the town centre of Velas.

the ocean, the old lighthouse at the Ponta dos Rosais marks the westernmost tip of the island. On the way westward, pass Beira, home to a large cheese-makers' cooperative and then reach the local recreational area of Sete Fontes with a little labyrinth of walking trails. Tolêdo, Santo António, Norte Pequeno and Norte Grande are all little secluded villages on the northern coast, mostly characterised by agriculture. Many old footpaths descend to the seaside and the abandoned *fajãs* there. A high level route along the mountainous ridgeline in the middle of the island can be driven and affords marvellous views of the island and the neighbouring islands. Along the southern route, pass Velas, former centre for the orange industry with plantations still surrounding the present-day airport at Fajã de Santo Amaro. Past this, reach the little settlement of Urzelina with its surviving bell tower, some old windmills and the sea cave Furna das Pombas. Heading eastward, settlements are even more few and far between. In Manadas, the church Santa Bárbara merits a visit, one of the most splendid examples of Baroque architecture on the entire archipelago. The unique lagoon at Fajã da Caldeira de Santo Cristo boasts clam-growing and is a popular spot for surfers. In Calheta, a long journey begins, crossing over the uninhabited high plateau of the Serra do Topo on the eastern side then to the secluded settlements of Santo Antão and Topo with the islet of Ilhéu do Topo lying offshore; the islet is a protected nature reserve.

São Jorge ↗ 360m | ↘ 360m | 13.3km

62 Ponta dos Rosais

3.40 hrs

Excursion to the western tip

A lonely lighthouse is the highlight on the western tip of São Jorge. From the woodland park Sete Fontes, farming trails and a long track lead directly to the old lighthouse on the Ponta dos Rosais; the lighthouse was severely damaged by the 1980 earthquake. On the way back, you walk on dirt trails south of Monte Trigo and through pastureland with grazing cattle.

Starting point: Parque Florestal das Sete Fontes, Largo das Sete Fontes, 410m (next bus stop Ponta at the end of the village of Ponta de Rosais).
Grade: mostly an easy walk via broad gravel trails, dusty trail to the lighthouse.
Refreshment: bar Vieira in Ponta de Rosais.

Alternative: excursion to Miradouro do Pico da Velha (2.1km, 45 mins there and back): from the square at the starting point at the fork, follow a dirt trail southward (sign: Miradouro). The trail ascends in bends to climb up to the Pico da Velha and then circles the summit. Return along the approach route.

From the central square with the Capela de São João Baptista in the woodland park **Sete Fontes** ❶, at first follow the red-coloured track westward (sign: Farol) and, not quite 10 mins later and past the reservoir, turn right onto a **dirt trail** ❷. Some mins later, the trail ends at a stable and an intersecting trail. Turn right onto the trail and follow this for 30 mins, continuing over pastureland, to finally reach a dusty **track road** ❸, which you follow to the right. After 15 mins,

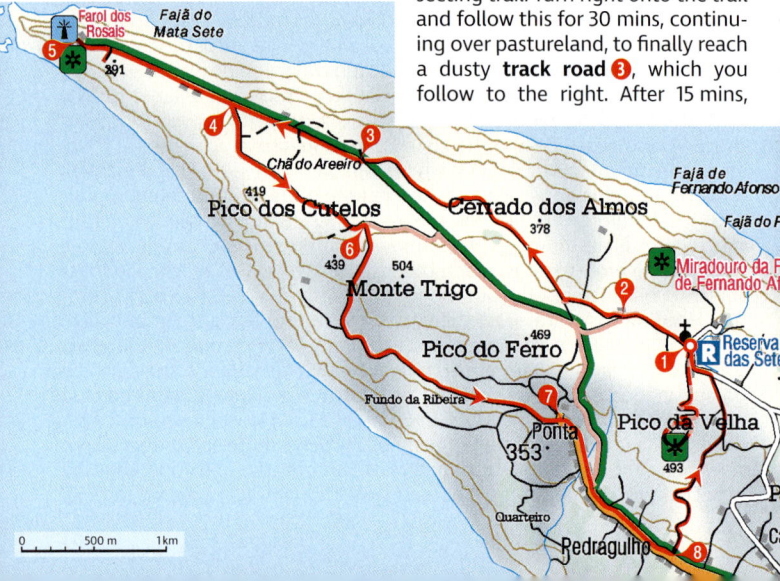

Clear view of the lighthouse at Ponta dos Rosais from the old vigía.

pass a **turn-off** ❹, which you will take later to return to the starting point. Stay on the track that ends at the lighthouse **Farol da Ponta dos Rosais** ❺ (1.20 hrs). Just before the end of the long straight, a concrete stepped trail leads left to ascent to a *vigía* boasting a lovely view. The ruin of the derelict lighthouse is closed and all viewpoints to the wild western tip have been bricked up and are no longer accessible due to the risk of collapse.

After this excursion, return to the track and at the **turn-off** ❹ turn right onto the first dirt trail, which heads directly toward the two hills of Pico da Baleia and Monte Trigo. 25 mins after that, just before the trail reaches its highest point, at the fork, turn right onto a **dirt trail** ❻ which crosses over the saddle between the two hills and, on the other side, becomes a splendid panoramic trail for the southern coast. After a total of 2.45 hrs, reach the street at the village limits of **Ponta de Rosais** ❼.

Turn right onto the street and pass a washing site and a fountain (1887). After 20 mins, turn sharply left at the end of the village of Ponta, opposite house no. 59, and follow the **Canada do Miradouro** ❽, which is paved for the first 100m, uphill. It quickly turns into an old mule path. After 30 mins, you reach a road again where you turn left to return to the **Sete Fontes** ❶ woodland park.

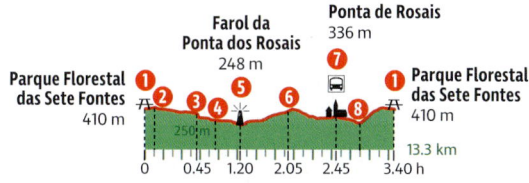

São Jorge ↗ 650m | ↘ 650m | 13.4km

63 Fajã de João Dias

4.40 hrs

Pleasant descent to the northern coastline

Only a few fajãs are so easily reached as Fajã de João Dias. From Rosais, at the outset, supply roads lead to the trailhead. Starting here, a pleasant donkey path zigzags down in many bends to the coastline. One of the easiest descents down the steep cliffs of the island!

Starting point: the church in Rosais, 245m (bus stop Rosais/Igreja).
Grade: until reaching the edge of the cliff, mostly via gravel trails. Descent along a broad donkey path; sure-footedness is required. Sometimes somewhat muddy when wet.
Refreshment: cafés in Rosais.
Bathing: small pebble beach in Fajã de João Dias.

Past the church in **Rosais** ❶ and at the little football pitch, climb up the Caminho de Cima. After a good 5 mins, a detour which starts to the left at house no. 56 and leads to a **windmill** ❷ is well worth it.
Another good 5 mins later, turn left at the Loural sign. 10 mins later, reach a **water reservoir** ❸ and then at a trough, turn left onto a country lane to continue ascending. The lane climbs up along the streambed of the

Descent to Fajã de João Dias.

Ribeira da Canada das Faias and soon meets up with a road. Turn right onto the road and then take a left onto a **dirt trail** ❹ at the next possible turn-off (tiled sign: Fajã do João Dias). Follow this trail until it ends at a **cul-de-sac** ❺ (55 mins). The descent begins beyond the iron gate along a broad, well-constructed donkey path. At the beginning, the path is even paved in places. The path climbs quickly downward in bends but is never too steep. 50 mins later, you are at the bottom and turn left to follow the seaside until reaching the little Ermida de São João Evangelista in **Fajã de João Dias** ❻ (1.55 hrs), a settlement with three dozen holiday homes, all of which are lovingly cared-for but not always inhabited year-round. Past the chapel, continue left to cross through the settlement then pass two fountains to reach the white pebble bay on the ocean.

On the way back, follow the coastal path to the chapel. Pass the junction of the descent path and reach the end of a steep gravel track. Via this new access road, which is suitable for all-terrain vehicles, you will reach a **viewpoint** ❼ with a swing on the high plateau after about 1 hr (3.20 hrs). From here, continue inland along the red track which soon turns into a road that joins a crossroad ❽. Continue right on this road. After about 30 mins, you reach a **fork** ❾ where you continue straight ahead. In about 5 mins, you reach the **water reservoir** ❸ and rejoin the path you took on the way out. Follow it back to the starting point in **Rosais** ❶.

TOP 64 — São Jorge — Fajã de Além

↗ 490m | ↘ 490m | 4.9km
2.50 hrs

Along the old access trails to Fajã de Além

No longer inhabited, Fajã de Além lies isolated and scattered along the northern coast. An ancient obscure access route brings you down to the western end of the settlement for a curious look at the gardens that are still under cultivation there. After this excursion, you will climb back up again but this time you will take the steeper path on the east side.

Starting point: Santo António, the chapel in the district of Ermida, 468m (bus stop Entrocamento – Caminho da Ermida 500m west on the ER 1).
Grade: steep, slippery path along a precipitous slope; the ascent is sometimes over steep steps of natural stone. Physical fitness and sure-footedness are required.
Refreshment: nothing en route.

Start off at the **Ermida de Nossa Senhora da Auxiliadora** ❶ (1936) in **Santo António**, pass the fountain (1903) and descend for 250m along the street. Soon reach a concrete bridge and immediately past this turn left onto the **footpath** ❷. The path leads along the upper edge of the pasture and 100m on, hooks off to the left and then descends along a watercourse that is dry in summer. 200m on, change over to the other bank at a small stone bridge and follow the traces of a path toward the coast. Soon the descent ❸ begins.

Climb down in numerous zigzags, passing a number of springs and, immediately at the outset, enjoy a marvellous view of the *fajãs* on the northern coastline. After a total of about 1 hr, reach the **first house** ❹.

A stream appears just after, diverted into a canal. A good 5 mins later, at a fork near the first cluster of houses, bear right to continue and before the patch of reeds and rushes that follow just after, bear right again. Two more streams are met and you continue above the coast following the edge of the reeds. The houses are scattered far apart from one another; grapes and vegetables are growing everywhere. Past a bridge (2004), reach a cable hoist and turn inland to reach another cluster of houses at **Fajã de Além** ❺ (1.25 hrs).

At this point, the trail ascends again to the right. Reach a little village square with a 'winter garden' and continue half left above it. 50m on, keep to the right after the concrete bridge and, a good 75m further on, still before reaching a house, climb up to the right. Starting now, ascend steadily along the main trail. The winding trail ascends via countless, sometimes very high, steps. The climb up the slope is very strenuous. On the way up, pass some waterfalls. A bench located past a stream gives you the chance to catch your breath before the final steep climb begins. Finally, at a cable hoist, arrive at the top ❻ (2.20 hrs).

Immediately behind the upper end of the wire cable at the Miradouro da Fajã de Além, a concrete road begins. Ascend along this road to the main road **ER 1** ❼. Turn right here to continue and 10 mins later, turn right again to enter **Santo António**. Here, keep straight ahead until returning to the **Ermida de Nossa Senhora da Auxiliadora** ❶.

On the trail through Fajã de Além.

São Jorge

↗ 390m | ↘ 390m | 6.5km
2.15 hrs

65 Fajã da Ribeira da Areia

Modern and ancient trails along the coast

A narrow but easily-driven trail descends from Ribeira da Areia to the fajã of the same name. For your descent, however, you will take the ancient footpath which climbs quickly down the steep, coastal cliff. After completing the brief tour of the settlement which has only been revived in recent years, take the pleasant road to climb back up again.

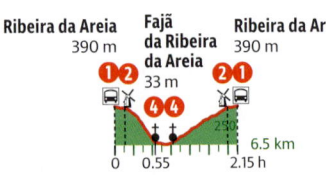

Starting point: Ribeira da Areia, the chapel São Miguel Arcanjo, 390m (bus stop Ribeira da Areia/Ermida).
Grade: descent along an ancient footpath. Easy ascent via a roadway. Otherwise, dirt and tarmac trails. Sure-footedness is required.
Refreshment: nothing en route.

On the way to Fajã da Ribeira da Areia.

From the Ermida de São Miguel Arcanjo in **Ribeira da Areia** ❶, follow the main street for a few metres eastward (right) and then, opposite the fountain (1899), turn left onto the concrete trail. 150m on, bear right and afterwards, follow a cart track which crosses a streambed 100m further on (old cartwheel tracks can be seen here). The trail continues straight on, heading for the stump marking the ruins of a windmill. At a **crossroad** ❷ past the windmill, turn left and, 100m further on, keep to the main trail by bearing left (sign: Fajã da Ribeira da Areia). Soon reach a cul-de-sac and 250m past this, the street hooks off to the right. Here, continue straight ahead to climb down along the old, initially somewhat overgrown **descent trail** ❸.
The footpath soon improves and descends along many bends through the forest. After 20 mins,

Rock arch in Fajã da Ribeira da Areia.

pass a roadside shrine and then emerge from the forest soon after. At this point, bear right. At a house with a painting of the Virgin Mary, you come to a street; turn left onto the street to continue to the little church close by, the Ermida de Nossa Senhora da Fátima (55 mins). You have already reached the first houses of **Fajã da Ribeira da Areia** ❹ which was more or less abandoned in 1980. A century before, about 500 people lived here. Continue by turning left onto the Caminho do Arco which turns into a dirt trail just outside the village and takes you to the coast where interesting rock formations and a rock arch have been created. At the most north-westerly corner of the loop, traces of a trail lead to the rock arches. From here, the main trail leads back to the village before it eventually returns to the fork below the chapel.

Take the road to ascend pleasantly back up again and then return along the approach route to the starting point in **Ribeira da Areia** ❶.

São Jorge ↗ 580m | ↘ 580m | 9.7km

66 Fajãs do Norte

3.45 hrs

Excursion to the forgotten fajãs on the northern coast

The fajãs on the northern side of the island are so close to one another that you can pass a number of them during this walk. Via a pumphouse, descend to Fajã do Mero. A refurbished connecting trail leads to Fajã da Penedia. From here, continue on a coastal path to Fajã das Pontas. At the end, a pleasant access road climbs back up again.

Starting point: Norte Pequeno, church, 464m (bus stop Norte Pequeno/Casa do Povo 75m east).
Grade: mostly along easy dirt and concrete-paved trails; descent via a narrow footpath. Exciting fishermen's path to Fajã das Pontas which is partly exposed. Sure-footedness is required.
Refreshment: café in Norte Pequeno. Nothing en route.
Alternative: excursion to Fajã da Neca (2.5km, 45 mins there and back): above the harbour in Fajã das Pontas, follow the gravel trail to the left until you reach the last houses. Beyond the houses, a coastal path continues for 15 mins. The detour ends at the ruins of Fajã da Neca. Afterwards, return along the same route.
Bathing: natural bathing area in Fajã das Pontas.

From the Igreja de São Lázaro in **Norte Pequeno** ❶, first follow the main street eastward for 60m and at the Casa do Povo, turn left onto the side street Canada da Igreja to continue. Some mins later, reach an **intersecting street** ❷ (info point A). Turn left to follow this street and then immediately bear left at the next fork. Soon, the street hooks off sharply to the left. At

View to Fajã da Penida.

this point, turn right onto a **dirt trail** ❸, following a stone wall through pastureland. 20 mins later, just after passing under the power lines, leave the dirt trail behind by turning right onto a **gravel trail** ❹. This descends through a forest to reach a viewpoint (info point D).

To the right, a broad, lit descending trail leads to the pumphouse for the springs **Sete Fontes** ❺ situated in the middle of the slope (50 mins). To the left, continue the descent along an old footpath through the forest until, at Fajã do Mero, you reach a **roadway** ❻ (1.25 hrs). Turn right to climb up this road. 15 mins later, pass the houses of Fajã das Fonduras. Now continue past a water reservoir and then cross over a stream. Past this point, the trail gradually improves and descends to **Fajã da Penedia** ❼ (1.50 hrs). At the village centre near a fountain (1972), you could turn left if you wish to make an excursion to the little chapel Santa Filomena. Many of the stone-built houses have been renovated in the meantime. Past the final houses, climb up again along bends via a pleasant track. Immediately at the first sharp right turn, go straight and follow a fishermen's path into the undergrowth (sign: Pontas) which leads to **Fajã das Pontas** ❽ in 20 mins. Just above the harbour to the right, you join the main trail (Alternative to the left). Follow the steep concrete path up to the right until you reach a track. A few steps to the right, you will find the **Miradouro da Linda** ❾.

For the way back, follow the well-maintained roadway leading up to a **turning area** ❿ (3.25 hrs). From here, continue ascending along the street. At the first junction near a little **bus stop shelter** ⓫, turn right. Cross over the next street at a fountain, join the trail that you took on the way out ❷ and turn left to return to the starting point in **Norte Pequeno** ❶.

São Jorge ↗ 280m | ↘ 1060m | 16.7km

67 Via Pico da Esperança to Fajã do Ouvidor

4.45 hrs

Panoramic tour over the central island ridge with a long descent to the northern coast

São Jorge looks like a needle in the Atlantic. This walk takes you across the central section of the island's long ridge, where one volcanic summit follows another. The trail continues across the highest point of the island, Pico da Esperança, and then descends to the northern coast, where you make your way down to the large Fajã do Ouvidor via Norte Grande.

Starting point: turn-off to Pico da Esperança at the highest point of ER 3, 783m.
Destination: Fajã do Ouvidor, harbour, 2m (the next bus stop is above in Norte Grande). Please pre-book a taxi for the return journey (there is no taxi stand at the destination).
Grade: wide, well-maintained gravel tracks up to Norte Grande; descent to the sea along an old footpath.
Refreshment: cafés in Norte Grande and a restaurant at Fajã do Ouvidor.
Alternative: 1. end of the route in Norte Pequeno (4.75km, 1.20 hrs): shortly after the road is paved again, follow the first dirt trail ❻ to the right (sign: Ribeira d'Areia). Stay on the main trail for 1.10 hrs and continue straight ahead to the ER 1. From here, turn right to the church in the centre of Norte Pequeno.
2. return to the starting point (5.3km, 1.30 hrs): from ❼, simply continue straight for 1.25 hrs until you reach the ER 3. Turn left and continue uphill to return to the starting point.
Bathing: natural bathing area Poça Simão Dias and the harbour basin at Fajã do Ouvidor.
Note: the high trail is often covered in clouds. Only do this walk on truly clear days.

View from Pico da Esperança across the Pico do Areeiro to the Serra do Topo.

The walk starts at the pass of the **ER 3** transverse road ❶. From here, a well-maintained track continues eastward, initially leading past a spring and around the northern flank of Pico do Pedro. There are several farm tracks branching off to some cattle pastures. On the southern slope of Morro Pelado, you will pass a **memorial** ❷ commemorating the 35 victims of the SATA plane crash in December 1999 (1.05 hrs). Beyond this point, the trail ascends toward **Pico da Esperança** ❸. If you feel like it, you can make a short detour from an information board on the western flank to reach the highest peak on the island (1.20 hrs). Continue past Pico do Areeiro and Pico Pinheiro to a **fork in the trail** ❹ (2.20 hrs). Turn left here and head downhill crossing a cattle grid. About 25 mins later, at another **junction** ❺, keep left again. The trail will soon be paved. After just under 15 mins, stay left on the **road** ❻ (Alternative 1 turns right). Another 100m on, cross another cattle grid and turn left again to join the Caminho Rural Longitudinal Norte. After 15 mins, just before a dip in the road, follow a **dirt**

215

Magnificent views of the North: Miradouro da Fajã do Ouvidor.

trail ❼ which turns sharply to the right. Descend this trail for 30 mins to go directly into the centre of **Norte Grande ❽** (4 hrs).
Turn right here and continue north along the village road (Canada da Igreja) just past the church which is opposite the bus stop. Passing two fountains (dated 1890), you will reach the **Miradouro da Fajã do Ouvidor ❾** after 10 mins. A few steps lead down to the left, and an old, partly cobbled footpath zigzags steeply downhill over many stone steps to a pumping station, before it joins the **main road ❿**.
Continue downhill on the side trail on the other side until you reach a junction with a tree at its centre. From here, go straight and once you have passed a small church, continue all the way down to the harbour of **Fajã do Ouvidor ⓫**. If you feel like it, you can take a detour that starts in the final bend – 150m before the harbour – by turning left just before two residential houses from where you join a marked path with a wooden railing. This path soon branches off to the left and leads to the beautiful natural bathing area of Poça Simão Dias in just a few mins.

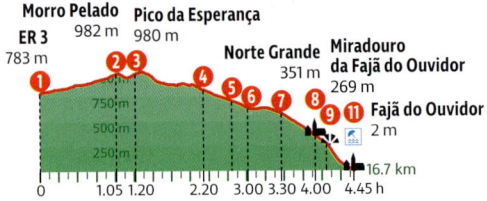

↗ 370m | ↘ 370m | 5.6km São Jorge

1.50 hrs

From Biscoitos to Fajã Grande   68

Descent into a tourist village with typical windmills

An ancient connecting trail descend in hardly any time at all from the farming village of Biscoitos into the quiet and remote Fajã Grande. In summer, it's bustling with young people because here, the youth hostel and the campsite are very popular. The Caminho da Fonte follows several springs. After a quick swim, you will find the return way rather pleasant.

Starting point: Biscoitos, chapel, 327m (bus stop Biscoitos/Ermida).
Grade: the descent is partially extremely steep and exposed and very damp in places. Experience, sure-footedness and good footwear are essential. The ascent follows a comfortable dirt trail.
Refreshment: cafés in Biscoitos and at the campsite. Bar Portinhos at the campsite.
Alternative: descent to Fajã Grande on the Caminho da Atalhada (section 660m, 20 mins): at the junction of the descent trail, follow the Caminho da Atalhada to the left. It is much more comfortable and an easier alternative to the main trail. At the bottom of the village street, go left and after 250m turn right down to the campsite.
Bathing: natural bathing area at the campsite.

The ancient woodland trail to Fajã Grande.

Fajã Grande in view – descent along the Caminho da Fonte.

The starting point is the Ermida de Nossa Senhora do Socorro in **Biscoitos** ❶. Starting here, follow the ER 1 while passing the fountain (1877) and heading towards Velas. At km23, turn left along the concrete trail Canada da Fonte. This soon becomes a grassy trail and, shortly afterwards, crosses over a red-coloured **gravel trail** ❷. Straight ahead, follow the cobbled hollow way. After 50m at the junction, continue straight (Alternative to the left). Soon reach the first spring captures, beyond which the path becomes very narrow. You will soon be able to enjoy a magnificent view of Fajã Grande. From here, the steep descent leads you across stone steps for a short while which requires full concentration. After you pass a first water house, you have to cross a damp yam field after which you will walk past a rock with a natural hole and more water houses. Finally, you reach the end of the roadway from where you continue straight into the village of **Fajã Grande** ❸. At house no. 70, a narrow concrete trail descends to the sea, where you find a **campsite** ❹ and a natural bathing area (45 mins).

Afterwards, return to the village street and then turn right. About 10 mins later, at a **fountain** ❺ next to house no. 56a turn left onto the narrow street climbing upwards. At the junction 100m on, bear to the right. At the last house, the street becomes a gravel trail. It bends and leads back towards Biscoitos. Keep ascending steadily straight on until reaching the junction ❷ with the approach route, just past the edge of the wood. Here, take the grassy trail to climb up to the main road and return to the starting point in **Biscoitos** ❶.

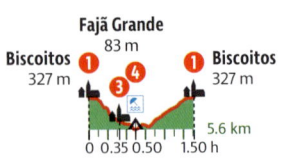

↗ 210m | ↘ 880m | 9.8km
3.40 hrs

São Jorge

From the Serra do Topo to the Fajã dos Cubres

TOP 69

The most frequently walked route on São Jorge

No other walk is as popular as the descent from the high plateau to Fajã da Caldeira de Santo Cristo. From the wind farm on the Serra do Topo, follow a donkey path to this unique coastal settlement with a deep blue lagoon, often used as the cover photo for many a picture book. Via a trail that has been broadened and flattened by quad bikers, the route continues in easy up-and-down walking to finally reach Fajã dos Cubres.

Starting point: the car park at km7.3 on the ER 2, 673m (bus stop).
Destination: Fajã dos Cubres, Nossa Senhora de Lourdes chapel, 7m. Prebook the taxi for the return journey (no taxi stand at the destination).
Grade: descent along an ancient, slippery footpath. Along the coast via a broad dirt trail (heavily frequented by quad bikes). Sure-footedness is required.
Refreshment: restaurant and snack bar in Fajã da Caldeira de Santo Cristo. Snack bars in Fajã dos Cubres.
Linking tip: Walk 71.
Bathing: pebble beach and lagoon in Fajã da Caldeira de Santo Cristo.

From the car park at km7.3 of the **ER 2** ❶, just past the turn-off to the wind farm (Parque Eólico), a trail crossing the pasture climbs up along a hydrangea hedge. Past a cattle trough, the trail ends on a **ridge** ❷. Here, the descending trail begins to the right, at first as a broad trodden-down, but slippery, walking path, climbing down along hydrangea hedges. Pass a cave shelter and soon reach the first wooden gate. Two other gates follow in 10-minute intervals. Afterward, the route continues along zigzags through the forest, sometimes as a trodden-down path, sometimes as a stepped path. After 40 mins of descent, the first view opens up, taking in the lower valley where you will cross a meadow in a wide serpentine further along the route. The trail has narrowed to a trodden-down path. At the lower end of the meadow and

Fajã da Caldeira de Cima.

A walker's heart leaps for joy: view of Fajã da Caldeira de Santo Cristo.

in the valley bottom, reach a fourth gate (1.10 hrs). Cross over a **bridge** ❸ spanning a stream. Here, the trail broadens and leads along an ancient cart track, sometimes showing old cobbles as it follows the stream down the valley. Always stay on the main trail. At a concrete bridge, reach the upper limits of **Fajã da Caldeira de Cima** ❹, abandoned at the end of 1980. Tumbledown watermills lie to the right. Just past the bridge, you could turn right onto a path to take a short excursion climbing down to a waterfall. 5 mins later, reach another bridge (built 2005) and get to a **fountain** ❺ yet another 5 mins later. At this point, an old cart track (Caminho das Polegadas) turns off to the left to ascend back again to the high plateau.

However, continue straight on along the main trail which soon bends to the left and from a viewpoint, it leads directly towards **Fajã da Caldeira de Santo Cristo**. Upon reaching the first houses, continue straight along the main trail until you reach the visitor centre. Here, turn right at the fountain and head towards the coast. At the end of this path, by a large fountain, turn left behind the stone wall to go directly to the centre near the **church** ❻ (2.10 hrs). Since 1984, the entire settlement is a protected natural reserve – so please be sure to scrupulously remove your rubbish!

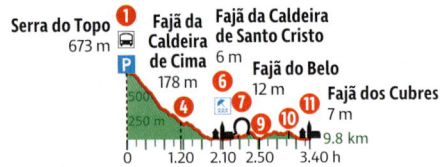

To the right, a very clear-cut path provides an excursion along the outer breakwater of the lagoon to the opening at the ocean (30 mins there and back).

Passing the church, continue straight ahead along a stone wall and bear right at the fork following immediately after. At an information board in front of the boathouse, continue to walk inland again and past a tide-powered well before you ascend to the main trail. Turn right onto the trail which leads you directly to the lagoon before you pass a steep cliff along a concrete-paved stretch. Shortly afterward a detour along a dirt trail turns left to ascend to the face of the cliff (sign: car park); at the foot of the cliff, you can find the entrance to the cave **Furna do Poio** ❼ (from the outside, this appears as a small hole in the basalt rock face but, on the inside, there is sometimes a little lake).

Next, pass **Fajã dos Tijolos** ❽ with a tide-powered well (2.30 hrs). The main trail now goes past the tiny settlement. Afterwards, a short stretch of ascent follows and, 20 mins later, reach **Fajã do Belo** ❾.

A century ago, over one hundred people lived here.

Just after, cross over the Ribeira do Belo (bridge) and 20 mins later cross over the Ribeira do Ferro (bridge). Past the river, you will soon reach a **cul-de-sac** ❿. Up to this point, the trail can only be driven with a quad bike. However, the trail turns into a more comofortable track which continues to a car park and then directly enters the settlement of **Fajã dos Cubres** ⓫, where, at the Ermida de Nossa Senhora de Lourdes you have reached your destination.

São Jorge ↗ 490m | ↘ 490m | 8.3km

70 Portal – Fajã dos Vimes

3.10 hrs

A short circular walk including a pleasant stretch of coastline

On the way to the idyllic Fajã dos Vimes, you pass the hamlet of Portal, the starting point of this circular walk. Right at the beginning, walk down to the tiny Fajã da Fragueira with its fertile orchards. From here, follow a quad trail along the coastline to Fajã dos Vimes, where the island's unique coffee is cultivated.

Starting point: Portal, the chapel Nossa Senhora da Boa Viagem, 208m.
Grade: descent to the seaside along dirt trails and a steep footpath. Sure-footedness is required.
Refreshment: cafés in Fajã dos Vimes.
Alternative: return along the road (section 3.3km; 1 hr): from Fajã dos Vimes, along the main road and pass the viewpoint, Miradouro da Fajã da Fragueira. From here, it is 35 mins to Portal.

Linking tip: Walk 71.
Bathing: pebble beach and natural bathing area at the Portinho in Fajã dos Vimes.

Just a few metres below the chapel at the exit for the village of **Portal** ❶, turn left to follow a red gravel trail with street lanterns (trail board). This descends, at first, until reaching an initial fork. Turn diagonally left here to continue while keeping on the level. Pass two watering troughs and get to a cul-de-sac. A footpath continues past this point. Soon reach a bridge spanning the Ribeira do Briador. The descending trail starts at a **stone cross** ❷. It quickly descends via steep serpentines and across some natural steps. In no time at all, reach the little **Fajã da Fragueira** ❸, which is used by the inhabitants of Portal for their gardens (35 mins).

View across Fajã da Fragueira towards Pico.

Turn right at a fountain. 20m further on, turn left through a breach in the wall to meet a meadow. Past a bridge, a quad bike trail sets off. 15 mins later, cross over a streambed that is dry in summer. Another 15 mins later, after numerous up-and-downs, the trail ends at a bend at the first houses of **Fajã dos Vimes** ❹. Now turn right along the street. At the bridge spanning the Ribeira dos Vimes, 10 mins later, you can climb up to the left for a break at the Café Nunes and sample the locally-grown coffee. Weavers are at work on the first storey above the café. Directly in front of the little chapel São Sebastião (1.15 hrs) turn left to continue along the **street** ❺.

After 100m, the street bends to the right. Turn half left to join the gravel trail. In the upper section, the trail narrows and turns into an old cobbled stepped trail. After a short stretch on a concrete trail, you will rejoin the **main road** ❻ at the village sign. Follow the serpentines uphill towards the left. A good 10 mins later, cross a bridge spanning the Ribeira dos Vimes. Continue by crossing the bridge spanning the Ribeira do Capadinho. 150m further on, where electric lines intersect overhead, at a steel cable, turn left along a **country lane** ❼ to descend (the Alternative continues straight on). Above the first houses of Fajã dos Vimes, 10 mins later, get to a concrete trail and turn sharp right to continue. After 150m, you reach the road at the end of the village. At the bend, you get to your approach trail ❹. Return along the cobbled cart track, via **Fajã da Fragueira** ❸, pass the **stone cross** ❷ and return to **Portal** ❶.

São Jorge ↗ 680m | ↘ 1300m | 15.7km

71 Serra do Topo – Fajã dos Vimes – Fajã de São João

6.00 hrs

A walkers' dream on the southern island

This walk in the island's south-east is a classic example of São Jorge's renown as a paradise for walkers. From the wind farm at the Serra do Topo, at first climb down along an ancient stepped trail to Fajã dos Vimes where carpet weavers and coffee plantation owners make their home. Via Fajã dos Bodes, ascend along the old coastline path to reach Loural where the tour can be divided into two individual walks. The dream walk ends in Fajã de São João.

Starting point: the car park at km7.3 on the ER 2, 673m (bus stop).
Destination: Fajã de São João, Café Águeda at the chapel, 49m. Pre-book the taxi for the return trip (no taxi stand at the destination).
Grade: much of the route is along steep, ancient footpaths. Near the settlements, mostly along track roads. A high degree of sure-footedness, an excellent head for heights and sufficient physical fitness are required.

Refreshment: cafés in Fajã dos Vimes, café Águeda in Fajã de São João.
Alternative: via Loural 2° (section 840m, 15 mins): on the road through Loural 3° ⑪, turn left up to the Ermida de Nossa Senhora do Livramento in Loural 2° (15 mins). You can either finish the walk here or start the second section by heading east down the road, where a trail board at ⑪ indicates the continuation of the main walk. If you decide to finish the walk in Loural, you must book a taxi in advance.
Linking tip: Walks 68, 70 and 72.
Notes: this tour can be easily interrupted, for example in Loural, and simply divided into two separate walks.
In 2024, this walk was cut off by a landslide between ⑧ and ⑨. It is uncertain when it will reopen. Signposted detour (1.10 hrs – 2.20 hrs shorter): at ④, turn left and follow the signposted grassy path. It is mostly level and widens into a comfortable country lane. After 45 mins, turn right down to the road, and after 10 mins, continue left at the church. After a quarter of an hour, you will reach ⑪ and follow the main walk straight ahead.
Bathing: pebble beaches and natural bathing areas in the tiny harbours of Fajã dos Vimes and Fajã de São João.

Descent from the highlands.

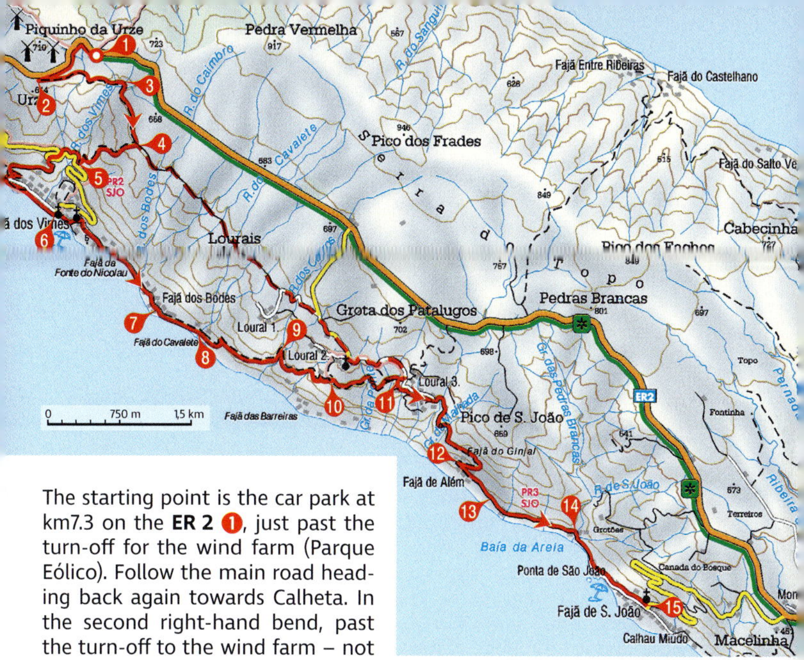

The starting point is the car park at km7.3 on the **ER 2** ❶, just past the turn-off for the wind farm (Parque Eólico). Follow the main road heading back again towards Calheta. In the second right-hand bend, past the turn-off to the wind farm – not quite 100m after crossing under power lines – turn sharp left onto a **country lane** ❷. After 30m, the lane hooks off to the left, narrows and while following a wall of hydrangea, crosses under the power lines. 10 mins later, it reaches the streambed of the Ribeira do Capadinho. Behind a first cattle gate, walk up briefly along a pasture fence. At another cattle gate, you reach the end of the fence. From here, walk down on a narrow, sloping footpath along a barbed wire fence. After 50m, turn away from the fence and follow the clearly defined traces of a path down to a depression. From here, the path gets a bit confusing for a short while. Cross three more cattle gates to reach a meadow and a heavily eroded course of a **stream** ❸. Turn right here. Once in the juniper forest, the path climbs up again. The entrance to the forest is somewhat difficult

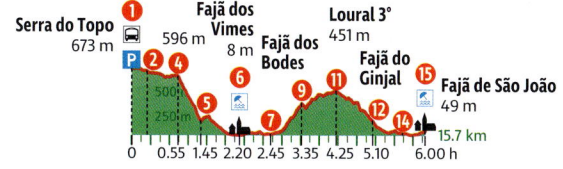

225

Along the trail to Fajã dos Vimes.

to find. An old sunken trail leads you uphill through the forest, and after 10 mins, you reach yet another, old, cattle gate. 5 mins later, be careful not to miss the **narrow path** ❹ going down to your right (55 mins).
This ancient stepped trail with countless stone steps is often very steep. You need about 50 mins for the descent to a **road** ❺. Then, turn right onto the road to continue and 100m on, reach the bridge spanning the Ribeira dos Vimes. A second bridge follows and 100m past this, a cable hoist. Just after the hoist, where the power line crosses overhead, descend to the left along a dirt trail. Above the first houses 10 mins later, get to a concrete trail and continue by turning sharp to the right. At the village limits, reach a roadway and follow it until coming to the Capela de São Sebastião in the village centre of **Fajã dos Vimes** ❻ (2.20 hrs). Between the bridge and the schoolhouse, you can also turn left for an excursion to see the weavers in the first storey above the Café Nunes or to enjoy a cup of the locally-produced coffee.
Beginning at the little church, continue along a track at the seaside. Past the small harbour and then a fountain, turn left onto the first track to ascend. At the end of the track a couple of mins later, turn right to continue. Pass the cemetery and, 10 mins later a spring, the Fonte do Nicolau. Cross over the Ribeira dos Bodes with its old watermills along the banks. The roadway ends at the cul-de-sac in **Fajã dos Bodes** ❼ (2.45 hrs). From here, a dirt trail continues towards the east and quickly takes you out of the village.
10 mins later, you reach **Fajã do Cavalete** ❽ which has been converted into a tourist resort. Cross the Ribeira do Cavalete and its waterfall on a suspension bridge. Now the path becomes steeper and the tiring ascent to Loural starts in the forest. 15 mins later, pass a reinforced landslip. 20 mins

later, reach the deep-cut valley of the **Ribeira dos Cedros** ❾ and its tributary stream. Another 25 mins later, the forest opens up and you have finally reached the end of the ascent ❿ (4.05 hrs). At a big stone block, turn right onto a flat trail. 15 mins later, reach the street through **Loural 3°** ⓫ (4.25 hrs). If you want to finish the walk in Loural, ascend to the left here (Alternative).

Descend along the street to the right until reaching a cul-de-sac and then continue along a dirt trail. At the outset, the trail leads through the untamed valley cleft of the Ribeira do Salto with a waterfall and some natural rock pools. More streambeds follow. The old paving is well preserved in places. Soon get to the first *adegas* and, after a zigzag bend, reach **Fajã do Ginjal** ⓬ which is still being cultivated (5.10 hrs). Steep sections of the trail have been reinforced with concrete paving. Small *adegas* are scattered all around. Ahead, you can already see your destination.

Now **Fajã de Além** ⓭ follows with some vineyards. The trail ascends steeply again for a short way and then reaches **Ribeira de São João** ⓮, which empties into the ocean at the sweeping bay Baía da Areia with a pebble beach. To the left are some tumbledown watermills which are also scattered far upstream. At the first house of **Fajã de São João** a concrete track begins. Now pass the little harbour boasting a bathing area, ascend along the street to the Ermida de São João and just a few paces away, you can recharge your batteries in the **café Águeda** ⓯ with a mini market.

View from Loural 2° towards Fajã de São João.

São Jorge ↗ 460m | ↘ 460m | 7.0km

72 From São Tomé via Fajã de Saramagueira to Fajã de São João

2.40 hrs

Alternative circular walk in the remote eastern island

The eastern part of São Jorge is only sparsely inhabited and characterised by animal husbandry. Because of this, the villages tend to be very small and tourists are hardly ever seen. Along a former connecting trail, you will descend to Fajã de Saramagueira and then follow a coastal trail into the sprawling Fajã de São João, where fruit, vegetables and grapes are cultivated. In many sections, the ascent follows the narrow access road.

Starting point: São Tomé, chapel, 428m (bus stop São Tomé/Centro 200m east).
Grade: the descent is made via a pleasant, ancient connecting trail. Stones overgrown with grass are slippery when it's wet. Sure-footedness is required. The ascent follows a steep access road and a dirt trail.
Refreshment: café in Fajã de São João.
Linking tip: Walks 71 and 73.

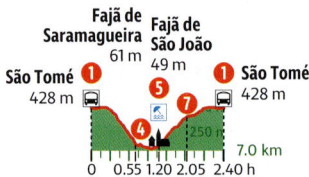

Bathing: at the harbour from São João.

The starting point is the chapel in **São Tomé** ❶ at km18 on the ER 2. Follow the main road westwards, heading towards Velas until reaching the **turn-off** ❷ for Fajã de São João. Afterwards, ascend to the left along a broad dirt trail. Flanked by hortensia, the trail hooks away to the left, 5 mins later, at the edge of the high plateau ❸. Here, turn right and follow the country

Remote: along the road through Fajã de Saramagueira.

Just like a picture postcard: the little chapel in the village centre of Fajã de São João.

lane which is initially covered in rough gravel and later turns into an old paved trail. 10 mins later, the pastureland comes to an end and the woodland phase begins. Three bends later, reach the upper limits of the village with the first cultivated fields. Take the steps of undressed stone to reach the village street in **Fajã de Saramagueira** ❹; turn right along this street (55 mins).

The settlement ends when the street becomes a track and, past the concrete-paved ford at the first power pylon, reach the eastern limits of **Fajã de São João**. After a total of 1.20 hrs, at the fountain (1896), get to the village centre with the **café Águeda** ❺. If you would like to take a dip, go past the chapel for another 10 mins heading straight on to reach the harbour. However, turn right to ascend steeply along the access road. Behind the end of the village, 100m after the tiled picture, take a sharp left turn (Ladeira Velha). Once you are up on the road, go left and turn immediately right again at the fountain to join a **grassy trail** ❻ going uphill. At the **roadway** ❼, turn right and continue to the main road ❷ to turn right again and return to the starting point in **São Tomé** ❶.

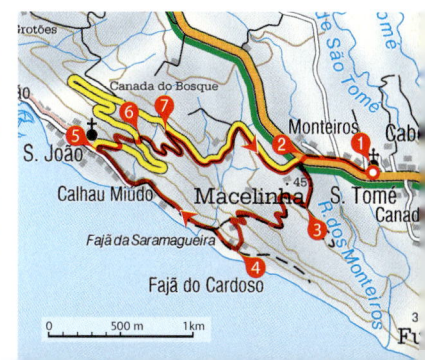

São Jorge   ↗ 150m | ↘ 480m | 9.2km

73 From São Tomé to Topo

2.50 hrs

Walk through the most remote and rural part of the island

Cattle farming and peasant life dominate the most south-eastern tip of the island of São Jorge. Away from all villages and streets, this walk follows various farm roads as well as old connecting trails between valleys. After a break in Santa Antão, this walk finally finishes in the most eastern village of the island Topo.

Starting point: São Tomé, chapel, 428m (bus stop São Tomé/Centro 200m east).
Destination: Topo, 100m, church (bus stop Topo/Escola).
Grade: mostly good and pleasant gravel trails. Several ascents from valley to valley.
Refreshment: cafés and snack bars in Topo.
Linking tip: Walk 72.

From the chapel in **São Tomé** ❶ at km18 on the ER 2, follow the main street towards the east and turn right onto the side road after 200m at the bus stop. You get quickly out of the village and follow the main trail all the way down.

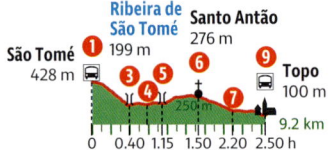

15 mins after the last houses, the road flattens out briefly. At a waymarker, turn left onto a **country lane** ❷ (there are two dirt trails on the left just before). Following two bends, the path finally leads into the valley, narrowing briefly into a mule track and at the bottom of the valley crosses the **Ribeira de São Tomé** ❸ on a concrete bridge (40 mins).

Adventurous bridge at the Ribeira do Meio.

Behind it, a dirt trail ascends again; always stay on this main trail. After 10 mins, you reach the crest from where you descend into the next valley. Cross the **Ribeira do Meio** ❹ in a ford (1 hr).
After a short ascent, you reach a roadway. Follow it at the same altitude for a short while to a farm. From here, continue straight on the dirt trail into the next valley and cross the stream via a **concrete bridge** ❺. After a 15 mins ascent, you reach another road that leads into the village. A good 10 mins later, take the third street in the village on the left and walk to the church in **Santo Antão** ❻ (1.50 hrs).

Turn right and follow the main street straight on out of the village. Behind two threshing floors, a red track continues. After 15 mins, keep left at the **fork** ❼ in the depression of the track (if you go right, you'll get down to Fajã do Labaçal).
Finally, you reach a **cemetery** ❽ where you follow the road to the right and pass the whale-observation station Vigía do Outeirao. In the village, take the first road on the left and continue to the Igreja de Nossa Senhora do Rósario in **Topo** ❾.

Terceira – the Holy Spirit island

- population: 53,200
- county seats: Angra do Heroísmo, 10,100 inhabitants; Praia da Vitória, 6000
- area: 400km²
- length: 30km, width: 18km
- coastline: 124km
- highest points: Serra de Santa Bárbara, 1021m; Pico Alto, 808m

Terceira most certainly merits a visit even though tourism has not quite taken hold here. This is an island with history and tradition; the capital Angra do Heroísmo is without a doubt the most beautiful city in the entire archipelago. For centuries, the islanders profited from an advantageous location along the Atlantic trading route and the city centre is still stamped today by the very image of affluence. Terceira is only populated along the coastline; settlements stretch out like single main street towns, one after other. The countryside is used primarily for raising livestock and the rural landscape is divided into parcels in a checkerboard pattern. In the secluded interior, fighting bulls rest up after taking part in the bloodless bullfights which are held in the town centres with the bull being tethered on a rope.

Azorean weather: both rain and sunshine bathe Angra do Heroísmo.

The island was formed by three volcanic systems. The entire western half is dominated by the Santa Bárbara range which last erupted in 1761. Countless small volcanic cones and also two lava tunnels give witness to continuous volcanic activity. There are plenty of recreational activities available to the holidaymaker but cultural ones are also high on the list. No other Azorean island can match the beauty of the chapels dedicated to the Holy Spirit found here, and only on Terceira are there lavish festivals almost every day. The presumed date for the discovery of Terceira is the year 1445. At the time, the island appears on the maps as Ilha de Jesus Cristo; the present name was given somewhat later on. Jácome de Bruges from Flanders brought prosperity to the island through grain cultivation and the export of plants for dyeing purposes. Also playing a major role was the island's central location along the Atlantic trading route. From the end of the 15th century, Terceira was one of Portugal's most important hubs for maritime trade. Pirates soon caught wind of the wealth and began to plunder regularly. A town charter was granted to Angra in 1534 and a diocese was established there. In the 16th century, during the Spanish rule of Portugal under Philipp II, the islanders put up a lengthy resistance and, in 1581, fought the Spanish forces near Salga, driving them to the sea with the help of fighting bulls. Nonetheless, from 1583, Terceira was also occupied by the Spanish. Bastions were established throughout the island; maritime trade was safeguarded and became the driving force for prosperity. In the 19th century, during the Portuguese civil war, the islanders aligned with the liberal movement and again offered a lengthy front of resistance.

The airport was established during World War II and, even today, is used for both civilian and military aircraft. Since 1947, the USA maintains a military base here. In 1980, the island was rocked by a devastating earthquake and some people died. A majority of the buildings were destroyed. In

TERCEIRA

Getting there
From the mainland with TAP, SATA or Ryanair. Some direct flights from the USA and Canada. Direct flights within the Azores are provided by SATA to all of the islands except Santa Maria. The airport is located in Lajes, 3km outside of Praia da Vitória. The ferry harbour is situated in Praia. In summer, a ferry operates to the *Triângulo* four times a week, twice via Graciosa.

Bathing
Lovely sandy beaches in Angra and Praia da Vitória. Natural bathing areas in Porto Martins, Salga, Salgueiros, Porto Judeu, Vila Nova, Quatro Ribeiras, Biscoitos, Cinco Ribeiras, São Mateus (Negrito) and in the Silveira bay near Angra. An enclosed swimming pool in Angra.

Festivities
Annual Carnival celebrations on the island can be compared with a street theatre. Holy Spirit Celebrations from Whitsun until summer. Sanjoaninas in Angra end of June with a culture festival and processions. Cultural Week, Festas da Praia, beginning of August. Wine festival in Biscoitos, 1st week in Sept. Jazz festival AngraJazz beginning of Oct. In the summer, almost daily bullfights in the street with the bull tethered to a rope (*tourada a corda*).

Medical services
Hospital in Angra, tel +351 295 403 200. Clinic in Praia, tel +351 295 545 000.

Tourist information
Turismo with a city office in Angra, tel +351 295 404 800, angradoheroismo.pt and cmpv.pt. Branch office in the airport, tel +351 295 513 140, pt.ae.ter@azores.gov.pt.

Cultural activities
The island museum Museu de Angra with historical exhibits. Museu Vulcanoespeleológico from the friends of nature organisation Os Montanheiros (information regarding geology and caves). Museu do Vinho in the Adega Brum in Biscoitos. A small ethnographical museum Casa Etno in Cinco Ribeiras. Well worth seeing are the colourful Holy Ghost Chapels (*impérios*) in every settlement.

Public transport
A modern, well-developed bus network has been created with scheduled connections throughout the island. The bus lines from Angra to Biscoitos and from Praia to Biscoitos are less frequent and run only along the coastal roads, not through the highlands.

Accommodation
Star-rated hotels and hostels in Angra and Praia. Private accommodation is scattered across the island: from a few high-standard *quintas* to farm stays. Campsites in Salga, Salgueiros, Quatro Ribeiras, Biscoitos, Raminho and Cinco Ribeiras. A youth hostel in São Mateus.

Walking note
Bulls could be met in any pasture in the highlands. In case of a chance meeting, it is advisable to turn back or give the animals a wide berth!

1983, Angra's centre was added to UNESCO's World Heritage List.

The Renaissance city **Angra do Heroísmo** is worth a visit all by itself. The cathedral Sé is the largest sacred building in the entire archipelago. The municipal museum in the old Franciscan monastery boasts a collection of historical documents and other exhibits. The churches of São Gonçalo and Misericordia are good examples of Baroque architecture. Countless palaces of the ruling families are still intact or have been restored. A walk through the centrally-located municipal park leads to the obelisk at the Alto da Memória with a sweeping view over the entire city. The Forte de São João Baptista at the foot of Monte Brasil is a relic from the time of the Spanish occupation and a military base even today. The Monte Brasil itself has become a 'green lung' for the city and a place to while away the time.

A modern motorway leads to **Praia da Vitória**, the second county seat with a lovely town centre. The churches of Matriz de Santa Cruz and Santo Cristo merit a visit as does the newly-renovated Casa das Tias. However, the city's real pride and joy is the endless sandy beach found here.

Império in São Sebastião.

Not far from Porto Judeu, the two rocky islets Ilhéus das Cabras lie offshore from Terceira's southern coast. The best view sweeping over the entire north-east can be enjoyed from the mountain ridge of the Serra do Cume. Praia da Vitoria is situated in a broad bay, protected by two breakwaters. Because of the military base there, Americans are settled around the airport at Lajes. The northern coast is primarily agricultural. In Biscoitos, grapevines flourish along a broad lava flow to produce the typical Terceira wine. The lush woodland park of Serreta is just on the western tip of the island. The former district of the well-to-do is located to the west of Angra; countless villas give witness to affluence. In São Mateus da Calheta, the most important fishing harbour finds its port of call. In the highlands, you will hardly ever encounter another person. Worth visiting are the volcanic vent Algar do Carvão and the lava cave Gruta do Natal as well as the fumaroles of Furnas do Enxofre.

Terceira ↗ 470m | ↘ 470m | 10.6km

74 Fajãs and Mata da Serreta

3.45 hrs

Excursion on the western tip of Terceira

The viewpoint Miradouro do Raminho towers high above the coast. Hidden old cart tracks take you to a remote forest area, where the refreshing scent of eucalyptus accompanies you for most of the way. Beyond the forest, descend to Serreta and cross a volcanic eruption area on ancient, forgotten paths that run underneath gnarled Metrosideros trees. The old vineyard plots have been overgrown for decades. Towards the end of the walk, you pass the secluded fields of the fajã and a whale-spotters' lookout.

Starting point: the viewpoint Miradouro do Raminho, 149m (next bus stop in Raminho, 700m away).
Grade: large parts of this walk follow adventurous forest paths across loose rocks and exposed roots, which can be slippery when wet. The rest runs along easy tracks and forest trails.
Refreshment: nothing en route.

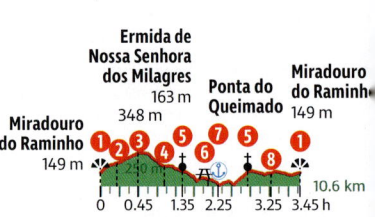

From the **Miradouro do Raminho** ❶, follow the main road southward and after about 50m, turn left onto an old footpath that leads uphill into the forest. Just after having crossed a power line, keep right at the first fork. A few mins later, the path forks again. Turn left here and walk against the direction of the trail markers. This takes you to a small **clearing** ❷ where you continue straight on the main trail. About 25m after a trail joins from the left, you have to push aside some wild ginger which grows over the trail for the first few metres. This ancient connecting path slowly gains in elevation. At the only fork along the way, keep right to stay on the main trail. 15 mins later, you will reach a road which you follow uphill to the left until you come to a **crossroad** ❸ (45 mins).

Turn right here and follow a forest path which takes a diagonal right turn after 10 mins. The trail descends over rocky ground and reaches the **EN 1** ❹ main road after 20 mins. Continue left here. At the first houses of À Vila, turn right onto the gravel track Canada da Fajã. After just 150m, take an old forest path to the left which runs parallel to the roadway. After 50m, the path bends left and after 5 mins, it joins a cross trail which you follow to the right. Eventually, your mule track meets a dirt trail and arrives at the **Ermida de Nossa Senhora dos Milagres** ❺ (1.35 hrs). Continue left until you reach a road and a viewpoint after 5 mins. Another mule track heads downhill on the left. Where it ends at the pastureland, a tangled forest trail continues through long-overgrown terraced fields. For the next half hour, closely observe the trail markers and follow them until eventually, you get back to the road. Diagonally opposite, you can see a **picnic area** ❻ with a **lighthouse**.

Continue downhill on the road. After a good 5 mins, you reach a small viewpoint on the headland behind which exposed steps descend to the old harbour platform of **Ponta do Queimado** ❼. This is a popular fishing spot which is located high above the sea (2.25 hrs).

From here, return on the road. About 75m before you reach the **picnic area** ❻, an adventure trail turns off to the left (signpost) leading into the undergrowth. The path soon offers spectacular views of the wild cliffs and winds its way uphill along the rugged coastline. This stretch also feels like being on a treasure hunt for trail markers.

After 30 mins, you are back on the outward route near the **Ermida de Nossa Senhora dos Milagres** ❺. Turn left here and stay on the wide dirt trail. 10 mins later, you reach a rough cross trail. Turn left again and follow the cross trail along the forest edge with the pastures of the Fajã da Serreta lying below you. A few mins after you pass a cattle trough, you will pass another one (Fonte da Fajã). Just beyond the second trough at the **fork** ❽, take the main trail to the right. The trail continues to wind its way through the forest with gentle ups and downs before it ends at a parking area just below a stone cross. On your left is the Raminho **grill and campsite** ❾ with a small, former whale-spotters' lookout. Turn right onto the gravel track and follow it back to the **Miradouro do Raminho** ❶.

Walking trail through the Fajãs da Serreta.

Terceira ↗ 435m | ↘ 435m | 6.7km

75 Pico da Lagoínha

2.45 hrs

Unspoiled ascent route to a hidden crater lake

The little Lagoínha lies concealed and secluded high above on the western flank of the volcanic Santa Bárbara mountain range. It is often covered in thick cloud or mist. Old cart tracks and narrow footpaths ascend steeply along the Ribeira da Lapa all the way to the crater lake. The return route follows above the deeply cut Ribeira de Além passing through pastureland.

Starting point: hikers' car park of the PRC3TER above Serreta, 360m. Access: in northern Serreta, turn off the EN 1 at the Trilho Turistico sign and follow the steep Canada da Fonte inland (bus stop: Serreta – Canada da Fonte). After 800m, you will reach the hikers' car park.
Grade: the ascent to Lagoínha along a slippery forest path. Sure-footedness required. Avoid this route during rainy periods. Hiking boots with ankle support recommended.
Refreshment: nothing en route.

At the **hikers' car park** ❶ high above Serreta, follow the dirt trail inland on the left. It soon bends sharply to the right and immediately turns sharply left again. After a short ascent, turn left at level with an iron gate onto a forest trail. At the edge of the forest, this becomes a sunken trail and climbs up through the dense forest. The terrain is wet and slippery. 10 mins later, at a fork, bear right and ascend through a gully. A level stretch follows, along which two streams are crossed and then a dense grove of trees with towering Japanese cedars. After another stretch of ascent, meet up finally with a narrow road where it bends and turn right onto a **gravel trail** ❷ (50 mins) until it ends at a geological outcrop. Directly in front of us, the knoll of the Lagoínha is rising up.

Rarely fog-free: the hidden crater lake of Lagoínha.

To the left, over wooden steps, reach a footpath that is rather indistinct at the outset to begin the ascent. The steps seem to go on endlessly in places. A good 10 mins later, descend into a washed-out gully and climb up along this to reach a red **dirt trail** ❸. Turn right onto the trail until, 10 mins later, a steep footpath with countless adventurously constructed wooden steps continues the ascent onto the **Pico da Lagoínha** ❹ where the little crater lake Lagoínha da Serreta is embedded (1.30 hrs). At the summit you can enjoy a view of the old lava flow between Serreta and Raminho which is now covered in trees.

Afterwards, return to the track and follow it to the left. At the edge of the forest, leave the trail behind, and, at the first meadow, go right through two gates onto a **pasture trail** ❺. At the same height as a watering trough, go left in a depression and head towards the edge of the pasture. Past the pasture gate, the distinct traces of a path above the edge of the pasture lead downwards along the **Ribeira d'Além**. When the pasture comes to an end, turn left below the Pico Negrão.

Here starts a rocky descent path which is secured with wooden steps in the steep sections. Pass a **viewpoint** ❻ perched above the river valley. You have to skirt around the terminus of a deep, washed-out gully by bearing right for a short stretch through the wood. You then reach another pasture, which you descend along an old fence on the left hand side. Below the pasture, the path bends sharply right and joins the end of a **dirt trail** ❼. Continue on the dirt trail along a hydrangea hedge and finally join the approach route which you follow all the way to the **hikers' car park** ❶.

Terceira ↗ 90m | ↘ 90m | 6.1km

76 Vinhas dos Biscoitos

2.00 hrs

Ramble through the vineyards at the popular seaside resort

A splendid opportunity for bathing and the Verdelho wine create a goldmine for the traditional winegrowing settlement of Biscoitos in the northern island. From the guarded bathing area, at first follow the coastal trail. Afterwards, turn off into the vineyards (vinhas), following the scattered waymarkers. On a hot summer's day, you could take a cooling dip in the Atlantic at the end of the walk.

Starting point: Biscoitos, car park at the bathing area Belo Abismo, 6m (next bus stop Biscoitos/Canada do Porto up above, on the main road).
Grade: in the vineyards, sometimes cross-country walking along agricultural paths. Watch out for waymarkers. In residential areas, along a street.
Refreshment: restaurants at the bathing area and at Biscoitos' harbour.
Note: several sections of the waymarked trail lead through privately-owned vineyards. Please be careful and respect the grapevines!
Bathing: natural bathing pool with lifeguards as well as numerous bathing areas in Biscoitos.
Linking tip: Walk 79.

From the car park at the bathing area (with lifeguards) in **Biscoitos** ❶, at first follow the seaside road past the fishermen's harbour inland and, at the red beacon light, turn right onto the Caminho do Canto do Feno. 100 m on, at the Forte de São Pedro, turn right to continue and, past the artistic monument, straight ahead, always following the coastline. The roadway becomes a gravel track. 5 mins later, after the fourth individual building, you leave the gravel track and turn left through an inconspicuous **gap in the stone wall** ❷. Directly afterwards, keep left at an old shooting stand and reach the vineyards (info point 3). To the right of the stone wall, climb up along the supply path. 80m further on, hook off to the right and immediately go left again at the same height as an *adega*. Leave this plot of land through a wooden gate in the upper left-hand corner and continue left up and down on a footpath to the upcoming vineyard, which you cross going straight on. Below a residence, leave the vineyard behind by passing through an **iron gate** ❸ and follow the red concrete trail straight on. 5 mins later, at the intersecting trail, turn left and, 5 mins more, at the end of the tarmac road, turn right. At the next **intersecting road** ❹ another 5 mins later

Blue/red waymarkers indicate the way through the vineyards.

(50 mins), turn left to descend to the sea. Halfway up, pass an old *adega* on the left side of the road.

At the Forte, at first turn right to continue and, 100m further, at the junction, head straight on (Caminho de Santo António). Passing a chapel, reach a large car park. At the access road for the **campsite** ❺ (stone arch), a gravel trail leads eastwards for 60m, heading towards a house. Just before the driveway of the house a supply route starts on the right, ascending through a little wood. At the same height as the football pitch, get to a **street** ❻. Turn left here and, 15m on, turn right to follow the supply path that leads along the playing field. Seawards, the path hooks off and leads once again into the vineyards. Starting here, be sure to pay close attention to waymarking! 50m from the football pitch, at some stone steps, bear right, then, 25m on, bear left and immediately bear right again. A short stretch of zigzags follows before the route heads straight ahead again towards the sea. At the end of this stretch, 80m further on, the continuation of the route hooks again to the right. Finally, reach a gravel trail at info point 8 and turn left to continue to the road (1.40 hrs). Here, turn left to descend and, passing picnic tables, reach a **natural bathing area** ❼. Past this, on your right-hand side at the edge of the road, an old military position (*trincheiras*) can be seen. Past the campsite, continue steadily along the coast to return to the bathing area Belo Abismo in **Biscoitos** ❶.

77 Baías da Agualva

Terceira ↗ 350m | ↘ 350m | 7.5km
2.30 hrs

Interesting coastal walk along the coves below Agualva

Only a few trails lead along the untamed, often inaccessible coastline of Terceira. Crossing over the silt bank of the Alagoa da Fajãzinha with its rough rock walls, a seaside footpath brings you to the promontory Ponta do Mistério. Afterwards, return via the forest-blanketed eruption zone Biscoito das Calmeiras.

Starting point: the turn-off to Alagoa da Fajãzinha on the EN 1 west of Agualva, 115m (next bus stop Farroco/Canada das Baleeiras on the EN 1 in Farroco).
Grade: the narrow coastal path requires sure-footedness. The second leg of the route follows tracks and country lanes.
Refreshment: nothing en route.
Note: as the entire area around the coast has been declared a nature reserve, it presents an excellent opportunity for bird-watching.

Begin the walk on the main road **EN 1** ❶ at the turn-off to Alagoa da Fajãzinha and follow the side road Canada da Baleeira along the painted retaining wall leading towards the coast. Soon, you will pass a **viewpoint** ❷ and reach a fork a little later. From the fork, continue straight ahead on the metalled road. After a good 5 mins, the concrete road ends in another fork from where you continue on the dirt trail to the left which will soon take you to the rocky bay of the small coastal plain known as Fajãzinha (20 mins). From here, a slippery path leading across wooden steps climbs up the slope on the left. After a short scramble, you reach a viewpoint and join a mule track, which you follow to the right until it merges with a broader track. Keep to the right here. A few moments later, you will arrive at the **Miradouro da Alagoa da Fajãzinha** ❸ on the headland.

Those who feel like it and are absolutely sure-footed can make a short detour along a sloping path to a dramatic fishing spot which is located high above the Baía da Ferradura.

On the Ponta do Mistério.

Follow the same track to return to the road and turn right uphill. In the first left-hand bend, near the **viewpoint** ❷, an old fishermen's path disappears into the undergrowth. It initially leads over loose rocks below a stone wall and eventually swings right at a pasture descending toward the coast. In the thicket, near info point 5, the trail becomes visible again and climbs up the slope to the left. Before continuing, however, first walk straight ahead for another 50m to reach a **viewpoint** ❹ perched precipitously above the rugged coastline; to the right and down at the seaside, you can spot the opening for the lava cave **Furna das Pombas** (55 mins).

Now return to the path and climb steeply up the slope in zigzags which is partially a scramble. At the high plateau, continue along the edge of cattle pastures following a stone wall to reach the promontory **Ponta do Mistério** ❺. Turn left at a fork. Afterwards, the path veers landwards again and ascends to a country lane. Turn left onto this for a few metres of ascent and then turn right. Now, past a residence, a roadway (Canada das Baleeiras) climbs up again to the main road EN 1 in **Farroco** ❻ (1.35 hrs). Here, turn left at a fountain (1894) and 50m on, turn right again onto the Caminho do Farroco to ascend. After 20 mins of climbing, shortly before a right-hand bend, turn left onto the first broad **gravel trail** ❼ and soon reach a patch of woods perched on the old lava flow of the **Biscoito das Calmeiras**. At the point where you leave the forest, turn sharp left onto a **gravel trail** ❽ which descends and keeps to the edge of the forest until returning to the starting point on the **EN 1** ❶.

TOP 78 — Terceira ↗ 160m | ↘ 160m | 5.3km **2.10 hrs**

Místerios Negros

Adventurous path along little lakes and over rugged volcanic cones

If you enjoy battling your way by hand and foot through a dense tropical forest in the highlands, this is exactly the tour of your dreams. The challenging path begins at the lava cave Gruta do Natal and passes little marsh lakes. The path narrows rapidly but is always marked and always distinct. Then reach the raven-black hills Mistérios Negros and the beginning of a much more comfortable descent along paths and forest trails passing through a lush natural landscape. This is the most untamed walk presented in this guide!

Starting point: Gruta do Natal, 548m.
Grade: a very demanding path through the forest requiring absolute sure-footedness and a little acrobatic skill. Very unpleasant when wet. A sense of direction is helpful.
Refreshment: nothing en route.

From the natural stone-built house at the **Gruta do Natal** ❶ at the Lagoa do Negro, follow the road westwards but, only 50m on, at the hikers' car park turn off to the right along the dirt trail. The trail soon ends at a pasture. Traces of a path lead straight to a trough before entering the forest ❷. The path winds along in steady up-and-down walking. Wet stretches are supported by wooden log walkways. You will soon reach a lake that is often dried-up in summer and skirt around it to the right in a semi-circle. 10 mins later, you will get to a fork. By bearing right, you can take a short excursion to the marsh lake **Lagoínha do Vale Fundo** ❸.

Continue along the main trail. Soon, another side path branches off to the right leading down to the Lagoínha. After that, keep left at the next junction. Soon, you will reach a third lake, which also often dries up in summer and is half-circled counterclockwise. Past this point, the trail becomes more narrow and untamed then begins an ascent through the dense undergrowth. Some stretches even require easy scrambling. After negotiating a last ascent (slippery under foot) the

Spectacular: the Gruta do Natal   *The small Lagoínha do Vale Fundo.*

wood opens up and the trail improves. Now you are right in the midst of the black volcanic hunch-backed hills of the **Mistérios Negros** ❹, which were formed during the eruption of the Santa Bárbara massif in 1761 and appear like giant molehills in the landscape (1.10 hrs).

The faint path now continues outside the forest and leads downhill. After about 10 mins on the path, take the **faint path** ❺ on the left at the second right-hand bend and follow a wooden boardwalk into the undergrowth beneath the Japanese cedars. The forest path climbs in a tight zigzag through tree trunks along the forest edge, leading up to the elevation marker at **Pico da Cancela** ❻ (1.30 hrs).

Beyond this point, the well-worn path turns to the left. From here on, keep an eye out for trail markers on the trees. Five mins after the elevation marker, the path leaves the pastureland and continues downhill as a wider forest trail. After another good 5 mins, leave this trail and follow a path to the left, which runs alongside an old dry-stone wall. The path crosses from one side of the wall to the other several times before ending at a **road** ❼. Turn left here. A few metres further on, where the forest opens up on the right, you can take a short detour to climb Pico do Gaspar (20 mins there and back; information board).

Along the road, return to the starting point at the **Gruta do Natal** ❶.

79 Malha Grande – Biscoitos

Terceira ↗ 230m | ↘ 705m | 14.7km 5.10 hrs

Demanding walk along a high ridge and ancient paths

This walk displays clearly how the island was shaped by volcanic activity. It can be divided into two parts: the upper section promises magnificent views across the central highlands, while the second part is more of an adventure trail. After a scenic start at the Rocha do Chambre massif, you walk through the Vale do Azinhal and along open pastureland to reach the northern coast and the protected landscape of Vinhas dos Biscoitos, where the island's wine is produced. Parts of this walk follow wild and romantic centuries-old mule tracks.

Starting point: from the EN 3 in the highlands turn off towards Biscoitos (Canada do Caldeiro), at km-stone 1, turn right through the second iron gate, 482m (sign: Trilho do Chambre).
Destination: Biscoitos, car park at the Abismo bathing area, 6m (next bus stop Biscoitos/Canada do Porto up on the main road; return only by taxi).
Grade: in the hinterland, the route follows footpaths and pathless terrain. A short, steep descent from the Rocha do Chambre. Sure-footedness and a good sense of direction required. The middle section is mostly on dirt trails. Due to the demanding lower section, this walk is rated difficult.
Refreshment: restaurant at the Biscoitos bathing area. Nothing en route.
Alternative: short walk without Rocha do Chambre (section 1.3km; 25 mins; saves 2 hrs compared to the main route): at the fork ❷ after 20 mins, keep left. The dirt trail ends after 5 mins. Beyond that, a rough and rocky footpath continues through the undergrowth. After 15 mins, you reach a junction. Instead of following the markers, continue straight along the grassy path which joins a red dirt trail 5 mins later. Continue straight to reach a junction with the main route ❽. Turn left to stay on the main trail.
Bathing: guarded natural bathing area and several swimming spots in Biscoitos.
Linking tip: Walk 81.

View across the protected nature reserve in the central highlands around Pico Alto.

Start at the **Canada do Caldeiro** ❶ which is the road leading from the EN 3 to Biscoitos, just at the second green iron gate (trail board). From here, follow the red gravel trail straight inland. Ignore all side tracks. After 20 mins, you reach a **fork** ❷ where you turn right following the trail markers for 100m, then continue on the main trail along a long natural stone wall. After 10 mins, you reach its end where you can find a gap in the wall. Pass through it and follow the gravel trail to the right which leads to a **farmstead** ❸ (45 mins).

Just before reaching the farmstead, turn left and walk through a gate to join a wide pasture track that ascends alongside a row of trees. After 20 mins, you reach the top where you are rewarded with the first panoramic views of the central highlands. A short detour to the right leads to a **viewpoint** ❹. To the left, the rocky edge of the Rocha do Chambre massif drops steeply into the Biscoito da Ferraria basin. From here, continue to climb to the left along a natural stone wall and a deep trench directly on the ridge until you reach the survey point at **Pico do Juncal** ❺ (1.25 hrs).

Soon, the trench veers to the left. Here, walk across the steps on the faint footpath and continue straight ahead through the Japanese cedar trees. Cross another trench via a footbridge. The path now descends quickly on

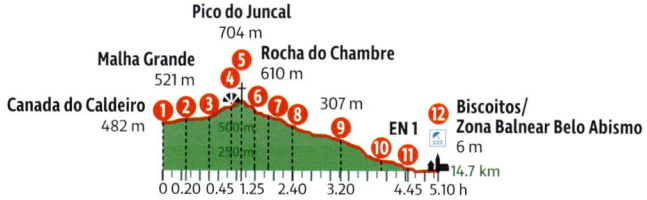

247

The old farming terraces above Biscoitos are now pretty overgrown.

an imposing wooden walkway. Beyond a dip, climb the steps on the opposite slope and at the top, bear slightly right towards a forest of Japanese cedars. About 20m before reaching the trees, just below the right embankment, the trail continues into the forest. From here on, keep a lookout for waymarkers carved into the tree trunks. At first, the path heads slightly to the right and soon continues alongside a rampart. Through a clearing ❻, you will get a view of the steep drop at the edge of the Rocha do Chambre. Next comes a steep section which is secured with ropes and iron steps and is challenging to climb. Eventually, the trail veers sharply to the left and leads through dense forest where you have to pay close attention to the waymarkers. The mossy ground makes for a soft, springy walk. After crossing two streams, you finally reach the **end of a forest track** ❼ (2.10 hrs). Stay on this track for just under 10 mins until a country lane branches off. After a few mins, the country lane turns into a heavily eroded, slippery footpath that eventually meets three dirt trails. Continue on the far-left trail which is more comfortable to walk on. After 200m, the Alternative comes in from the left ❽. Continue straight ahead. After another 100m, keep right at the fork. The now wide gravel track starts to descend. After 15 mins, stay on the main trail which soon bends left at a water reservoir. A good 5 mins later, at level with a barn, leave the main trail and turn right onto the red dirt track which leads towards the north coast. After a quarter of an hour, you reach a crossing **gravel track** ❾ (3.20 hrs).

Follow this gravel track to the right. After a good 10 mins, leave it just after a right-hand bend and follow an ancient footpath down to the left. Large sections of this mule track have collapsed. After 20 mins, you reach the end of a paved road (Canada da Fonte). Continue to the right along the farm track which passes a few remote orchards. After a quarter of an hour, leave the main trail, **Caminho Novo**, at a **green wooden gate** ❿ and follow a footpath leading into the forest on the left.
After 5 mins, leave the old mule track by walking through an opening in the stone wall to the right and continue on a narrow, old supply path (trail marker). This is the start of the most demanding and strenuous section of the walk which requires some scrambling through the rugged volcanic area. After 15 mins, a power line crosses the trail beyond which the trail becomes wider and easier for a short while. After 5 mins, where the main trail is overgrown again, the final part of the adventure trail starts on the left. Once again, a rocky supply path continues for 15 mins. The final section is a very steep descent leading down to a side road (Rua Longa). At an old washing site, turn right. The side road takes you to the main road **EN 1** ⓫, which you have to cross.
Of the two roads, take the right one (Canada da Rua Longa) and walk towards the coast. The road meets the coastal road Avenida do Mar. Turn right here and continue along the coast. Walking past an old fortification with picnic tables, a natural bathing area at Baía das Pombas and old World War II structures, you will finally reach the large natural bathing area of **Biscoitos** ⓬ after 15 mins.

Having fun in the evening light in the sheltered seawater pool of Biscoitos.

Terceira ↗ 290m | ↘ 290m | 9.1km

80 Rocha do Chambre

3.20 hrs

Varied high mountain walk along narrow paths

Countless volcanic cones make up the highlands of Terceira. This walk, rich in diversity but also quite strenuous, is an excellent means to get truly acquainted with this volcanic landscape. At the outset, ascend to the summit of Pico do Juncal and then continue the walk along the edge of the sheer drop of the Rocha do Chambre massif. A difficult descent path brings you back down again. Through dense forest and over open pastureland, you finally make your return.

Starting point: from the EN 3 in the highlands, take the turn-off to Biscoitos (Canada do Caldeiro), at Km-stone 1, turn right through the second iron gate, 482m (sign: Trilho do Chambre).
Grade: at the outset, along dirt trails. In the interior, along trodden paths and sometimes pathless. Short, steep descent at the Rocha do Chambre. Sure-footedness and orientation skills required.
Refreshment: nothing en route.
Linking tip: Walk 79.

Start at the **Canada do Caldeiro** ❶, the road from the EN 3 to Biscoitos, on the right at the second green-coloured iron gate (trail board). Beyond it, go straight inland on the red gravel trail. Ignore all side tracks. After 20 mins, reach a **fork** ❷ where your return path comes in from the left. Go right following the waymarking for another 100m and then follow the main trail along the long natural stone wall. After 10 mins, you reach the end of the wall where you find a **gap** in the wall. Pass through it and follow the gravel trail to the right until you reach a **farmstead** ❸ (45 mins).

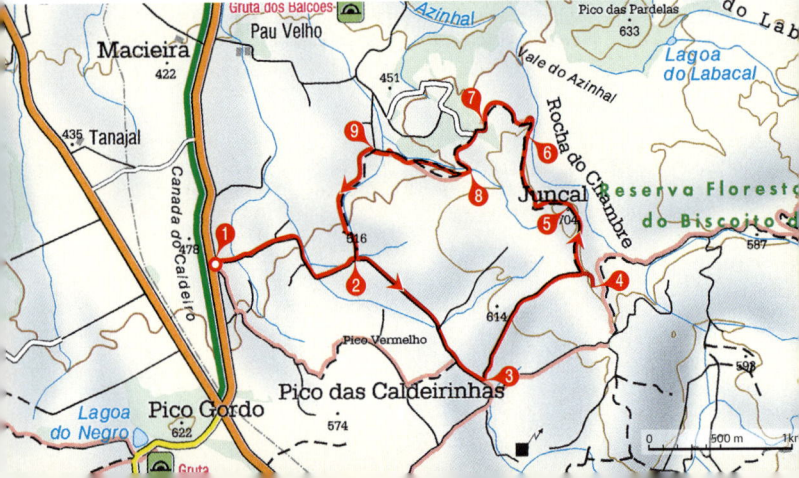

The massif of the Rocha do Chambre (right) is a sheer drop.

Just ahead of the farm, go left through a gate and follow the broad pasture trail that runs uphill alongside a row of trees. After 20 mins, you reach the top from where you can enjoy the first panoramic view of the central highlands. A short detour to your right leads to a **viewpoint** ❹. To the left, the rocky edge of the Rocha do Chambre massif drops steeply into the basin of Biscoito da Ferraria. Afterwards, turn left and ascend along a natural stone wall and along the edge of a deep trench until you arrive at the altitude survey point at **Pico do Juncal** ❺ (1.25 hrs).

Soon, the trench veers to the left. Follow the traces of a path over steps, go straight through the Japanese cedar trees and cross another trench via a footbridge. On an impressive wooden walkway the descent is pretty fast. Behind a dip, climb up the steps on the opposite slope and once on the hill, turn half right towards a forest of Japanese cedars. 20m ahead, directly below the right slope, the trail continues into the forest. From here on, look for waymarkers that are carved into the tree trunks. At first, the path heads slightly to the right and then leads along an old rampart.

Through a clearing ❻, you can see the steep slope of **Rocha do Chambre**. You reach a steep passage, which is difficult to overcome despite being secured with ropes and iron steps. Finally, the path bends sharply to the left and leads through a thick forest, where you have to pay attention to waymarkers again. The mossy ground is soft and pleasant

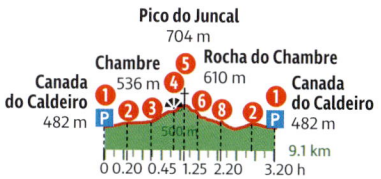

Narrow trails lead along the pastureland through the highlands.

to walk on. There are two watercourse crossings before you reach the **end of a forest track** ❼ (2.10 hrs). After 200m, leave it again and go through a wooden gate on your left. Behind it, a well-trodden path continues through a grove of young cedar trees. It runs largely flat over a fern meadow and leads to another **stream** ❽ that you have to cross. Immediately beyond, an old connecting path begins on the right. It leads you along the deeply incised course of the stream through the forest and across wooden bridges before it ends at a small footbridge after about 10 mins.
From the bridge, turn to the right side of the stream and continue down the valley. For a short stretch, the way becomes somewhat confusing; the way-markers help you find your bearings: after 50m, turn left, cross the streambed on another walkway and go back on the left side of the stream for another 25m until you reach an open area. If the streambed is dry, you can walk through it from the footbridge and turn left after 50m.
At the open area, another roadway starts and crosses a power line. Behind it, the country lane continues straight. After 100m, you reach a **T-junction** ❾. Go down the gravel path to your left. It immediately turns into a slightly overgrown track on loose ground. Once you reach a stone wall, follow the path through the undergrowth until you reach another country lane at an animal loading station. Continue straight until you reach the **fork** ❷ where you meet the outward path. Turn right here and return to the **Canada do Caldeiro** ❶.

The steep descent through the Chambre massif is well secured.

Terceira ↗ 200m | ↘ 200m | 7.9km

81 Algar do Carvão – Furnas do Enxofre
2.50 hrs

Remote highland trails and alternative energy sources

This circular walk takes you to the secluded highlands, large parts of which are protected nature reserve. Along the way, you pass the two natural monuments of Furnas do Enxofre and Algar do Carvão. At the edge of the protected zone, you will encounter a wide variety of endemic plants, accompanied throughout by the scent of wild mint. At the end of this walk, make sure to have an extra hour to visit the volcanic vent. The visitor centre is only open in the afternoons, even in summer.

Starting point: car park at Algar do Carvão, 561m.
Grade: large parts of this walk follow grassy paths or restored farm tracks with little elevation gain. Depending on maintenance, the trail may appear as a narrow footpath through grass or a wide groomed track. Do not attempt this walk in foggy conditions.
Refreshment: nothing en route.

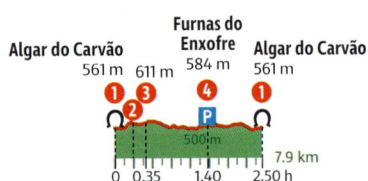

The volcanic vent of Algar do Carvão.

This walk starts at the large car park at **Algar do Carvão** ❶. Follow the access road for 120m, then turn right onto the gravel track just before the cattle grid (sign: Agualva). After 5 mins, turn left at an iron gate and follow the footpath beyond, which soon climbs up via some wooden steps. After a wooden footbridge, you reach a broad **cross trail** ❷ where you turn left. A wide view opens up across the central highlands, with the Serra de Santa Bárbara straight ahead and the Rocha do Chambre massif to the right. After 5 mins at a fork, keep left and 75m later turn left again. The trail now climbs up again and leads to a **geothermal borehole** ❸ (35 mins).
Continue straight ahead. The broad footpath leads through the remote, unspoilt highlands. After about 10 mins, the geothermal power station at Pico Alto comes into view. The trail winds its way forward in zigzags. Just under an hour after the geothermal borehole, leave the main trail and

A grassy trail runs alongside lush highland meadows – with constant views of the Serra de Santa Bárbara.

follow a faint footpath to the left, climbing 25m to a gap in a stone wall. Beyond the gap, turn left onto the road.

After 100m, your onward route later continues through another gap on the opposite side. But for now, you continue straight ahead, cross a cattle grid and follow the dirt track to its end. At the small car park, a 10-minute circular walk begins leading clockwise around the steaming sulphur fumaroles of **Furnas do Enxofre** ❹ (1.40 hrs).

From here, return along the track to the upper gap in the stone wall. The trail continues from here as a faint grassy footpath which ascends for the next quarter of an hour before it descends again. Steeper sections are reinforced with wooden steps. After around 40 mins, you reach a road at an iron gate. Follow it uphill to the left and return to the car park at **Algar do Carvão** ❶.

Terceira ↗ 200m | ↘ 200m | 4.1km

82 Passagem das Bestas

2.00 hrs

Hidden viewpoints and old cart tracks in the heart of the island

This circular walk crosses two vast volcanic areas in the central highlands. At just 23,000 years old, the Caldeira de Guilherme Moniz is still geologically young and plays a key role in storing the island's groundwater with its peatlands. The walk follows hidden connecting paths through this protected area – an enchanted forest of tree heather and juniper accompanied by a beautiful chorus of birdsong.

Starting point: grassy area (hikers' car park) 300m above the large reservoir, 442m.
Grade: mostly forest footpaths and an old cart track. Can be muddy in places when wet.
Refreshment: nothing en route.

	Miradouro da Fajã Redonda	Miradouro da Caldeira
	501 m	484 m
442 m	❺❻	442 m
❶		❶
	500	
0	1.15	2.00 h 4.1 km

The **trail board** ❶ directly at the main street about 300m above the big reservoir near the Furna de Água is the starting point of this walk. Cross the large grassy area behind, which serves as a hikers' car park. At the far end, an inconspicuous footpath begins which initially runs along a stone wall. After a few mins, you reach an ancient **ox-cart track (Passagem das Bestas)** ❷. Follow this track to the left. Here you can still see the track grooves *(relheiras)* of the old ox carts. After a few mins, the trail continues under sickle trees in a narrow, sunken gully. At an **aqueduct** ❸, leave the gully and climb up to the right. You will immediately reach some wooden steps that lead steeply up the slope at the edge of the forest. After an exhausting and sweaty quarter of an hour, you reach the hilltop from where you can enjoy a magnificent view across the expansive caldera of the Cinco Picos massif to the left (35 mins).

The old cart track Passagem das Bestas.

Amazing view at the Miradouro da Caldeira de Guilherme Moniz.

At the left edge of the pasture, a loose faint footpath gently descends and crosses a row of trees before turning right after 10 mins. After a short ascent, the path continues away from the pasture running directly beneath tall sickle trees along the edge of the Serra do Morião. 10 mins later, the path descends again ❹ and soon becomes more comfortable to walk on. After about 15 mins, a side path leads left to the exposed viewpoint of **Miradouro da Fajã Redonda** ❺. 5 mins later, another side path leads to the viewpoint of **Miradouro da Caldeira de Guilherme Moniz** ❻. Just a little bit further on, you will reach a third viewpoint, shortly after which, a 10-min descent begins with numerous wooden steps until you finally reach a wide, deep **hollow path** ❼ (1.35 hrs).

This section of the island's old trail network runs straight back to the start. After 15 mins, you reach a country lane which you follow straight ahead for 50m. Where it turns left, continue straight on the faint footpath. You will immediately return to the cart track which you took on the outward journey and turn left to head back to the **starting point** ❶.

83 Rota da Água

Terceira — ↗ 400m | ↘ 400m | 5.4km | 2.45 hrs

Ascent along old water collection points to the Serra do Morião

High above Angra, countless springs have long been used for both water supply and energy production. During the ascent, you will follow this route of water. After a strenuous final climb, you can enjoy a stunning panoramic view of the city from the ridgeline of the Serra do Morião.

Starting point: Quinta da Nasce-Água, 178m (bus stop Canada das Algas 150m west).
Grade: initially dirt trail which later turns into a steep and narrow forest trail. Sure-footedness required. Walking poles are very helpful. The ascent should not be underestimated.
Refreshment: nothing en route.
Note: The high plateau is generally used for grazing bulls. Please be careful and avoid wandering around aimlessly.

Water house at the Mãe-de-Água.

Just next to the entrance of the **Quinta da Nasce-Água** ❶ above Angra do Heroísmo, follow the narrow concrete road inland on the right. After 5 mins, you reach some water reservoirs and, before the ruins of a building, turn left onto an old cart track. After 50m, a footpath leads down to the ruins of old watermills in the streambed. Back at the water reservoirs, continue along the concrete road. After 100m, the road forks. Here, stay left on the main trail which soon turns into a gravel trail and passes the hydroelectric power plant **Central Hidroeléctrica Nasce-Água** ❷.
Above the power plant, the trail narrows and meets a green pipeline after 5 mins. Climb up to the right of the pipe and, without a trail, make your way up to the open pasture. 100m above the edge of the pasture, you have to crawl underneath the pipeline and continue up the last stretch via many concrete steps. Finally, you reach a **storage reservoir (Tanque das Costaneiras)** ❸ (50 mins).
A few metres further on, about halfway around the reservoir to the right, hidden earth steps lead into the forest to the left.

From the Tanque das Costaneiras, the view stretches across the Angra do Heroísmo and the Monte Brasil.

This is the place where the ascent trail leading up to the plateau begins with a stone cross immediately along the way. After 30 mins of ascent, you reach a viewpoint. The path leads further up to the high plateau. Above to the left, is the elevation point of the nearly 600-metre-high **Serra do Morião** ❹ (1.25 hrs).

Return along the same route to the hydroelectric **power plant** ❷. From here, descend the access road behind the iron gate, turn right at the Mãe-de-Água spring intake, cross the aqueduct and follow the forest trail downhill. At the bottom, you will meet the main trail again. Follow it back to the **Quinta da Nasce-Água** ❶.

Terceira ↗ 440m | ↘ 440m | 10km

84 Monte Brasil

3.00 hrs

Spanish forts, World War-era relics and a charming local recreation area

Monte Brasil, the local mountain of Angra do Heroísmo, is the perfect spot for some rest and recreation. Those heading up will pass the Spanish fort of Fortaleza de São João Batista, dating back to the 16th century. At the heart of a true maze of paths lies a beautifully located picnic and recreation area. Along the way, you'll come across old military posts, even older forts, and stunning viewpoints. A city walk which is definitely demanding – but well worth the effort.

Starting point: Angra do Heroísmo, Largo da Boa Nova, 39m (next bus stop at Alto das Covas).
Grade: mostly on dirt trails and challenging footpaths. Walking boots are highly recommended. This walk can be extended into a full-day outing with a picnic.
Refreshment: cafés and restaurants in Angra. Nothing en route.

This walk starts at the large water basin on **Largo da Boa Nova** ❶ and follows the plane tree-lined avenue to the entrance gate of the **Fortaleza de São João Batista**. Just inside the gate, turn left at the guard post. Shortly after the first left-hand bend in the road, take the narrow track to the left behind the barrier. This turns into a dirt trail near the **Ermida de Santo António**. After 5 mins, a grassy trail branches off sharply uphill to the right. For now, however, you stay on the dirt trail continuing straight ahead to the viewpoint at the end of the trail ❷.

Return to the junction and climb up the steep grassy trail. After about 5 mins, the trail gets flatter. Where power lines cross overhead, leave the main trail and follow the wooden steps up to the left continuing until you reach the top where a large boulder with a wooden sign marks the entrance to the **Reserva Florestal de Recreio do Monte Brasil** ❸, and where you meet the road (40 mins).

Turn left here and after 50m, take the left-hand dirt trail uphill. Eventually, you will reach a turning circle from where you continue on the middle path, which is paved at the beginning and leads you back over the **Pico do Facho** ❹ with its old fortifications and signal mast. After 10 mins, you will rejoin the

track. The route continues diagonally opposite to the left where you descend the slope in three wide switchbacks. 50m after the second right-hand bend, leave the main trail and follow a slippery footpath via wooden steps down to the left. Here you often have to walk over bare rock. In the hollow, you reach a junction. First, go left and follow the rugged wooden steps down to the old **Forte da Quebrada** ❺ (1.20 hrs).

Afterwards, return to the junction and climb the slope on the left. After a little over 10 mins, you reach another dirt trail. At first, turn left un-

At the Miradouro do Pico das Cruzinhas.

til you come to a crossing trail where you continue right. After a good 5 mins, you reach a turning circle from where a rocky footpath takes you the final stretch up to **Pico do Zimbreiro** ❻ with its World War-era fortifications and the casemates below.

Afterwards, return to the last junction and continue straight on to the **Pico da Quebrada** ❼ with its exposed whale-spotters' lookout *(vigia)*. Then, head back to the track and follow it until it joins a road. Just on the right, you will see the viewpoint overlooking the wide Caldeira (2.20 hrs).

The road continues to ascend. After 5 mins, follow a few stone steps going up on the left. 50m further up, turn sharp left onto a faint grassy footpath which leads to a few picnic tables and a big army building. Behind it, stone steps lead up to old artillery pieces and the obelisk on the **Pico das Cruzinhas** ❽.

Descend via stone steps to the monument of Dom Afonso VI and continue to the right along the road. Just past the aviaries, follow the narrow road to the left downhill through the picnic area (dead end). Where it bends sharply

to the right, take the footpath down to the left which leads to the road. First turn left here and walk to the **Miradouro do Caminho Florestal Monte Brasil** which is located above the Fortaleza de São João Batista. Afterwards, follow the road back to the **Largo da Boa Nova** ❶.

TOP 85 — Terceira ↗ 235m | ↘ 235m | 7.3km

Fortresses of São Sebastião

2.30 hrs

Historic walk through the east of the island

This coastal walk through the east takes you back to the time of the Spanish occupation. Along the rugged coast, pass several old and mostly collapsed fortresses of the 16th and 17th centuries. The magnificent view over the bay of Baía da Mina as well as its rocky islands will accompany you most of the way.

Starting point: Ermida de Maria Vieira, 87m, car park below the chapel.
Grade: partially narrow gravel trails. There are several steep ascents on this walk. Sure-footedness required. The way back is on the road.
Refreshment: nothing en route.
Bathing: lava pools at Poça dos Tremoços.

From the car park below the chapel of **Ermida de Maria Vieira** ❶, follow the road down to the coast, where it turns right and continues along the sea for a while. After 15 mins, descend to the left directly at a trail board above several greenhouses. The left trail leads to a tiled painting above the ruins of the **Forte de Santa Catarina das Mós**. A short detour leads to a viewpoint and a tiled picture. Traces of a path continue to the headland. After 100m, take the path to your left. At the tip of the headland, you reach the **Forte da Greta** ❷. The path is briefly exposed on a bare rock but it is secured by a rope. From here, it goes back inland to a viewpoint across the south-east coast and the Ilhéus das Cabras in front of it. The continuation of the walk takes you back to the trail board on the road.

First, go back on the road for 10 mins until it goes noticeably uphill again after it bends to the left. Immediately after the green iron gate, turn right onto a mule track which disappears after 100m on the meadow. Stay on the lower edge of the meadow and walk down to the right to the tip of the headland. Down there, you reach the **Forte de Bom Jesus** ❸ and in front of it, the Ilhéus da Mina in the bay with the same name. Return to the meadow and ascend anticlockwise to the right along the edge. At the upper end, wooden steps lead into the

Panoramic view towards Porto Martins from the viewpoint.

forest. After a steep ascent, you reach the first viewpoint. The second viewpoint is 100m farther down the path. The forest path ends at a pasture. After you have crossed it, you reach a magnificent **viewpoint** ❹ with seating on the upper right (1.15 hrs).

At the altitude survey point, turn to the north side of the slope and walk down the steep, pathless pasture directly along a stone wall. At level with a trough, leave the pasture below by walking across high concrete steps and keep to the left edge of the field. After 150m at a gate, you reach a cart track. Follow it 200m inland and then take the first mule track down to your right. It ends at a wooden gate, behind which you get to a fork. Here, a short detour to a hill with two viewpoints is well worth it.

The coastal walk continues on traces of a path along the landside of the hill. Turn left at the sea and climb up the rocky slope on the opposite side. Stay on the edge of the rim across pastures. Finally, you reach the **Forte do Pesqueiro dos Meninos** ❺. The lava pools of the Poça dos Tremoços are located below it (1.50 hrs).

From here cross the meadow, go inland and at the gate after 50m, turn right onto the mule track, which merges with a concrete trail farther up. Follow the trail left up the hill to reach the district of **Arrabalde** ❻, where you turn left again at the main street. Continue straight on to get back to the **Ermida de Maria Vieira** ❶ after 20 mins.

Terceira ↗ 110m | ↘ 110m | 5.9km
2.15 hrs

86 Relheiras de São Brás

Easy walk on an old ox cart track

Until just half a century ago, many goods were still transported by ox cart on the Azores. The oxen may have disappeared, however, their traces are still visible. From a picnic area nestled in lush greenery, this walk takes you along the foot of the Serra do Cume through the densely forested lava field of Biscoito das Fontinhas. The return is on an old cart track where you pass deeply carved wheel ruts (relheiras). Much of the route along this well-worn forest path feels like a cross between a treasure hunt and an adventurous stroll through an enchanted forest.

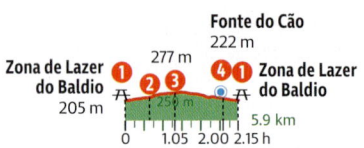

Starting point: picnic area Zona de Lazer do Baldio near São Brás, 205m.
Grade: very earthy and unpaved footpath winding through the forest. Sturdy footwear essential. Return via an old cart track.
Refreshment: nothing en route.

The 200-year-old cart tracks are pretty well-preserved.

From the car park at the **Zona de Lazer do Baldio** picnic site ❶, follow the road 100m west and turn left onto a mule track just before you reach a power line. After 5 mins, pass a green iron gate beyond which the path takes you into the forest. A few mins later, leave the main trail and turn left onto a forest path (waymarked). It winds in zig-zags through the wooded lava field of the **Biscoito das Fontinhas**. After

Mostly dry: the Fonte do Cão.

30 mins, you will get a brief glimpse of the Serra do Cume ridge. Five mins later, you reach a **fork** ❷. If you want to do a shortcut, you can turn right here and join the return route after 50m where you turn right. But if you want to continue this walk, keep left at the fork and meet a broad footpath 25 mins later. Turn left here. After another 10 mins, the forest opens up and you reach a **gravel track** ❸ at an iron gate (1.05 hrs).

Turn right onto it. After about 5 mins, where the road is paved again, take a dirt trail to the right. Five mins later, leave the dirt trail and pass through a gap in a dry stone wall to enter the forest. Your path merges after a few mins with a wide main trail which you follow to the left. There are some old watering troughs hidden in the woods. After 35 mins, you will come across the first wheel tracks. Shortly afterwards, you pass an old goat shed and the **Fonte do Cão** spring ❹.

Stay now always on the main trail which follows the exposed old ruts of the ox carts. After 5 mins, you reach a restored cart axle behind a stone gate where you will find yourself back on the road. Turn right here to return to the **picnic area** ❶.

Graciosa – island of windmills

- population: 4100
- capital: Santa Cruz, 1700 inhabitants
- area: 61km²
- length: 12km, width: 8km
- coastline: 43km
- highest points: Caldeira, 402m; Pico Timão, 398m; Pico do Facho, 375m

A windmill in Fontes.

Graciosa is the second smallest island of the Azores and because of that, life here is simple and quiet. The capital is more like a provincial backwater; in the countryside, life continues at the same pace as it has for decades. Farmers still use horse-drawn carriages and in many areas, wooden ploughs are still used to till the soil. The emblem of the island is the windmill; these appear in every settlement and many have been renovated, some are even inhabitable.

On Graciosa, one is not only assured of the lowest amount of precipitation on all of the nine islands but also of a truly relaxing holiday sojourn! In the meantime, the isle has also been added to the UNESCO Biosphere Reserve listing.

The exact date of Graciosa's discovery is not to be found in history books but, in 1440, Henry the Navigator brought livestock to the island. 10 years later, Vasco Gil Sodré became the first settler and founded the island's first settlement – Carapacho. The population increased quickly with settlers arriving from Portugal and Flanders and, in 1486, Santa Cruz was given a city charter. The island developed into a veritable granary and sacks of grain were shipped via Terceira all over the globe. In the 16th and 17th centuries, pirates frequently raided the prosperous island and a number of fortifications were established along the coast. In the late 19th century, phylloxera put a sudden end to the flourishing viniculture. Many of the island's inhabitants emigrated. In 1879, Prince Albert I from Monaco made a stopover on Graciosa and climbed down into the Furna do Enxofre using a rope ladder.

Santa Cruz, the capital of Graciosa, exudes the flair of a small village. The passages here are narrow and crooked; all of them lead to the central square Praça de Fontes Pereira de Melo. Here, at 'Rossio' during the day, one sits to make an appearance and to

Country life on Graciosa.

View of Santa Cruz da Graciosa from the Monte da Ajuda.

watch the passers-by; you can always find a shady spot under the towering araucaria pines. In a 100m radius, you can find anything you could possibly need: shops, supermarkets, restaurants, post office, banks, pharmacies, the city hall and also a taxi rank. Only a few steps away, the bell tower of the old Franciscan monastery stands alone. The two churches Matriz de Santa Cruz and the Igreja da Misericordia are located at the edge of the town centre. A visit to the island museum is worthwhile in any case, as well as an excursion to the old boathouse only a few metres away. On the Monte da Ajuda high above the town, visitors will find three chapels and a marvellous viewpoint taking in the town. The bullring which comes alive every August, is located in the crater nestled in the mountain top.

From Santa Cruz, a circular route leads at first northward along the coast to reach the secluded lighthouse on the Ponta da Barca. Next to it, the island Ilhéu da Baleia lies offshore and resembles a sleeping whale. The northern island is relatively flat for the most part and is used in many areas for the cultivation of grapevines for wine-making. The spine of the island is supported by three mountain ranges: the Serra Branca with its wind turbines, the Serra Dormida and the Serra das Fontes with what is considered the oldest rock stratum on the island. These mountains form a natural barrier between north and south. On the east coast, halfway down, lies Praia de São Mateus. Here, you will not only find a small cluster of churches and chapels but also a cake shop offering the island's speciality, the biscuits *Queijadas da Graciosa*. High above the little town, the Ermida de Nossa Senhora da Ajuda is enthroned on a rise and affords a lovely panoramic view. The south is reigned over by the immense crater of the Caldeira, a lovely spot to take a break and also boasting the sulphur cave Furna do Enxofre: in a tower built into the volcanic cave, you first have to descend a seemingly endless flight of steps. Right at the southernmost tip of the island, the seaside resort Carapacho boasts a lovely natural bathing area and a quaint little thermal pool.

GRACIOSA

Getting there
Regular connections within the Azores with SATA to Terceira. There are also occasional direct flights to São Miguel. The airport is situated 2km from the Santa Cruz city limits. The ferry harbour is located in Praia de São Mateus. In summer, there are connections to Terceira and to the *Triângulo*.

Bathing
Sandy beach in Praia de São Mateus. Pebble beach at Barro Vermelho on the north coast. Sea water pools in Carapacho and in Santa Cruz. Natural bathing areas in Vitória, at the Porto Afonso and in the bay at Folga. Thermal bath in Carapacho. Santa Cruz boasts a lovely municipal open-air seawater swimming pool.

Festivities
Carnival in winter. Holy Spirit Celebrations from Whitsun until summer. Festa de São João (Santa Cruz), June 24. Festa do Senhor Santo Cristo dos Milagres (Santa Cruz), beginning of August.

Medical services
First aid facility in Santa Cruz, tel +351 295 730 070.

Tourist information
Turismo da Graciosa with an office in Santa Cruz, tel +351 295 712 430, pt.gra@azores.gov.pt, cm-graciosa.pt. Free Wi-Fi in Santa Cruz's centre and Praia de São Mateus, as well as at the airport.

Cultural activities
Museu da Graciosa and a handicrafts centre in Santa Cruz. The windmill in Fontes and the whalers' museum in Praia de São Mateus are only open upon special request. The wine cellars Terra do Conde near Santa Cruz with wine-tasting. Furna do Enxofre with an information centre in the caldeira. Casa Museu Bettencourt in the style of an old general store in Guadalupe.

Public transport
Bus service during the day between all the settlements. Taxi ranks in Santa Cruz, Praia de São Mateus and Luz. Since travelling distances are short, a hire car is not really necessary.

Accommodation
There is a limited selection of accommodation. Hotels in Santa Cruz. Some private rooms and small holiday homes are scattered throughout the island. There is a lovely campsite near Praia de São Mateus, others are situated in Carapacho, at Barro Vermelho and near Santa Cruz.

TOP 87 — From Bom Jesus to the Barro Vermelho

Graciosa

↗ 50m | ↘ 70m | 6.8km
2.40 hrs

A stroll through vineyards with a spectacular section along the coast

The flat northern part of the island is still used for growing wine. Carefully stacked basalt walls protect the delicate vines, while windmills seem like bright red dots across the landscape. We experience the contrast on the north coast. The rugged rocky islands offer stunning photo opportunities and are home to numerous seabirds.

Starting point: Bom Jesus, the future Vineyard Interpretive Centre, 24m (bus stop Caminho do Bom Jesus).
Destination: Barro Vermelho, 9m. Return either by taxi or via the Alternative route back to the starting point.
Grade: initially comfortable mule tracks. Partially narrow and rocky vintners' paths. The coastal section is pathless and leads across ash deposits and lava rubble.
Refreshment: nothing en route.
Alternative: circular walk back to Bom Jesus (section 1.3km, 25 mins): from Barro Vermelho, follow the main road for about 10 mins towards the lighthouse, then turn left at the animal shelter. Just beyond it, a dirt trail goes around the airfield. Where the fence bends left at the southwestern corner (after about 5 mins), turn right to rejoin the path you took on the way in. Keep right, pass the windmill and return to the starting point.
Bathing: sheltered natural pools at the Barro Vermelho.

From the future Vineyard Interpretive Centre in **Bom Jesus** ❶, first follow the main road ER 5 (Caminho do Barroso) towards Santa Cruz and turn left onto a mule track 200m after house no. 151. After 5 mins, you reach a fork. This is where you will continue to the left later. But for now, you keep right and after 75m – at the same height as the **Moinho da Achada** windmill ❷ – you turn right again.

Where the trail becomes paved again after a little over 5 mins, turn left onto a mule track. At its end, a narrow supply path continues half-right into the vineyard fields. It ends just before the airfield, where two **roadways** ❸ join from the right. Here, continue slightly to the left along another mule track for 75m. Beyond that point, the trail is sometimes heavily eroded and leads through dense undergrowth. Keep to the left along the fence of the airfield and stay on the path that leads through the reed. Just above some wooden steps, turn left onto a grassy path and pass some ruins. The mule track curves back towards the south. After 5 mins, at a fork, keep left towards the windmill. Follow the mule track back to the **Moinho da Achada** ❷ and the fork behind it.

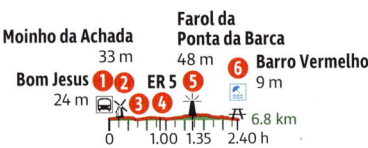

Altitude measuring point at the Pico Negro – behind the Farol da Ponta da Barca.

Turn right here and pass the water reservoir Tanque da Achada. Shortly after the reservoir, you reach the **main road ER 5** ❹ (1 hr). Continue straight for 20m and, opposite house no. 180, turn right onto a narrow vintners' path heading towards the coast. After 5 mins, the path bends to the left, then swings north again after 150m and eventually joins the coastal road. Follow it left for 100m, then take the sandy track to the right just after the junction to the lighthouse. A few metres on the left, you will get an amazing view of the Baía do Forno. Climb the embankment to the road and walk up to the **Farol da Ponta da Barca** lighthouse ❺. From here you have a splendid view all the way across the Ilhéu da Baleia (1.35 hrs).

Walk 75m back along the access road, then turn left and pass through a gap in the wall. This is the start of the coastal trail. For the most part pathless, it follows the markers across Pico Negro through the dusty volcanic landscape. There are several viewpoints along the way. After 1 hr, the markers continue on the road. Once you continue left you have almost reached your destination – the picnic and bathing area of **Barro Vermelho** ❻.

Graciosa ↗ 500m | ↘ 500m | 14.5km

88 From Praia de São Mateus to Fontes

4.30 hrs

A walk along old cart tracks in the island's east

Graciosa has been shaped by farming and livestock breeding. This walk starts in the port town of Praia and leads up to the farming village of Fontes via ancient mule tracks. Up here, you will come across several windmills and get wide views over the island's northern part. Return to the south in a wide loop. If you prefer, you can also end the tour in the island's main town, Santa Cruz.

Starting point: Praia de São Mateus, town gate by the beach, 5m (bus stop Praia/Rua Dr. Brito de Albuquerque 100m west).
Grade: mostly well-maintained cart and farm tracks. Part of the walk leads across enclosed pastureland (you are likely to get close up and personal with the cows) and along mule tracks which are not always in the best condition. Unfortunately, some sections are often overgrown with knee-high grass.
Refreshment: cafés, bars, restaurant in Praia de São Mateus. Nothing en route.

Alternative: end the walk in Santa Cruz (section 3.3km, 50 mins): follow the concrete trail ❼ down to the left. Once down at the road, go straight ahead before it merges with the main road ER 1. Follow it left to a crossroads with a stone cross (Cruz da Barra). Turn right at the old washhouse down towards the sea and turn left at the Porto da Barra. Continue along the seafront for 25 mins to reach the centre of Santa Cruz.
Linking tip: Walks 89 and 90.
Bathing: lovely sandy beach and seawater pool in Praia de São Mateus.

From the town gate at the beach of **Praia de São Mateus** ❶, start off by following the road past the harbour heading north. Pass a few charming windmills and continue on the coastal road (Passeio Marítimo). After 15 mins, it bends inland into the suburb of Lagoa. At the crossroad with the **bus stop** ❷, turn right and leave the settlement 100m beyond, at the Casa da Fonte, on a road that leads uphill. At the **Saibreira do Quitadouro** quarry ❸, turn sharply left and follow the dirt trail uphill. After 15 mins, it meets the **ER 1** ❹. A few steps to the right, slightly uphill, you will see a viewpoint. Diagonally opposite, an old cobbled mule track with ruts of ancient cart wheels continues. After a 10-min ascent, the track reaches an iron gate. 120m further up on the right, you will reach the **road** ❺ again (1.15 hrs).

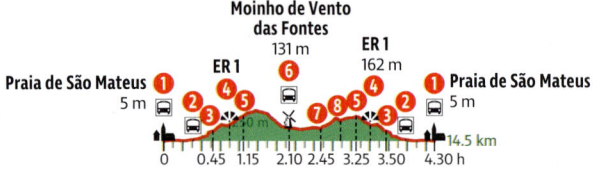

Follow the road uphill to the left and pass a stable building. Where the road eventually bends left, continue to the right for 100m on a country lane until you reach a watering trough. Here, go through a cattle barrier to the right and stay on the pasture to the right of the stone wall. After 75m, cross to the left side of the wall. Continue straight ahead, now along the right edge of the pasture, following the stone wall downhill without a path.

View across the Caldeira massif.

The way leads directly toward a solar panel plant below on the coast. Further down, you will reach an old mule track which you follow to the left. After 100m, it bends left at an iron gate and broadens into a lush cart track. Continue on the main path until you reach the farming village of **Fontes** on the Canada da Vela Latina. At the crossroad, turn right and immediately – after the Holy Spirit chapel at house no. 61 – turn left again to reach the beautiful windmill **Moinho de Vento das Fontes** ❻ (2.10 hrs).

Afterwards, return to the chapel and walk down through the village on the cobbled street. After 5 mins, turn right just behind house no. 18 to join the narrow paved Canada de Trás do Pico. At the last house, the small road turns into a country lane. Here, a grassy trail branches off to the right – a short detour to another windmill.

The country lane continues on the same level, narrows to a footpath, and joins a **concrete trail** ❼ (for the Alternative, turn left). Turn right here and climb steeply uphill. The concrete trail passes two water tanks and becomes a country lane, which leads to two green iron gates 100m above. Turn left here onto an old cart track, which soon bends right. Follow the old drovers' path all the way up. At the end, keep left and follow a piled stone wall for about 100m. The footpath then turns left again, descends, and ends at a **road** ❽.

Follow it to the right. After 15 mins, you meet your original route ❺ which you follow back to your starting point at **Praia de São Mateus** ❶.

89 — From the Serra Branca to Praia de São Mateus

Graciosa ↗ 70m | ↘ 380m | 11km — 3.15 hrs

Descent from the island's wind farm to a small seaside resort

High above, on the Serra Branca, wind turbines tower to the heavens. Just next to them, the maw of the Caldeirinha plummets down like a funnel to hell. Once at the Serra Dormida, you first pass the Pico Timão and a little later some abandoned and overgrown fruit tree plantations. A cart track finally leads back toward the coast.

Starting point: the turn-off from the ER 1 at km13 to the Parque Eólico, 317m.
Destination: Praia de São Mateus, town gate at the beach, 5m (bus stop Praia/Rua Dr. Brito de Albuquerque 100m west).
Grade: mostly cart and donkey trails good for walking. Sometimes over tarmac. At the Pico Timão, the scree path is narrow and sloping.
Refreshment: cafés, bars, restaurant in Praia de São Mateus. Nothing en route.
Linking tip: Walks 88, 90 and 93.
Note: circumvent the difficult section across the Pico Timão: below the Pico Timão just before the ascent, follow the country lane to the right and after a good 5 mins, turn left onto the crossing path ❺).
Bathing: lovely, sandy beach and a seawater pool in Praia de São Mateus.

Begin the walk at km13 on the main road **ER 1** ❶. Here, climb up the Caminho do Canadão da Serra Branca. Opposite the gate to the wind farm, turn left onto a **gravel trail** ❷. If you wish, you can first circle round the Caldeirinha. From the iron gate, the continuation leads northwards directly below the crater rim trail. Where the trail drops down steeply on the north side, go through a cattle barrier and follow a faint footpath. Partly across wooden steps, you will reach the ochre-coloured **Tanque Velho** ❸.

On the dirt trail, go right uphill, passing a water house, until you reach the concrete road to the wind farm. Continue straight ahead on the asphalt road (Caminho Rural da Canada da Fajã), which turns left as a concrete trail after about 5 mins (Caminho dos Picheleiros). After another 5 mins, an asphalt road joins from the right. However, you continue straight ahead

on the concrete trail, which soon turns into a dirt trail. After another 5 mins, a concrete trail goes uphill to the left. Initially, stay straight on the country lane which turns right after 250m. At this point, turn left onto an old mule track which goes uphill and turns right at the top. The track ends after 5 mins at a pasture, where you continue left along the stone wall without a path heading towards Pico Timão. At the upper end of the pasture, a country lane starts to the right (take note of the sign). Turn left through a gap in the

Wind farm on the Serra Branca – in the foreground the vent of Caldeirinha.

stone wall and follow it for about 100m. Then, climb steeply and partly via wooden steps until you reach a wooden **lookout** ❹ at **Pico Timão**.
A narrow gravel path continues counterclockwise along the crater rim. Pass the elevation point and later descend steeply on the east side via many wooden steps. Further down, stay along the left edge of the pasture until you finally reach a country lane and an **iron gate** ❺.
Beyond the gate, you will reach the end of a road where you continue right on a gravel trail. 10 mins later, at the point where the road, now tarmaced again, hooks sharp to the left, continue straight on through the wood along a mule track which climbs directly down to the **ER 3** ❻ (1.50 hrs). 50m to the right, a gravel trail on the opposite side continues the route (stop sign). It leads along stone walls in a forest, passing long-abandoned and overgrown gardens. 15 mins later, get to an abandoned **quinta** ❼ and continue straight on. A good 5 mins later, the country lane hooks away sharp to the left below stone-supported terraces at the foot of the Serra das Fontes. At this point, turn right onto a **footpath** ❽ overgrown with grass. Soon the path widens to become a vehicle track and at the end meets up with the **ER 1** ❾ (2.30 hrs). Follow the road to the right. After 5 mins, just before it descends again, turn left onto an old narrow supply path. After 5 mins in the forest, you will reach a turning circle. Go right at the next crossing road towards **Lagoa** ❿ where you turn right at an ancient kiln.
At the junction 80m further on, turn left onto the Caminho da Beira Mar da Rochela. This street leads to the coastline, then hooks to the right and becomes a seaside promenade which leads to the refurbished **windmills** ⓫ and two ancient kilns. Pass the harbour and continue straight on into the centre of **Praia de São Mateus** ⓬.

Graciosa ↗ 530m | ↘ 530m | 13.9km

90 From Praia de São Mateus to Carapacho
3.50 hrs

Panoramic walk on the southern tip of the island

From Praia de São Mateus, climb at first strenuously up to the circular trail around the Caldeira. Along this trail, you can enjoy a view stretching over the entire southern half of Graciosa. When skies are clear, the other islands of the central group can be seen. Before climbing down to Carapacho and its thermal bath, take a panoramic excursion to the lighthouse and a whale-spotters' post above the Ponta da Restinga.

Starting point: Praia de São Mateus, town gate at the beach, 5m (bus stop Praia/Rua Dr. Brito de Albuquerque 100m west).
Destination: the thermal bath in Carapacho, 6m (bus stop Carapacho/Largo where the access road joins the ER 1).
Grade: the walk route follows cart tracks and donkey trails which are good for walking. Some stretches along tarmac. The descent to Carapacho may be overgrown (if need be, you can also stay on the road).
Refreshment: cafés, bars and restaurant in Praia de São Mateus, snack bar Dolphin in Carapacho. Nothing en route.
Linking tip: Walks 88, 89 and 91.
Bathing: lovely sandy beach and seawater swimming pools in Praia de São Mateus. Thermal bath and seawater swimming pool in Carapacho.

Starting at the town gate at the beach in **Praia de São Mateus** ❶, first follow the main street for a good 10 mins toward Carapacho. 200m past the chapel, turn right onto the **Caminho da Ventosa** ❷, a country lane that is pleasant at the beginning but later becomes steeper as it follows the course of a stream, crosses over an intersecting trail on the slope and then ends when meeting the **track** ❸ circling the Caldeira (45 mins).

Descent to the Fonte da Rocha.

Turn right and pass a trail ascending to the left via wooden steps to the Furna da Maria Encantada. At the **fork** ❹ which follows, keep left to continue the circular walk. Now pass a viewpoint above Luz and soon enjoy views of the neighbouring islands of Faial, São Jorge and Pico in the background and later, also Terceira on the horizon. There is another viewpoint. After 1.10 hrs along the circular route (a total of 1.55 hrs in all), a **road** ❺ ascends from the right (Caminho Rural das Rilheiras). Take this road along the eastern side of the crater to descend and meet up again 20 mins later with the **ER 1** ❻.

Turn left and, 70m on, turn sharp right onto a country lane which leads southward along the coast. After 10 mins, you reach a fork where you first stay half left on the main trail which soon ends and continues as a wooden stepped trail down to the coast ending at the **Fonte da Rocha** ❼.

Afterwards, return to the fork and follow the grassy trail up to the left. Eventually, you reach a lifestock gathering area and rejoin the **main road** ❽, which you follow to the left for 20 mins towards Carapacho. Above the seaside village, first take the access road to the **lighthouse** ❾ (sign: Farol). Further on, at the rim of the cliff, enjoy a lovely view of the Ilhéu de Baixo.

Return to the main road and turn left to continue. At the first green iron gate, a **grassy trail** ❿ turns sharp left to descend. After 50m, traces of a path, which might be difficult to see depending on how overgrown it is, turns off to the right and joins an old, often overgrown shepherds' path, heading towards Carapacho. At the first houses, the trail has become concrete-paved. Turn left onto the first street and then turn left again. Passing a snack bar and crossing the campsite, you first reach the thermal bath and and then the bathing area of **Carapacho** ⓫.

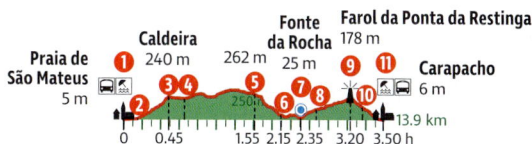

Graciosa ↗ 350m | ↘ 350m | 9.5km

91 Volta à Caldeira

2.50 hrs

Leisurely circular walk around the giant crater with a cave excursion

From the farming village of Luz, first ascend to the Caldeira circuit. During the subsequent loop around the crater, you can enjoy views of the southern part of Graciosa and the neighbouring islands of the central group. In the north, there is a lava tunnel and a viewpoint high above the Caldeira. Those interested can also descend to the sulphur cave of Furna do Enxofre via a long spiral staircase.

Starting point: Luz, central Largo 1° de Dezembro, 80m (bus stop Luz/Rua 6 de Janeiro 70m north).
Grade: mostly wide tracks or paved roads without major difficulties. Some sections of the ascent are quite steep.
Refreshment: nothing en route.
Alternative: Caldeira high route and sulphur cave (section 5km, 2 hrs): 100m after the cattle gate below the viewpoint, just before an open cistern, a hidden descent path leads down from the crater rim into the Caldeira basin. After 10 mins, leave the forest and turn left. After 100m, at the end of the cryptomeria grove, follow a faint footpath to the right to reach the Caldeira road. Turn right and follow it to the turning circle. From here, descend countless wooden steps through a stone gate to the cave Furna do Enxofre. Back at the turning circle, follow a footpath to the right along the stone wall. You pass a silted-up lake and reach the picnic area in the Parque da Caldeira. To the left of the barbecue huts, next to the Centro de Divulgação, a footpath starts zigzagging uphill to a stone wall. Beyond the wall, turn left and continue on the level grassy trail. After 150m, turn right and follow the stone wall uphill. At the top, you reach an iron gate and continue along the crater rim on the right-hand side of the pasture fence. The entire Caldeira slope is open pastureland. Watch out for the cows – they are likely to come close!! In several places, a wire fence separates the trail from the pastureland. In the south-east, you reach the highest point of this walk. From here, you can enjoy open views over Carapacho. Several collection cisterns follow. On the western side, near the green iron gate, you rejoin the main Caldeira circular walk. Beyond the gate, turn right to continue along the main route.
Linking tip: Walk 90.

From the central village square in **Luz** ❶, follow the Rua da Igreja towards the church and turn left just behind it. From here, go straight uphill. The road eventually becomes an old mule track at a watering trough which soon narrows and gets steeper. The steepest and most eroded sections can be bypassed on a footpath through the forest to the right of the track. At the top, you

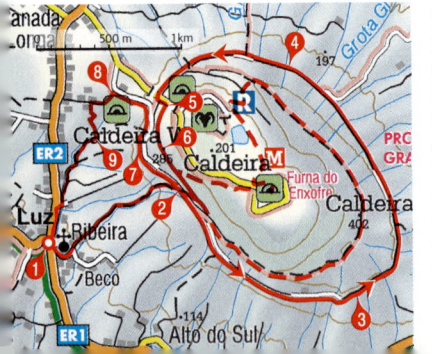

reach the Caldeira circular walk ❷ (30 mins). Continue to the right along the crater rim. Almost immediately, the return route joins from the left at the green iron gate.

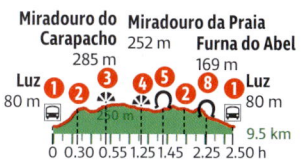

Soon you can enjoy views over the southern part of Graciosa and, on the horizon, spot the neighbouring islands of Faial, São Jorge, Pico behind them, and later Terceira. After 25 mins on the circular walk, you pass the **Miradouro do Carapacho** ❸, and 30 mins later the **Miradouro da Praia** ❹. Another 15 mins on, at the spot where a power line crosses the trail, a wooden staircase leads left up to the crater rim. At the top, turn left onto a small loop path to reach the **Furna da Maria Encantada** ❺. Behind the lava pipe, there is a hidden viewpoint into the Caldeira's interior with a nice spot to rest (1.45 hrs).

From the lava pipe, follow the path along the outer crater rim counter-clockwise passing a wooden statue. After 10 mins, reach a wooden **lookout tower** ❻. Stay on the grassy trail and go through a pasture gate to reach open grazing land (100m ahead, the Alternative branches off to the left). After 5 mins walking across the pasture, you will reach a country lane. Turn right and descend passing through the iron gate to rejoin your outbound route.

Follow the gravel track to the right, pass the **Miradouro da Luz** ❼ and reach a fork. Take the left-hand path downhill. After 5 mins, where the road bends, turn left onto a mule track. After a few metres, pass the entrance to the **Furna do Abel** ❽. Continue along the mule track until you get to a road. Stay left on the old track and, after 100m at a crossroad, turn left again. As the path descends, a short detour to the left leads to the pond at **Fonte de Nesquim** ❾. The main trail, which is very eroded on the following section, joins the main road **ER 2** after 10 mins.

Turn left to reach the **starting point** ❶ after 5 mins.

From the wooden lookout tower on the Caldeira rim, you have a good view of the entire crater.

Graciosa ↗ 90m | ↘ 90m | 3.2km

92 Baía da Folga

1.00 hrs

Short excursion to the rugged coast and the popular fishing harbour

Ancient windmills, partially abandoned vineyards and a rugged coastline await you along this interesting but short walk. An old cart track leads down to the coast. Then walk above the rugged coastline along a footpath to reach the fishing harbour on the Baía da Folga. Here you can find a pleasant inn at the harbour and, in the morning, freshly-caught fish and seafood.

Starting point: Luz, central square Largo 1° de Dezembro, 80m (bus stop Luz/Rua 6 de Janeiro 70m north).
Grade: an old cart track and a distinct coastal footpath. Return along a tarmac road.
Refreshment: restaurant Estrela do Mar at the harbour at Baía da Folga.
Alternative: a longer route via Beira Mar (3.1km, 1 hr): after descending out of the Folga bay, turn left onto the main street. 70m on, past the bus stop at house no. 86, a narrow passageway leads to the seaside. It immediately becomes a cart track and, 10 mins later, hooks off to the right, afterwards to the left. 50m further on, the trail ends. A narrow access trail continues through the undergrowth to reach the seaside and a coastal path. Turn right on this path. 100m further on, a 50m-long stretch follows that has broken away. Afterwards, the cart track, in better condition at this point, ascends to Beira Mar. Climb up the access road, at the main street, bear right. In the settlement, bear right again and return to the starting point.
Linking tip: Walk 93.
Bathing: in the small harbour at Baía da Folga.

From the centrally-located village square in **Luz** ❶ at first follow the main street in the direction of Ribeirinha and 150m on, turn left onto the Canada dos Padres. At the end of the side street, reach a cul-de-sac at an old renovated **windmill** ❷ to find the beginning of an old cart track. Following drystone walls, the track heads straight ahead and climbs down to the coast. Ignore all of the forks which fork off to the left and right.

At the end of the main trail, a distinct **coastal path** ❸ turns right above the coast to continue, keeps straight ahead and in 10 mins reaches the **fishing harbour** ❹ on the Baía da Folga (35 mins). Here, you can take an excursion along a narrow path to the tiny harbour light with a lovely viewpoint.

Turn right onto the cobblestone street to climb up the slope, pass a chapel on the way and finally return to the **main street** ❺ (the Alternative turns left). Turn right again onto the street and then head back to the starting point in **Luz** ❶.

From the small fishing bay of Baía da Folga, you can see all the way to the Serra Branca.

Graciosa ↗ 380m | ↘ 380m | 8.3km

93 Ascent from Beira Mar to the Serra Branca
2.30 hrs

Ascent from a summer residence to the island's wind farm

At the newly-renovated stone-built houses of Beira Mar on the Baía do Filipe, it is only lively during the summer months. A pleasant trail climbs up to the wind farm on the Serra Branca. Passing the precipitous sheer drop at the rim of the Caldeirinha crater, continue to the abandoned hamlet of Fajã and via numerous fields and pastures, return to the starting point.

Starting point: Beira Mar, 30m.
Grade: dirt trails and country lanes which are good for walking. The ascent is sometimes over tarmac. A very steep ascent to the Serra Branca.
Refreshment: nothing en route.
Linking tip: Walk 92.

From the picnic spot in Beira Mar you get a magnificent view of the cliffs in the west.

From the picnic area in **Beira Mar** ❶, at first climb up the street toward the ER 1. After a good 5 mins, underneath a high natural stone wall turn sharp left onto a country lane which joins a dirt trail after another 5 mins. Follow it to the left and continue on an old cart track all the way to an old threshing yard ❷ at the ER 1 (25 mins). The cart track continues onward on the other side of the road. A few mins later, get to yet another road. At the cattle pen, turn right onto this road and follow it for 25 mins until it comes to an end ❸. A concrete path continues to the left. At the next **fork** ❹ a good 5 mins later, follow the road to the right (your way back later leads to the left). A few mins later, reach a narrow **concrete road** ❺. Turn left onto this road which climbs extremely steep up to the wind generators on the Serra Branca (1.15 hrs). Arriving at the top, turn diagonally right in front of the gate for the wind farm and onto a **country lane** ❻. If you wish, you could first circle the Caldeirinha crater.

The trail continues a bit below the crater path heading north. Where it drops off steeply on the north side, turn right through a cattle gate and follow some traces of a path. Partly over wooden steps, you reach the ochre-coloured **Tanque Velho** ❼. On the dirt trail, head up to the right, and pass a water station until you reach the concrete road leading to the wind farm.

Here you rejoin your ascent route ❺. First, cross the road to the wind farm and continue straight back to the **fork** ❹. Here, bear diagonally right along the gravel trail which leads straight on to the abandoned village of **Fajã** ❽ which lies in ruins (1.55 hrs). Cross over the ER 1 and descend further along an old cart track, cobbled at the beginning. Returning to the main road, turn right for a few paces and then immediately left to ascend along the Canada do Sul. 50m on, at a cattle pen, meet up again with the cart track used on the approach route. Take this back to return to **Beira Mar** ❶.

Flores – the flower island

- population: 3400
- county seats: Santa Cruz, 1600 inhabitants; Lajes, 560
- area: 141km²
- length: 17km, width: 12km
- coastline: 72km
- highest points: Morro Alto, 914m; Pico da Burrinha, 886m; Pico dos Sete Pés, 849m

Flores is the most westerly of the Azorean islands and a paradise for walkers and nature-lovers alike thanks to its lush natural landscape. There are only a few settlements to choose from but the mountain highlands – a mixture of woodland and marsh – and a few crater lakes make up for that. Month after month, trails are flanked by a profusion of bright and colourful flora – a compensation for being the island with the highest annual precipitation in the entire archipelago. The little villages are mostly situated above the coastline which consists of steep cliffs dropping sheerly to the sea; very few access routes lead to the seaside. The flanks of the countless deep-cleft valleys are just as steep. In any case, a day trip by ferry to the neighbouring island of Corvo is worthwhile. If the opportunity arises to take a boat trip around the island, you should definitely take it up.

Enchanting landscape in the valley of the Ribeira d'Além.

The Portuguese Diogo de Teive discovered Flores in 1452. In 1470, Wilhelm van der Hagen from Flanders tried his luck with plants used in dyeing but soon gave up on the enterprise. Starting in the south, settlement of the island first began in 1504, initiated by the Captain General João da Fonseca. Due to its secluded location, trading was only aimed at the islands of the central group. Lajes was given a city charter in 1515. Santa Cruz followed in 1548 and became the island's capital in the 17th century. Countless pirate raids plagued the islands in the 16th and 17th centuries. In 1860, the first whaling ship with an all-Azorean crew set sail from Flores. The ocean liner Slavonia sank off the coast in 1906 and was the first ship to send out the signal 'SOS'. The

French set up a communications centre in the isolated north in 1963; this was in service until 1994. Since 2009, the entire island, including offshore waters, has been declared a UNESCO Biosphere Reserve.

Santa Cruz, the main town, is easy to explore; the little town centre is settled around the square Praça do Marquês de Pombal in front of the city hall. The main church Matriz de Nossa Senhora da Conceição, boasting a magnificent facade, is standing not far away as is the old Franciscan monastery São Boaventura. At the seaside, you can walk past three separate harbours: Poças, Velho and Boqueirão. The latter is the location of the old whale-processing plant which has been converted into a museum with an attached visitor centre. The airport is situated on the outskirts of town. The hill Monte das Cruzes towers above the town and affords a lovely view. The second county seat **Lajes** is situated at the southernmost tip. Lajes becomes lively once a year during the Emigrants' Celebrations. The church Matriz de Nossa Senhora do Rosário, boasting a pleasant, panoramic forecourt, is worth a visit. The reconstruction of the harbour, which was destroyed by a hurricane in 2019, will be another highlight over the next few years.

FLORES

Getting there
Scheduled SATA flights within the Azores are provided frequently during the week from Flores to Corvo, Faial, Terceira and São Miguel. The airport is located in Santa Cruz. At the time of writing, there was no ferry connection available. The little Corvo ship and also speed boats (in summer) start off at Porto das Poças in Santa Cruz.

Bathing
A small sandy beach in Lajes. Fine pebble beach at Fajã de Lopo Vaz. Lovely natural bathing area in Santa Cruz. Bathing areas in Fajã Grande and at the harbour in Ponta Delgada. A bathing pond with a waterfall at the Poço do Bacalhau. Secluded bathing spots on isolated pebble-beach coves, especially on the east coast.

Festivities
Good Friday Procession at Easter. Holy Spirit Celebrations starting on Whitsun and continuing until summer. Sanjoaninas in Santa Cruz, June 24. Festa do Emigrante (Lajes), 2nd week in July.

Medical services
A clinic in Santa Cruz, tel +351 292 590 270.

Tourist information
Turismo das Flores in Santa Cruz, tel +351 292 592 369, pt.flo@azores.gov.pt; cmscflores.pt and cmlajesdasflores.pt. A small branch office is at the airport. Free Wi-Fi in Santa Cruz's town gardens, at the airport, in Fajã Grande's town centre as well as numerous other hotspots (WIFI4EU).

Cultural activities
Modern island museum in Santa Cruz. Centro de Interpretação Ambiental do Boqueirão and Museu Fábrica da Baleia in Santa Cruz. Modern island museum, the little Casa Museu do Lavrador, with agricultural implements and the Casa Museu dos Lacticínios, focusing on dairy production, in the old cooperative in Lajes. The little privately-owned cheese factory Queijaria Pico Redondo in Fajãzinha. Moinho da Alagoa, an intact water mill, near Fajãzinha.

Public transport
In the meantime, the bus network operated by UTC is well-developed with numerous connections crisscrossing the island all day through. Bus schedules available at the *turismo*. Without a hire car, however, most of the attractive spots on the island are hard to reach. There are taxi ranks in Santa Cruz, Lajes and Fajã Grande but very few are found on the western side of the island.

Accommodation
Accommodation on Flores is limited; besides a few hotels, only family-run guesthouses, private rooms, and a handful of holiday homes are available. A rejuvenated village in Cuada offers a holiday experience in 19th century style. There are areas for camping in Fajã Grande, Lajes, Santa Cruz and Ponta Delgada.

View of the little capital Santa Cruz from the Monte das Cruzes.

Flores is marked by emigration – the population is only half of what it was in 1950. Settlements outside of the little capital resemble small farming villages and seldom count more than 100 inhabitants. In the meantime, a coastal road has been constructed circling the southern half of the island. Starting out from Santa Cruz, you can touch on every settlement on the island in an hour's drive. Fajãzinha and Fajã Grande are located on the west coast at the foot of steep cliffs from which, especially in the winter months, countless spectacular waterfalls tumble down. Lying offshore, the tiny islet of Ilhéu de Monchique boasts of being Europe's most western point. Also on the west coast, you will find the rock formation Rocha dos Bordões whose frozen lava flow resembles organ pipes.

The island's interior is uninhabited. In summer, hydrangea hedges light up the landscape with blue and provide natural borders for extensive pastureland. Tracks lead to the shimmering turquoise crater lakes of Branca, Comprida, Lomba, Funda, Rasa and Seca, nestled away in the hilly countryside. Rain often falls in the highlands and it is not rare that the heart of the island lies hidden under thick cloud cover.

On the north coast, a road climbs up from Santa Cruz, thanks to the French who built it. The road ends in Ponta Delgada, a farming village lacking in appeal at the northernmost tip. Countless caves and rock formations are scattered along the island's coastline but can only be seen from out to sea. One of the most striking examples is the Gruta do Galo to the north as well as the Gruta das Enxaréus to the east, a pirate hide-out in the past. In any case, the local recreational area, Luís Paulo Camacho, is a worthwhile stopover.

| TOP | Flores | ↗ 580m | ↘ 760m | 14.2km |

94 From Costa to Fajã Grande

5.00 hrs

From village to village along the west coast

An old connecting trail runs along the entire western coastline. From its southernmost end in Costa, the trail leads in steady up and down walking through all of the settlements located on the island's west coast. En route, you can enjoy many lovely views of the rugged coastline and the offshore islands.

Starting point: Costa do Lajedo, chapel, 192m (bus stop Costa do Lajedo 100m above the chapel).
Destination: Fajã Grande, harbour, 7m (bus stop Fajã Grande/Fim).
Grade: mostly along cobbled cart tracks that are overgrown with grass. Very slippery when wet. In the settlements, along streets.
Refreshment: bars and restaurants in Fajã Grande. Nothing en route.
Alternative: to Poço da Ribeira do Ferreiro (1.3km; 40 mins): in front of the Ribeira do Ferreiro, turn right to follow the grassy trail. This immediately becomes an ancient cobbled trail. Through the wood, a good 15 mins later, reach the shoreline of a lake known to the locals as the Poço das Patas. The lake owes its waters to the countless waterfalls of the Ribeira do Ferreiro. Afterwards, return along the same route.
Linking tip: Walks 95, 96 and 97.
Bathing: harbour area of Fajã Grande.

At the Poço da Ribeira do Ferreiro (Alternative).

Start off at the little chapel in **Costa do Lajedo** ❶. 20m below this, turn right along the narrow tarmac trail which ascends onto the height of the Rocha do Pico and, passing a cattle pen, descends again gently. When the trail begins another ascent, turn left onto a **country lane** ❷ and turn right onto the grassy path in front of the stables. The trail leads into the valley of the Ribeira do Campanário which you cross over below Lajedo. A cobblestone trail climbs up to the street, turn left and then reach the village centre of **Lajedo** ❸ (50 mins).

At the church, turn right and 40m on, turn left onto the Rua P. Dr. Caetano Tomáz. You have already crossed through the tiny village when you reach a picnic area. The road ends just past this area; now follow the country lane to the left to continue. At the fork 100m on, bear left again. From now on, keep following the old, cobbled mule track which leads in steady up and down walking across a number of streambeds. 30 mins of walking along the mule track, reach the old stone bridge spanning the **Ribeira da Lapa** ❹ with the basalt massif Rocha dos Bordões towering above. 15 mins later, reach the **Ribeira do Fundão** ❺ which must be forded via boulders. Past this point, the trail climbs up again and finally reaches the street in **Mosteiro** ❻ at a transformer house (2.05 hrs).

Turn left onto the street and descend past the church until the street hooks off to the right at the end of the village. Before reaching a rest area, continue along the con-

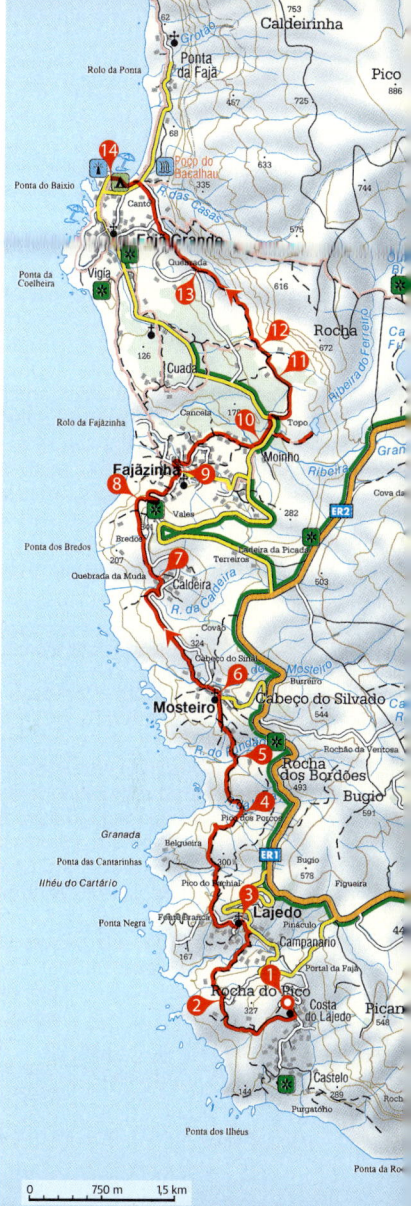

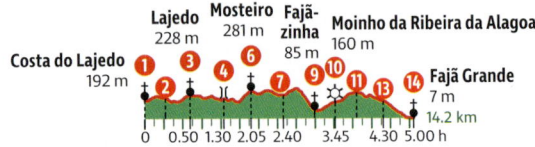

crete trail straight ahead until meeting the bridge spanning the Ribeira do Mosteiro. Past the bridge, a mule track continues, leading past hay barns and ascending to the road. Turn left onto the road. 10 mins later, the road veers to the right and climbs down to the hamlet of **Caldeira** ❼ abandoned since 1992; the natural stone-built houses have succumbed to the forces of nature (2.40 hrs).

After the trail levels out again and 50m before reaching a bridge, exactly in the hollow, turn left onto a grassy trail to continue towards a natural stone-built house. In the centre of the village in ruins, turn right onto a sunken trail to finally ascend to the road again. Turn left onto the road and ascend the slope for a somewhat strenuous 5-min climb. Where it levels out again, turn left onto a grassy trail. Soon reach the top ❽ and then begin the descent to Fajãzinha along old cobblestones (to the right, a short excursion ascending to the viewpoint taking in Fajãzinha is worthwhile).

Mosteiro at the foot of the rock formation Rocha dos Bordões.

Fajãzinha on Flores' dramatic west coast.

20 mins later, reach the first houses and also a concrete trail. Pass the church and now, after a total of 3.20 hrs, reach the village square (Rossio) in the village centre of **Fajãzinha** ❾. At a transformer house, turn left. 70m further on, at the little chapel, turn sharp right and, along the middle street, pass a total of three fountains in 5 mins until meeting up with a T-junction. Here, turn right and, 10m on, at the garage, immediately turn left into the narrow Rua do Espinhaço. Before reaching the residence, turn right onto an ancient cobbled trail to ascend and, 15 mins later, at the old watermill, **Moinho da Ribeira da Alagoa** ❿, merge with the main road to Fajã Grande (3.45 hrs).

Along the main road, turn left over the bridge spanning the Ribeira Grande. 150m on, you could take the opportunity to make an excursion to Poço da Ribeira do Ferreiro (Alternative). However, keep to the main road for a short time and then, past the bridge over the Ribeira do Ferreiro, turn right to ascend along the narrow street. A good 10 mins later, this ends at a **stable** ⓫. Here, a mule track continues. 100m further on, bear left. After an additional 200m, reach a **fork** ⓬.

To the left heads for Cuada but you turn right to descend and, 20 mins later, meet up again with a **road** ⓭. Here, turn right again to continue following the cart track. The mule track crosses over the road again and, at the end, above a junction, merges with the road. At the junction, turn right until reaching the bridge spanning the Ribeira das Casas. On the opposite side of the road, a cart track continues which follows the coastline, leading directly to the little harbour of **Fajã Grande** ⓮.

Flores ↗ 300m | ↘ 300m | 8.2km

95 Circling Fajã Grande

2.40 hrs

Circular route via old cart tracks along stonewall terraces

At the outset, this walk leads along the foot of a mighty sheer cliff, towering 400m above. Countless waterfalls plunge year-round over this height in wild surges and spurts. Along old cart tracks and mule tracks, pass carefully constructed stone walls created to provide terraces for pastureland and for old plantations of fruit trees. Via the idyllic tourist village Cuada, you make your return.

Starting point: Fajã Grande, harbour, 7m (bus stop Fajã Grande/Fim).
Grade: mostly along cart tracks overgrown with grass but still revealing ancient cobblestones. Extremely slippery when wet. Sure-footedness is required.
Refreshment: bars and restaurants in Fajã Grande. Restaurant in Cuada.
Alternatives: 1. longer route via Fajãzinha (4.7km; 1.30 hrs): at the fork ❹, stay left on the main trail. After 200m, keep right until you reach a stable. Follow the road from here. At the main road, continue left. 100m after the second bridge opposite the water mill, follow the cart track on the right. The main trail goes down to Fajãzinha in 15 mins. Continue on the road towards the right (Rua do Pico Redondo). After 200m, the road turns into a cobbled path. Keep left twice. At the restaurant, turn right at the road. You pass a picnic area. After 150m, follow the footpath that goes straight on in the left bend. Cross the Ribeira Grande on a wooden bridge. The opposite slope has slightly slod, but is easy to climb. From here, another old mule track continues. After 150m, there is a turn-off to Cuada (10 mins), however, continue straight on. Not quite 10 mins later, you reach two broken sections, which you can safely circumvent if you stay on the meadow. Soon after, a dirt trail begins and ends in the main route at waypoint ❽.
2. excursion to the *vigía* at Fajã Grande (750m; 20 mins): directly at the village limits ❽ of Fajã Grande take the first side street southwards and 150m past it, pick up the narrow footpath between the stone walls to climb up the hill. After a steep ascent, enjoy a marvellous view taking in the settlement. Return the same way.
Linking tip: Walks 94, 96 and 97.
Bathing: romantic rock pool Poça do Bacalhau at the foot of a waterfall. A quiet harbour basin and natural bathing areas are waiting in Fajã Grande.

At the **harbour** ❶ at **Fajã Grande**, start off at the car park, pass the picnic tables above the bathing area and then follow a cobblestone trail leading towards the waterfall. At the first fork, bear left and climb up to the bridge spanning the Ribeira das Casas. Just after crossing the bridge, follow a footpath along the left bank heading upstream. Passing the ruins of many watermills, reach the rock pool **Poça do Bacalhau** ❷ situated in an idyllic setting just below a waterfall.

Unspoilt nature idyll: bathing underneath the waterfall at the Poça do Bacalhau.

Return to the bridge and now turn left onto the street to ascend. At the following fork, turn left to continue climbing up. 150m on, in a left-hand bend, continue straight ahead along the cart track between stone walls. The cobblestone mule track ascends through pastureland, crosses over the road again and, not quite 10 mins later, meets up with the road once more at a cattle pen. Here, turn left along the continuation of the mule track ❸. The path now zigzags, climbing up below the cliff face of the Rocha da Fajã. 20 mins after leaving the road behind, the path noticeably steepens behind a watering trough for a short time. 100m past the trough, at a **fork** ❹ leave the main trail behind by continuing to the right (for the Alternative, go left).

Now the trail descends again and finally meets up with a road; turn right along the road for a few metres and then pick up the continuation of the cart track on the left-hand side of the road. The first few metres could be somewhat overgrown. 10 mins later, reach an old stone gate with a green door and yet another **fork** ❺. Here, turn left to continue descending and join the main road which heads for Fajã Grande. Cross over the main road; at the fork 50m on, bear right (this could be overgrown). 150m further, at the power pylon bear right once again. Get to a road and turn left. Soon after, reach the cul-de-sac at the holiday village **Cuada** ❻ (1.40 hrs).

Here, climb down along the cobblestone trail and at a fountain 50m on, bear diagonally right to continue and pass a cluster of natural stone-built houses. Soon you have left the village behind; the original inhabitants abandoned the village in the 1990s. Pick up a broad mule track to continue to the chapel **Santo António** ❼ situated on the main road. Diagonally to the left on the other side of the road and in front of a residence, the mule track continues by turning left. Reach the road again, turn right onto it and, a few mins later, at the same height as the settlement of holiday homes, 100m before reaching the sign for the village limits of Fajã Grande, turn right onto the continuation of the mule track, overgrown with grass.

Reach the first houses of **Fajã Grande** ❽ and meet up again with the road (the Alternative continues straight ahead); turn right onto the road to descend to the settlement. Shortly after passing a little park, turn left just before the yellow house 'Argonauta' onto the narrow **Rua das Courelas** ❾. Descend along this until reaching the seaside and then turn right onto the shore road. From now on, follow the seaside to return to the **harbour** ❶.

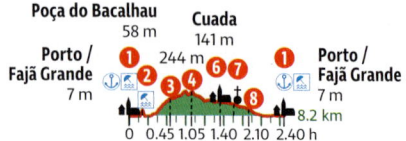

↗ 160m | ↘ 730m | 7.6km — Flores — **TOP 96**

3.10 hrs

From the Lagoas to Fajã Grande

Steep descent via ancient steps traversing the cliff face at Fajã Grande

Secluded highlands, hidden crater lakes, spectacular views and an extremely steep descent — these are the highlights of this walk. The route leads past four of the seven crater lakes that exist on the island; afterward, you must seek out your own path while walking cross-country over open pastures. After a steep descent via the Escada do Mar, the walk ends in Fajã Grande.

Starting point: viewpoint at the lakes Caldeira Funda and Comprida, 585m.
Destination: Fajã Grande, harbour, 7m (bus stop Fajã Grande/Fim).
Grade: before the descent begins, the walking trail is often slippery, sometimes precipitous and very marshy in the highlands. The descent route is extremely steep and even dangerous when wet. Absolute sure-footedness and an excellent head for heights are required. There is a danger of getting lost if foggy. Good footwear is absolutely necessary!

Refreshment: bars and restaurants in Fajã Grande. Nothing en route.
Linking tip: Walks 94, 95 and 97.
Bathing: harbour area in Fajã Grande, natural bathing area at Porto Velho.

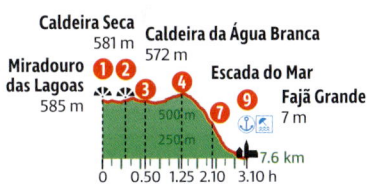

The deep blue Caldeira Comprida is part of the natural reserve park around the Morro Alto.

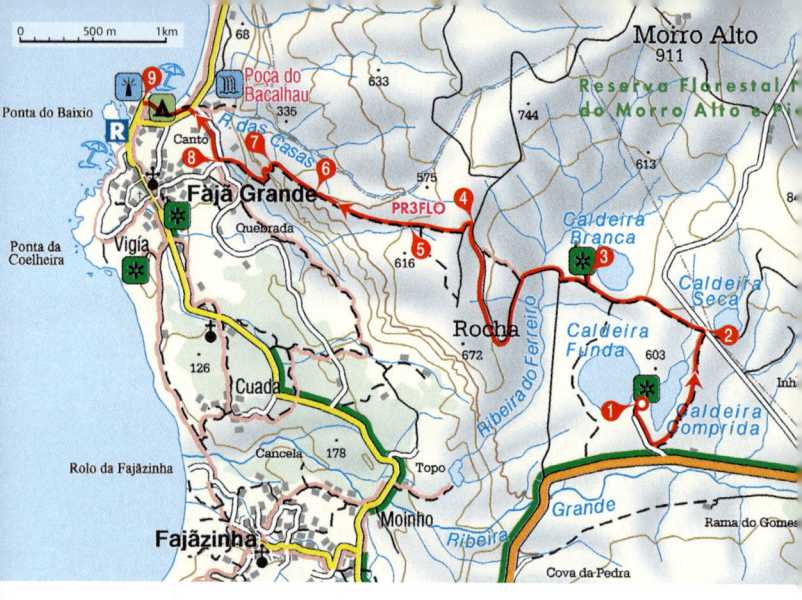

At the cul-de-sac at the viewpoint **Miradouro das Lagoas** ❶ for the lakes Lagoa Negra and Comprida, take the access road to descend and 100m before the main street, turn left onto a trodden path which veers northwards and 15 mins later, at the marshy **Caldeira Seca** ❷, meets up with a road. Turn left onto the road for 50m until you see a path to the left descending via steps. Along this path, pass the **Caldeira da Água Branca** and 20 mins later, reach a fork. Here, you could turn right to take an excursion to a well-camouflaged **bird-watchers' hide** ❸.

Continue straight on to reach a broad track which then leads over the Ribeira do Ferreiro. In a sweeping bend, the roadway ascends rapidly. After 30 mins on the track, a **gravel trail** ❹ turns off to the left. Follow it and bear to the right immediately. The trail crosses pastureland and bends sharply to the left about 10 mins later. Go straight through the **wooden gate** ❺. Past this, continue on the well-trodden path. At first, keep to the left, following a drystone wall. Waymarkers help in route-finding. After 20 mins of crossing solitary high meadows, reach a **rock gully** ❻. Immediately after, bear left and already catch a view of the harbour of Fajã Grande. Past this point, a second short stretch of descent as a hollow path follows. Afterwards, keep left yet again. For the following 300m, keep to the edge of the rim where a sheer face drops off abruptly.

After a total of 2.10 hrs, leave the pasture behind at a depression. At a gate, the clearly distinct descent trail begins, which is called **Escada do Mar** ❼.

Extremely steep steps climb down along the alpine route, traversing the steep cliff face of the Rocha da Fajã Grande for 35 mins via zigzags. Then the path levels out again, veers to the right and continues as a pleasant cart track following the course of the stream Ribeira dos Paus Brancos and finally meets up with a **road** ❽. Turn right onto the road to descend to the bridge spanning the Ribeira das Casas. On the other side of the road, a cart track continues, leading along the coast to reach the little **harbour** at **Fajã Grande** 🔴.

Steep descent to Fajã Grande.

97 From Fajã Grande to Ponta Delgada

↗ 600m | ↘ 590m | 13.2km
4.30 hrs

From the rugged west coast to the remote north

An ancient connecting trail leads from the popular Fajã Grande along the west coast. The extremely steep and strenuous ascent along the old shepherd's path through the steep cliff face transforms the walk into a spectacular one which should only be tackled by physically fit and experienced walkers. The reward is breathtaking views. Once at the top, the grassy trail becomes more pleasant but is often still slippery. The destination is the remote Ponta Delgada in Flores' north.

Starting point: Fajã Grande, harbour, 7m (bus stop Fajã Grande/Fim).
Destination: Ponta Delgada, picnic area at the harbour, 19m (bus stop Ponta Delgada/Fim 150m above the harbour).
Grade: the ascent trail is only for absolutely sure-footed, vertigo-free and physically fit walking fans. Sometimes sections with almost sheer drops! Often foggy and very slippery when wet. Never attempt this walk in the reverse direction.
Refreshment: bars and restaurants in Fajã Grande. Snack bar in Ponta Delgada. Nothing en route.
Alternative: Loop returning to Fajã Grande (11.3 km; 4.10 hrs): on the concrete road ❿ above the lighthouse, turn right and continue up. After 45 mins, the concrete surface ends. From here, a flatter track continues which ends after a total of 2.20 hrs at a crossroad. Here, turn right down and after 5 mins, take the first dirt trail on the right. Follow this trail and immediately keep right. The trail crosses pastureland and after about 10 mins, bends to the left. Go straight ahead through the wooden gate. Beyond that, continue straight without a clear path. Initially, stay left and walk along a drystone wall where waymarkers help for directions. After 20 mins across solitary high meadows, reach a rocky rock gully. Immediately after the gully, turn left and you will already see the harbour of Fajã Grande. After that, there's a second short descent in a rock gully, then turn left again. Continue along the cliff edge for the next 300m. After a total of 3.10 hrs, leave the pasture in the dip. At a gate, the clearly recognisable descent path Escada do Mar begins. On very steep steps, the mountain path descends in zigzags for 35 mins down the steep wall of Rocha da Fajã Grande. Then the path flattens out. It turns right and leads as a comfortable cart track along the stream of Ribeira dos Paus Brancos to a road. On this road, turn right down to the bridge over the Ribeira das Casas. On the other side of the road, a cart track continues along the coast directly to the small harbour of Fajã Grande.
Linking tip: Walks 94, 95 and 96.
Bathing: at the harbour area of Fajã Grande and the port basin of Ponta Delgada.
Note: in 2025, the path was closed due to safety concerns between ❹ and ❺.

View back to Fajã Grande.

Vista from the viewpoint to the Ponta do Albarnaz and to Corvo.

At the **harbour** at **Fajã Grande** ❶, start off at the car park and, passing the picnic tables above the bathing area, pick up a cobbled trail heading towards the waterfall. At the first fork, bear left and ascend to the bridge spanning the **Ribeira das Casas** ❷. Directly past the bridge, you could turn right along the stream for an excursion to the bathing pond, Poça do Bacalhau. The road leads straight ahead to Ponta da Fajã and ends just past the church at a **through** ❸ (45 mins).

Past this, a country lane continues. 150m on, at a concrete ford, continue left in the washed-out gully. After a few mins, reach the ancient cart track for the west coast and turn right along it. Soon, the track hooks to the right and takes you out of the valley. A few mins later, cross over a watercourse. 50m further on, leave the trail behind by turning right ❹ and climbing up the embankment. Now a strenuous ascent begins – it's less discouraging not to look up since the alpine path climbs all the way up to the top. After 30 sweat-provoking mins, a more level section follows and, past a spring, reach a lovely **viewpoint** ❺.

Past the viewpoint, the trail climbs further up along the rock face. A quarter of an hour later, reach a wooden stairway and use it to negotiate the last metres of height for the steep rock face. Then enjoy yet another marvellous view over the valley of Fajã Grande (1.45 hrs). Now another stretch of ascent follows, this time along terra firma. At a gate, reach the **highlands** ❻, and soon the path descends leisurely. After a total of 2.15 hrs, you reach a **small stream** ❼ and a goat gate. 5 mins later, you will reach the Ribeira do Monte Gordo. This stretch of trail is very eroded in some places.

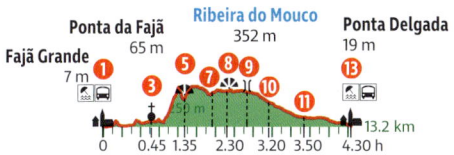

Cross over stone walls numerous times and then finally reach another lovely **viewpoint** ❽ directly at the rim (2.30 hrs).
The trail winds in steady up-and-down walking, heading towards Ponta Delgada. Yet another stone wall intersects the trail. 150m further on, reach a meadow; cross over this while ascending and following waymarkers. A few mins later, reach the course of a stream boasting a little rock pool. Soon arrive at another goat gate, and after 5 mins, you will reach the **Ribeira do Mouco** ❾ which always carries water. Past this, the terrain becomes level pastureland. 10 mins later, the trail descends through a wet, stony ravine along a concrete-paved ford. After the last, short section of mule track, reach a steep, concrete **road** ❿ (3.20 hrs; sign: Fajã Grande, the Alternative turns right). Here, you could arrange to be picked up.
Turn left onto the road to descend towards the lighthouse. At the **intersecting road** ⓫ at the bottom, turn right and continue along the seaside (just before you reach the road, it is worth taking a detour to your left leading to a viewpoint). 30 mins later, get to a **chapel** ⓬. Here, continue straight ahead and, 5 mins later, at the main road, turn left to descend to the **picnic area** above the harbour of **Ponta Delgada** ⓭.

The old mule track to the north coast.

Flores ↗ 370m | ↘ 370m | 6.6km

98 Trilho das Barrosas

2.30 hrs

Descent to a long-abandoned settlement on the northern coast

Only the older inhabitants of the island can still remember the good old days of Barrosas on the north coast because it has been decades since the hamlet was deserted. Before the road to Ponta Delgada was built, this was the only connecting trail for the northern island. If you take the extremely difficult alternative route to Ponta Delgada after the easier stretch to the Ponta das Barrosas, you can imagine how toilsome this must have been in the past.

Starting point: Ponta Ruiva, 259m, the end of the access road (bus stop Ponta Ruiva).
Grade: in residential areas, along roads. The descent follows an ancient cart track. The trail at the springs is muddy and damp. When wet, slippery throughout. Proper walking shoes are required.
Refreshment: snack bar in Ponta Delgada at the end of the Alternative. Noth-

Delightful: the view over the Ponta das Barrosas to Ponta Delgada.

ing en route. Restaurant in Ponta Ruiva.
Linking tip: Walk 99.
Alternative: the continued route to Ponta Delgada (6.2km, 2.35 hrs): past the viewpoint above the ruins ❺ continue along the footpath. This begins climbing up in broad bends. The path is sometimes only a narrow gully as it ascends steadily for 30 mins. Once at the top (total time: 35 mins), the trail continues on the level until, past a stone wall, it descends again through a mixed forest. An extremely steep section follows. Past a shelter, a stone wall intersects the trail. Soon, a grove of Japanese cedars follows; bear to the left and walk across several wooden steps. Cross over the course of a stream and join the old, broadly-laid, main trail for the northern coast (1 hr). The border for the municipalities is located here. More watercourses follow and, often, stretches of the trail are somewhat boggy. Stay always straight ahead along the main trail. The old cobblestone paving is often in excellent condition. When this becomes gravel, the adventurous leg ends (1.45 hrs), then a stretch of tarmac follows. When this ends, an excursion to the right is worth-while, leading to a tumbledown watermill, Moinho do Ilheu (sign: Ponta do Ilheu; 25 mins there and back). Continuing along the roadway, reach Ponta Delgada. Here, at the first fork, near a fountain, turn right to descend. At the bottom, at the intersecting street, turn left and, passing the church, continue steadily straight on, ascending to the town centre with a supermarket and a snack bar.

Note: the Alternative to Ponta Delgada is only fairly pleasant walking when it has been cleared. Otherwise, this first-class walk can turn into torture. Streams cross the trail in many places and numerous stretches are wet and muddy. Only for absolutely experienced and adventurous walkers!

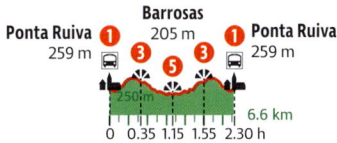

Reclaimed by nature: the ruins of Barrosas.

The starting point is the **Largo da Esperança** at the end of the access road to the hamlet of **Ponta Ruiva** ❶. At first, head southwards through the settlement. 250m on, the road hooks to the right (to the left, below: a small privately-owned museum); climb up the road until reaching the main road below the electric lines. On the other side, a concrete trail ascends and afterwards becomes cobblestone surfaced. At a **cattle pen** ❷, turn right onto the country lane which ends 250m further on and becomes a mule track. This leads sometimes over bare rock. You can already see Ponta Delgada and soon enjoy a delightful view taking in the northern coast ❸ (35 mins). Now the trail leads through a forest. Time and again, cross over rivulets and natural running springs. After a total of 1 hr, cross over the **Ribeira das Barrosas** ❹, which always carries water, hopping from stone to stone. From here, it is another 10 mins along a pleasant trail to reach the ruins of **Barrosas** ❺ (1.15 hrs). Between the first two buildings (gone back to nature), an overgrown flight of stone steps climbs up for 2 metres. Above the old buildings, once again enjoy a view of the northern coast. Afterwards, return again to the **starting point** ❶.

↗ 400m | ↘ 510m | 9.1km   Flores

3.20 hrs   **From Ponta Ruiva to**
🚌 ✕ ♒   **Fazenda de Santa Cruz**   99

From valley to valley on the eastern island

Deeply-cleft valleys cut through Flores' entire eastern side. From the tiny hamlet of Ponta Ruiva, a cart track leads to Cedros and continues to the picnic area on the Baía da Alagoa. Passing a marvellous viewpoint, follow a watercourse to the local recreational area above Fazenda. If you wish, you could continue via Monte to return to the island's capital.

Starting point: Ponta Ruiva, 259m, the end of the access road (bus stop Ponta Ruiva).
Destination: Parque Florestal Luís Paulo Camacho, 144m (next bus stop Fazenda, 1700m the access road from the forest park down to the ER 1).
Grade: mostly via cart tracks, overgrown with grass but with ancient, sometimes broken-up cobblestones. Quite slippery when wet. Numerous ascents and descents demand physical fitness. On the *levada*, a 5m stretch along the narrow wall.
Refreshment: small bar in Cedros. Restaurant in Ponta Ruiva.
Alternatives: 1. excursion to Fajã da Ponta Ruiva (a total of 1.9km, 1 hr): below the viewpoint with a view of the Ilhéu Furado climb down along an ancient donkey path to reach the extremely marshy Fajã da Ponta Ruiva where predominately fields of yams can be seen. 30m past a stone-built hut, bear right at a small stream. The path eventually fades out on a meadow. The old fishermen's path down to the mouth and the waterfall has since collapsed and is no longer passable. Climb back up again along the approach route. Instead of ascending back up the zigzag path, however, continue the final ascent by just keeping straight on.
2. extended route to Santa Cruz (5.9km, 1.40 hrs): from the Parque Florestal Luís Paulo Camacho ❾, ascend to the crossroad and turn right onto it. 200m further on, at the dairy at the fork, turn left to continue the ascent. Not quite 10 mins later, keep to the main trail on your left. 100m past this, turn left onto a road. It leads into the valley notch, crosses the Ribeira da Fazenda, and then climbs back up on the opposite side of the valley. After a long descent with a beautiful view of Santa Cruz, the road ends in Monte. At the first crossroad, turn right and at the viewpoint, turn sharp to the left. Now, turn right and immediately after, turn right again. Join the ER 1 and turn right onto it for a few paces. At the mirror, turn left onto a narrow passageway. Via a stairway, get to the old harbour, Porto de São Pedro at the northern end of the landing strip. Past the landing strip turn right and continue steadily along the enclosure for the airport until reaching the centre of town.
Linking tip: Walk 98.
Bathing: a pebble beach on the Baía da Alagoa.

Picnic area above the Baía da Alagoa.

View of Corvo from the Miradouro da Rocha dos Caimbros.

Begin this linear walk at the **Largo da Esperança** at the end of the access road to the hamlet of **Ponta Ruiva** ❶ and cross through the village by heading south. 250m on, the street hooks off to the right. At first, descend for about 75m at the nature park sign along the cobbled path to reach the Miradouro do Ilhéu Furado (turn-off for the Alternative). Afterwards, return to the road. Immediately after the bend, an old cobbled trail descends below a stone wall (trail board). 150m on, the trail forks. Turn left to continue descending along the main trail and pass an enclosed spring. On the way, enjoy a splendid view of the broad valley of the Ribeira Funda. 20 mins on, join a narrow concrete walkway crossing the **Ribeira Funda** ❷ (some waterfalls are located to the right). A little later, cross a second bridge spanning the Ribeira da Esguilhão.

The trail now ascends again and is sometimes extremely eroded. Watercourses cross the trail again and again. After 20 mins of climbing, pass a rock face. 5 mins after that, reach a **fork** ❸ below the summit of Burguilhão. Turn right to continue where the Cedros valley opens up. Keep steadily along the old cart track and finally pass the **ruins of ancient watermills** ❹. Right behind at the cemetery, a street begins which will take you to the main road ER 1 in **Cedros** ❺ (1.20 hrs). Cross over the main road and, following the Rua do Miradouro, bear left after 80m and thereby return to the main road.

First, make a 200m-detour to the right to the viewpoint Miradouro dos Cedros. Afterwards, continue the walk along the grassy trail along a stone wall, climbing downwards. The ancient, cobblestone connecting trail leads through the wooded slope (sometimes extremely steeply and very slip-

pery when wet) into the Bay of Alagoa and then, 20 mins later, ends at a house. Now pick up a narrow concrete trail to continue climbing down until reaching a road. Turn left to follow the road to a cul-de-sac. Now continue along a cobble trail and then cross over the Ribeira da Alagoa via a stone bridge to reach the idyllically-situated picnic area Parque de Lazer da Casa da Guarda at the **Baía da Alagoa** ❻ with a marvellous view of the rocky islets lying offshore (2.05 hrs). If you continue following the cart track, you will descend directly to the bay and a stony beach where you could enjoy a pause for bathing.

On the southern slope, at the same height as a building, a sometimes extremely steep footpath begins which gains altitude quickly as it winds in zigzags (Trilho dos Caímbros). Afterwards, reach a marvellous viewpoint and, just past this, join the ER 1. Turn left onto the ER 1 to reach the viewpoint **Miradouro da Rocha dos Caimbros** ❼ (2.30 hrs). Climb up the embankment and follow the opposite cart track towards the left. Once back on the road, continue right and after 80m, where the phone line crosses, turn left and walk down along a fence. At the bottom, a broad **water canal** ❽ crosses the trail. Follow the canal to the right and cross the main road.

You will soon reach a bridge. At the narrow sections, you need to change the side of the *levada* twice over a concrete crossing. 5 mins later, a watercourse spans over the canal. Just afterwards, reach a fern-blanketed meadow but continue following the canal which finally ends at a dam. On the southern side of the dam, a roadway sets off again. This leads directly to the **Parque Florestal Luís Paulo Camacho** ❾ with animal enclosures and a little labyrinth of trails.

Flores ↗ 330m | ↘ 330m | 6.8km

100 Fajã do Conde

2.10 hrs

Excursion to one of the island's oldest settlements

The stone-built houses of Fajã do Conde lie secluded along a small plateau high above the coast. This was one of Flores' oldest settlements but the village is now abandoned. Along the only approach road, cross over the Ribeira dos Barqueiros to reach this isolated paradise. The return is along an old cart track which passes abandoned terraced fields on the way back up.

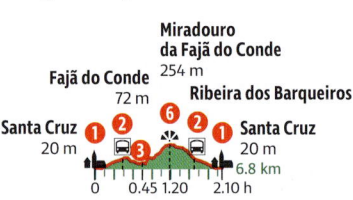

Starting point: Santa Cruz, municipal park, 20m (bus stop Santa Cruz/Jardim).
Grade: a mixture of roads and simple cobblestone trails. Ascent slippery when wet. Descent to the Ribeira da Cruz on a narrow footpath.
Refreshment: cafés, bars and restaurants in Santa Cruz. Nothing en route.

Fajã do Conde is situated on a small plain.

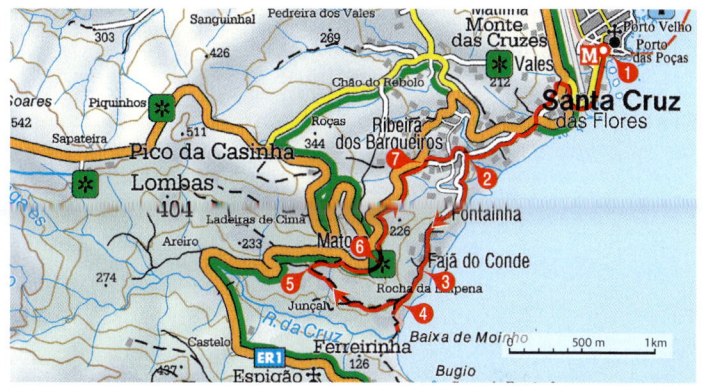

Starting from the little municipal park in **Santa Cruz** ❶, head south along the main street to leave the village and then, past the airfield, reach the island's main road ER 1. At the roundabout here, turn left and immediately at house no. 16, turn right to ascend along the secondary road. Back at the ER 1, now turn right again. At a fountain (1887) 200m on, turn left onto the secondary road. Shortly after passing the bridge in the settlement **Ribeira dos Barqueiros** ❷, the road ascends. At house no. 10, fork off to the left onto a side street.

This street leads out of the village again and a few mins later, to a sharp, right-hand bend. At this point, turn diagonally left onto a concrete trail to continue and descend directly to **Fajã do Conde** ❸, situated on a little plateau. The steep descending trail soon levels out and, after a total of 40 mins, ends. A dirt trail continues straight on, becomes an old footpath and ascends into a wood. 150m further, reach a **fork** ❹. If you want, you can descend – first via stone steps and later along a footpath overgrown with reeds and fern – to the mouth of the Ribeira da Cruz, where you will find a secluded bay with pebbles (there and back 25 mins).

Bear right, keeping to the main trail. This old connecting trail first leads through a dense forest in steady up and down walking. After the forest opens up, you reach a concrete path again. After 5 mins of ascent, right onto the **country lane** ❺ after the third concreted section and then turn immediately left onto the ancient cart track which ascends in 10 mins to reach the ER 1 (1.15 hrs). Turn right onto the ER 1 to head back toward Santa Cruz, passing the **Miradouro da Fajã do Conde** ❻. 15 mins later, at the first houses of the village **Ribeira dos Barqueiros**, turn right at a bus stop shelter and follow the **village main street** ❼ into the settlement. Continuing straight on, you rejoin the approach route which you follow back to **Santa Cruz** ❶.

Flores ↗ 280m | ↘ 280m | 3.4km

101 Ponta da Caveira

1.20 hrs

Short excursion to a ragged promontory with striking rock formations

The colourful rock formations on the Ponta da Caveira with a hidden pirates' cave are rough and spectacular. Via the lowermost district of Caveira, take a pleasant route to a cul-de-sac. Here, a steep fishermen's path descends to the headland and to the ocean.

Starting point: Caveira, church, 296m (bus stop Caveira below on the ER 1).
Grade: to the barbecue site, easy route along tarmac and concrete; very steep descent; at the seaside sometimes over broken steps. Absolute sure-footedness required.
Refreshment: nothing en route.

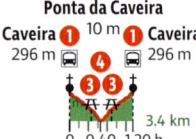

Next to the church above **Caveira ❶** at a transformer house, descend along the steep village main street Rua do Sul to reach the island's main road ER 1. Cross over to the other side of the road and descend via the Rua José Pereira Borges. At the final houses, the narrow street becomes a **concrete track ❷** which steepens steadily and then finally ends at a **barbecue site ❸** (20 mins). You could also drive to this point.

Now, an old stepped trail continues which brings you to the first fork; bear left. Beyond the fork, a small fishermen's path begins. After 5 mins, it joins a meadow, where the path peters out for a while. At the lower right end, the increasingly steep fishermen's path continues through the forest, passes a cross trail and leads directly to the promontory **Ponta da Caveira ❹**. Continue climbing down via stone steps to reach the seaside and a line of striking and colourful rock formations (40 mins). Beware: the final metres of this stretch have broken away!

Turn back to the cross trail, turn left and follow the ancient stepped trail steadily uphill. At the top, you are back on the route you took on the way out. Follow it back to **Caveira ❶**.

The final descent via steep steps.

Flores ↗ 240m | ↘ 240m | 4.1km

102 Porto da Lomba

1.35 hrs

Excursion to Lomba's secluded harbour

Lomba's harbour is old and tiny and no longer being used. It was protected by a small fortress built in the early 18th century. At the beginning of the walk, set off from Lomba to the end of the roadway on the Portal da Fajã. Here, your descent via an old cart track sets off.

Starting point: Lomba, church, 206m (bus stop Lomba/Terra Chã).
Grade: until reaching the cul-de-sac, along roads; descent via an ancient cobblestone trail which is slippery when wet.
Refreshment: nothing en route.
Bathing: tiny natural bathing area at the Porto da Lomba.

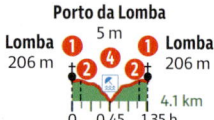

The boathouse on the Porto da Lomba has completely collapsed.

A pleasant trail descends to the bay.

From the church in **Lomba** ❶, follow the Rua do Cabeço northward, passing a chapel dedicated to the Holy Spirit. At the following fork, turn diagonally left to continue (Rua da Ribeirinha) and just afterwards, bear right (Rua do Porto). Now arrive directly at the island's main road **ER 1** ❷. Turn right for 50m then continue the walk along a narrow road on the other side of the ER 1 (sign: Porto da Lomba). Follow this narrow road all the way to the **cul-de-sac** ❸ where the road ends (25 mins). If you prefer a shorter walk, you could drive to this point (Warning: only room for one car!).

Now the descent begins via an old cobbled trail which is slippery when wet. A good 10 mins further along, at the only fork you will find along the way, bear right to reach the old harbour **Porto da Lomba** ❹ with an abandoned boathouse (45 mins).

Return to **Lomba** ❶ via the approach route.

Flores ↗ 390m | ↘ 390m | 9.2km

103 Fajã de Lopo Vaz

3.20 hrs

Coastal walk along a donkey path with a splendid panoramic view

Very few fajãs are as easy to reach as Fajã de Lopo Vaz. The descent route alone is a real pleasure. It opens up a long-lasting view taking in the rim of the steep coastal cliffs of the Quebrada Nova. Although no-one is living permanently at the foot of the 400-metre high coastal cliffs, the fields are still being cultivated. In this microclimate, even bananas, coffee and figs flourish.

Starting point: Lajes, municipal park, 64m (bus stop Lajes/Ponte).
Grade: to the picnic area, easy walking along roads and cart tracks; descent via a stony donkey path which is very slippery when wet. Sure-footedness and an excellent head for heights are required.
Refreshment: cafés, bars and restaurants in Lajes. Nothing en route.
Bathing: pebble beach in Fajã de Lopo Vaz.

Stone cross above the Ponta de Lopo Vaz at the picnic area.

Steep ascent over natural stone steps. *A guardian angel assures a safe descent.*

Begin at the centrally-located municipal park in **Lajes** ❶ and follow the island's main road ER 1 westward toward Fajã Grande. Pass the sports ground and 15 mins after starting off, turn left (Rua P. João Fraga Vieira). 150m past the **Chapel of the Holy Spirit** ❷, at the fountain, take the old cobblestone trail to the left. 50m on, keep diagonally right and, immediately after, bear left. Now follow the ancient mule track straight ahead for 10 mins and cross a gravel trail. Once you reach the crossroads, turn right to ascend to the **road** ❸, turn left onto it and continue until it ends at a **picnic area** ❹ (45 mins). If you are approaching with a vehicle, you could start here.

The descent begins along a donkey path at a stone cross. At first, the climb down is quite pleasant but 15 mins later, meeting up with some stone steps, the path becomes increasingly steeper. After a total of 35 mins descent, reach the bottom of **Fajã de Lopo Vaz** ❺ (1.20 hrs). As soon as you reach the beach house, turn right to follow the cart track for another 15 mins until it ends. Beyond the beach, the footpath continues for a short stretch through pastureland. Finally, descend via a scrambling path to the furthest **pebble bay** ❻. Then turn back to the beach house. Still at the seaside, you could, before beginning the strenuous climb back up, enjoy a bathing break at the pebble beach. In summer, some patches of fine sand may appear. Afterwards, ascend along the approach route to return.

Corvo – remote and lonely in the Atlantic Ocean

- population: 380
- capital: Vila Nova do Corvo, 380 inhabitants
- area: 17km^2
- length: 6.5km, width: 4km
- coastline: 21km
- highest point: Morro dos Homens, 718m

Corvo, the smallest Azorean island, is usually only visited as a daytrip for tourists from Flores. A mighty volcano with an impressive crater reigns over the island. On Corvo's southern flanks, the tiny village of Vila Nova, Portugal's smallest county seat and also the country's smallest town, clings to a slope. On Corvo, everyone knows everyone else and tourists stick out a mile. Continental European luxury is not to be found on the island. The population lives off the yields of their agriculture and depends quite a lot on improvisation.

CORVO

Getting there
Connections to and from Corvo are only offered via a 40-passenger plane serving Faial, Flores and Terceira. The tiny airport is situated directly below Vila Nova, only a short distance from the small harbour. The Atlanticoline company provides a ferry service to Santa Cruz on Flores the whole year round; during the summer months, the ferry service is extended and offers several trips per day via small hard-hull boats. There are no car ferries.

Bathing
Harbour basin at Porto da Casa. There are natural bathing areas at the Porto do Boqueirão and at the Portinho da Areia, west of the landing strip with a small sandy beach.

Festivities
Festa da Sagrada Familia, end of July. Festa de Nossa Senhora dos Milagres, August 15. Festival dos Moinhos, mid-August Festa da Senhora do Bom Caminho, beginning of September.

Medical services
A basic clinic in Vila Nova, tel +351 292 596 153.

Tourist information
The *turismo* is just above the harbour, half-way to the village; cm-corvo.pt.

Cultural activities
Centro de Interpretação Ambiental e Cultural and Ecomuseu in Vila Nova. The village, however, can be seen as a living ethnological museum.

Public transport
No taxis or buses. One or two share taxis await passengers embarking from incoming flights and ferries which take day visitors to the Caldeirão.

Accommodation
Only a few rooms in a mini hotel and in private accommodations. If you want to stay on Corvo for several days, you can be sure to find a family-like atmosphere. A small campsite (cold water showers) just west of the airport.

Along with the neighbouring island of Flores, Corvo was discovered in 1452 by the Portuguese navigator Diogo de Teive. Settlement only got started in the mid-16th century. During the 18th century, pirates were won over as friends and were rewarded for their services with a safe port and trading goods. Vila Nova received a town charter in 1832 and began to be self-sufficient in administration. The younger men in particular from Corvo were attracted by whaling and this caused a wave of emigration which lasted until the 20th century.

The first radio station in 1909 started off a new era in communication. Before that, smoke signals were used! Electricity was not available until 1963. The airport first began service in 1993.

Vila Nova is not only the capital but also the only inhabited settlement on the entire island – a hamlet with a miniscule old centre and countless, twisted passageways. Pigs grunt in the courtyards, cockerels crow at dawn and grain is still threshed by hand – one has the feeling here of being in a living farm museum. Vila Nova's population continues to shrink, and the villages has seen better times. The island's seclusion is even more evident during the winter months: when the storm season begins, ships may not be able to anchor for weeks on end and the reserves of life's necessities lessen day by day. The only site worth seeing is the main church of Igreja de Nossa Senhora dos Milagres in the centre.

Nevertheless, the island has a couple of highlights to offer. At the airport, you can see some renovated windmills in the Moorish mainland style. Three lovely viewpoints can be enjoyed: on the road above the village, at the crater of the Caldeirão and on the heights of the Morro do Pão de Açúcar. The interior is characterised by farming and livestock. Since 2007, the island is protected under the special auspices of UNESCO as a Biosphere Reserve.

Vila Nova de Corvo.

TOP 104 Corvo ↗ 200m | ↘ 200m | 4.8km
2.00 hrs

Caldeirão

Descent into the gigantic crater

The entire area around the crater of Caldeirão is used as open pastureland throughout the year. A pleasant footpath descends from the viewpoint at the end of the access road. You will circle the lakes by walking cross-country. Along the route to the lakes, at the floor of the crater, you are guaranteed close contact with cattle!

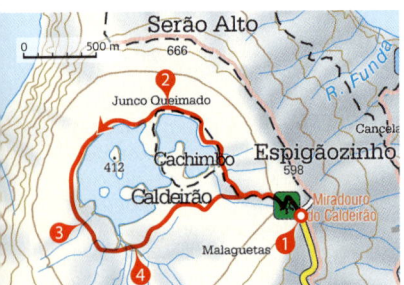

Starting point: viewpoint at the end of the road to the Caldeirão, 560m.
Grade: at first along a well-defined grassy trail. Whilst circling the lakes, cross-country walking along trodden-down, sometimes marshy, pastureland. On the southern side, a muddy trail. Do not attempt if foggy!
Refreshment: nothing en route.
Linking tip: Walk 105.
Note: starting at the harbour, when the boats dock, there is a shuttle service to the starting point (a fee is charged).

At the Poço da Velha.

Companion on the way in the Caldeirão.

The 'Monster' of Corvo sleeps peacefully in the crater lake of the Caldeirão.

At the **viewpoint** at the **Caldeirão** ❶ descend in zigzags along a grassy and stony serpentine trail into the crater and, 20 mins later, reach a large blocky boulder.

Starting here, the trail disappears. Turn towards the right and watch out for scattered waymarkers (wooden posts), that reveal the course of the route. At first, skirt around the easternmost of the two crater lakes in a semicircle heading anticlockwise. On the **northernmost point of the lake** ❷ veer to the right and thus cross over to the second lake across a hilltop. Depending on the water level, you could either continue directly along the shoreline or somewhat further upland.

On the southern side ❸ now veer away, leaving the lake behind you. Follow a wall of undressed stone for a stretch and, afterwards, continue away from the lake between the hill and the rim of the crater to pass the spring **Poço da Velha** ❹ (1.15 hrs).

Once you reach a watercourse, go left and climb up the hill in front of you. The circular walk then ends at the striking blocky boulder. From here, ascend back to the **viewpoint** ❶.

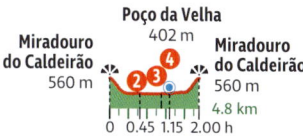

Corvo ↗ 130m | ↘ 680m | 6.9km

105 From the Caldeirão to Vila Nova

2.30 hrs

Descent from the island's dramatic gigantic crater

Just as the smallest of the Azorean islands is as tiny, just the more mighty seems the striking crater of the Caldeirão towering up above. From the viewpoint at the end of the only access road leading there, you will descend to the simply laid-out Vila Nova. During the descent, the panoramic view of Vila Nova is always with you.

Starting point: the viewpoint at the end of the road to the Caldeirão, 560m. Starting at the harbour, when the boats dock, there is a shuttle service to the starting point (a fee is charged).
Destination: Porto da Casa, 2m.
Grade: hardly-used road and gravel track.
Refreshment: restaurant O Caldeirão in Vila Nova. Nothing en route.
Alternatives: 1. extension via water reservoir (2.8km; 50 mins): from the wayside shrine, turn right and follow the gravel path uphill. After 5 mins, continue straight at the fork until you reach a reservoir. Leave the main trail at the gate and follow a pasture path downhill to the left. After 5 mins, turn left at the cross trail. 20 mins later, the main route continues in a left curve – 20m below the roadway and behind a livestock gate – along a mule track.
2. easy descent (1.1km; 20 mins): from the wayside shrine walk half left on the gravel trail and after the cattle grid, descend on a steep concrete path past some springs. Below the power plant, meet the road again. Turn right toward Vila Nova and soon reach the Miradouro do Sítio do Portão. From this point follow the main trail.
Linking tip: Walk 104.
Bathing: harbour basin at Porto da Casa.

From the viewpoint at the **Caldeirão** ❶, at first descend along the hardly-used access road for 40 mins until reaching a **stable building** ❷. Before reaching the cattle grid, turn right to climb down over the meadow. Cross over the concrete ford to turn right along the concrete road until, 10 mins later, at a **wayside shrine** ❸ this hooks to the right and begins to ascend (1 hr).

Descent to Vila Nova.

Follow the gravel trail around the bend for another 200m and climb up in a straight line across the meadow towards your left. At the top, walk through the cattle gate about 20m below the road. Beyond the gate, a clearly defined footpath begins which bends to the left after 200m. After 150m, leave the main trail towards the right and go right again after another 50m. Walk along the edge of the pasture along the drystone wall. From here, pay attention to waymarkers. Where the plateau breaks off towards the coast, you can see a **rock formation** ❹ of the head of an Indian (Cara do Índio) 100m below in the rockwall (1.25 hrs).

The path continues 50m farther to the left through a cattle gate and follows the stone walls at the edge of the pasture. You can soon enjoy a fantastic view over Vila Nova and Flores. 10 mins after the Indian view, descend on a path that is just wide enough for one person. At the bottom, the steep shepherd's path flattens out, continues to the left as a pleasant mule track and finally meets the road again. Walk 75m up on your left to reach the **Miradouro do Sítio do Portão** ❺ which offers a wonderful view to the headland with the village of Vila Nova (2 hrs).

Go back and take a shortcut via a grassy trail about 25m below the descent path to the left. At the edge of the village, turn left onto the cobbled stepped trail by the water house, pass the Largo da Fonte and continue downhill along the red-paved path through the village. In the centre, turn left onto Rua do Outeiro. A waterfront promenade then leads directly to the harbour of **Vila Nova** ❻.

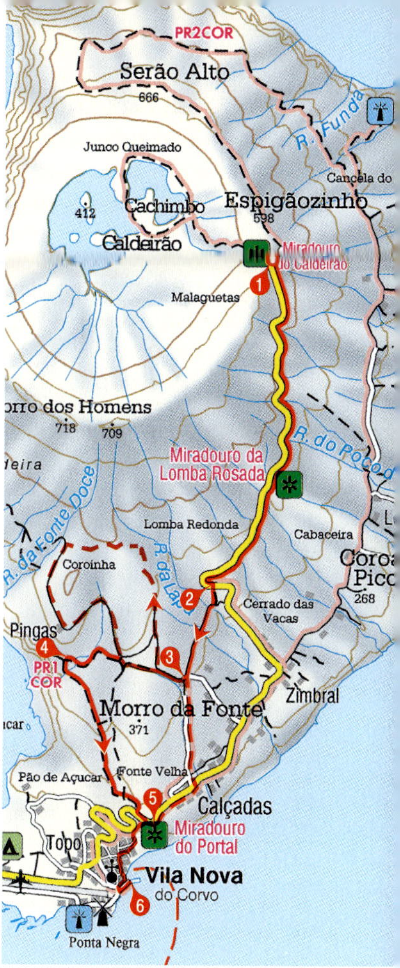

321

GEOGRAPHICAL DICTIONARY: PORTUGUESE – ENGLISH

Portuguese	English
adega	wine cellar
água	water
alto	high
algar	cave, grotto
amarelo	yellow
areal	sandy beach
areia	sand
avenida	avenue, boulevard
azenha	watermill
azul	blue
baía	bay
bairro	district, residential area
baixa	shoal, depression
baixo	deep/under
beco	dead-end street
biscoito	eruption area
cabeço	hill
cais	quay, wharf
caldeira	crater, basin
caminho	trail
canada	narrow trail/path
chã	level terrain, plain
chá	tea
chafariz	public fountain
cima	high
cruz	cross
eira	threshing yard
ermida	chapel
este	east
estrada	road
fajã	(coastal) plain
farol	lighthouse
fogo	fire
fonte	spring, fountain
forno	(baking) oven
foz	mouth of a river
frio	cold
furna	cave, lava tunnel
grande	large, big
grota	gorge
gruta	grotto, cave
igreja (matriz)	(main) church
ilha/ilhéu	island/islet
império	Holy Spirit Chapel
lagoa	lake
largo	small square
levada	watercourse
lomba	mountain ridge
mar	ocean
mata	woodland
meio	middle, half
miradouro	viewpoint
mistério	wooded lava flow
moinho	(wind) mill
monte	mountain
morro	hill
negro, preto	black
norte	north
novo	new
oeste	west
outeiro	height
parque eólico	wind farm
pedra	stone
pedreira	quarry
pequeno	small
pico	peak
pinhal	pine forest
piscina	swimming pool
planalto	high plateau
poço	well, pond
ponta	promontory
ponte	bridge
porto	harbour
praça	square
praia	beach
quebrada	cliff face
quente	warm
quinta	country estate
ribeira	stream, river
rocha	rock
rossio	central square
rua	street
serra	mountain spine
salto	waterfall
sul	south
terra	earth, terrain
travessa	passageway
vale	valley
velho	old
verde	green
vermelho	red
vigia	whale-spotters' post
vila	town
vinha	vineyard

INDEX

A
Achadinha 122, 124
Agrião 107
Água d'Alto 100
Água Retorta 111, 114
Alagoa da Fajãzinha 242
Além 59
Algar do Carvão 254
Algar do Pico Queimado 93
Almagreira 51
Alto do Brejo 186
Alto do Cabouco 186
Alto do Guarda-Sol 186
Ana Clara 142
Angra do Heroísmo 232, 258, 260
Anjos 62, 65
Arcos 148
Arrabalde 263
À Vila 236
Azenha 52

B
Baía da Alagoa 305
Baía da Folga 280
Baía de Canas 153
Baía do Canto 159
Baía do Filipe 282
Baía do Raposo 62
Baía do Tagarete 40
Baías da Agualva 242
Baixa da Ribeirinha 162
Barreiro da Piedade 59
Barreiro de Faneca 63
Barrosas 304
Barro Vermelho 270
Beira Mar 280, 282
Biscoito das Calmeiras 242
Biscoito das Fontinhas 265
Biscoitos (São Jorge) 217
Biscoitos (Terceira) 240, 246
Bom Jesus 270
Buraco de São Pedro 91

C
Cabeço do Fogo 191
Cabeço Gordo 185
Cabeços do Mistério 154
Cabeço Verde 195
Cais do Galego 166
Cais do Pico 153, 156
Caldeira da Água Branca 296
Caldeira da Graciosa 278
Caldeira das Sete Cidades 76
Caldeira de Guilherme Moniz 257
Caldeira (Faial) 183, 185, 187
Caldeira (Flores) 290
Caldeira Funda 295
Caldeira (Graciosa) 276
Caldeirão 318, 320
Caldeiras 94
Caldeiras da Lagoa das Furnas 104
Caldeira Seca 296
Caldeirinha 274, 282
Calhau 162, 166
Calhau da Areia 133
Calheta 55, 203
Calheta de Nesquim 170
Calhetas 90
Caminho dos Burros 153
Canada do Caldeiro 250
Candelária 142
Capela de Nossa Senhora das Vitórias 105
Capelo 190, 195
Cara do Índio 321
Carapacho 276
Cardal 57
Casa da Montanha 146
Cascata da Ribeira do Limbo 136
Cascata do Segredo 102
Caveira 310
Cedros 187, 305
Central Hidroeléctrica Nasce-Água 258
Chá Gorreana 134
Charcos de Pedro Miguel 183
Comprida 295
Comprido 195
Corvo 316
Costa do Lajedo 288
Criação Velha 143
Cruz dos Picos 46, 47
Cuada 292

E
Ermida de Maria Vieira 262
Ermida de Nossa Senhora dos Milagres 237
Ermida de Nossa Senhora do Socorro 218
Ermida de Santo António 260
Ermida Nossa Senhora da Guia 179
Escada do Mar 295
Espalhafatos 180

F
Faial 174
Faial da Terra 108, 111
Fajã 282
Fajã da Caldeira de Cima 220
Fajã da Caldeira de Santo Cristo 219, 220
Fajã da Neca 212
Fajã da Penedia 212
Fajã da Ponta Ruiva 305
Fajã da Praia do Norte 193
Fajã da Ribeira da Areia 210
Fajã da Serreta 237
Fajã das Fonduras 213
Fajã das Pontas 212, 213
Fajã de Além 208
Fajã de João Dias 206
Fajã de Lopo Vaz 314
Fajã de São João 224, 228
Fajã de Saramagueira 228
Fajã do Araújo 116, 118

Fajã do Belo 221
Fajã do Calhau 114
Fajã do Cavalete 226
Fajã do Conde 308
Fajã do Ginjal 227
Fajã do Labaçal 231
Fajã do Mero 212
Fajã do Ouvidor 214, 216
Fajã dos Bodes 224
Fajã dos Cubres 219
Fajã dos Tijolos 221
Fajã dos Vimes 222, 224
Fajã Grande (Flores) 288, 292, 295, 298
Fajã Grande (São Jorge) 217
Fajãs do Norte 212
Fajãzinha 242
Farol da Ponta da Barca 271
Farol da Ponta da Ilha 169
Farol da Ponta do Carapacho 277
Farol da Ponta do Malmerendo 67
Farol da Ribeirinha 180, 182
Farol de Gonçalo Velho 54
Farol do Vale Formoso 197
Farroco 243
Fazenda de Santa Cruz 305
Fenais d'Ajuda 126
Fenais da Luz 91
Fetais 171
Feteira 170
Flores 284
Fonte Clara 52
Fonte da Rocha 277
Fonte das Areias 191
Fonte da Silveira 173
Fonte de Nesquim 279
Fonte do Cão 265
Fonte do Nicolau 226
Fonte do Parol 180
Fonte dos Namorados 194
Fonte Grande 89

Fontes 272
Fonte Velha 123, 133
Forno 46
Forno de Cal 53
Fortaleza de São João Batista 260
Forte da Greta 262
Forte da Prainha 61
Forte da Quebrada 261
Forte de Bom Jesus 262
Forte de Santa Catarina das Mós 262
Forte de São Brás 60
Forte do Pesqueiro dos Meninos 263
Furna da Maria Encantada 276, 279
Furna das Pombas 243
Furna de Água 256
Furna de Frei Matias 144
Furna de Santana 65
Furna do Abel 279
Furna do Enxofre 278
Furna do Poio 221
Furna Ruim 196
Furnas 103
Furnas do Enxofre 254

G
Garden of Soul 136
Gorreana 135
Graciosa 266
Gruta das Canárias 157
Gruta do Cabeço do Canto 197
Gruta do Figueiral 60
Gruta do Natal 244

H
Horta 174, 178

I
Ilhéu da Baleia 271
Ilhéu da Vila 65

J
Janela do Inferno 97
João Bom 74

L
Ladeira da Velha 136
Lagoa Azul 76
Lagoa da Rosada 164
Lagoa das Furnas 103
Lagoa do Caiado 164

Lagoa do Canário 76, 79, 80
Lagoa do Capitão 153, 156, 164
Lagoa do Fogo 100
Lagoa do Negro 244
Lagoa do Peixinho 164
Lagoa (Graciosa) 272, 275
Lagoa Rasa 80
Lagoa (São Miguel) 70
Lagoas Empadadas 79
Lagoa Verde 76
Lagoínha da Serreta 239
Lagos 40, 44
Lajes das Flores 285, 314
Lajes do Pico 141
Lajido 148
Lapa de Baixo 54
Lomba 312
Lomba da Fazenda 118
Lomba da Maia 130
Lomba das Fagundas 114
Lomba de Baixo 127
Lomba d'El Rei 123
Lomba do Cavaleiro 107
Lomba do Pico 78
Lomba dos Homens 74
Lombega 198
Loural 2° 224
Luz 278, 280

M
Madalena 139, 144
Maia (Santa Maria) 54, 56
Maia (São Miguel) 130, 132
Malbusca 59
Malha Grande 246
Manhenha 166
Marquesa 41
Mata da Serreta 236
Mata-Jardím José do Canto 103
Mingato 142
Miradouro Alto dos Cedros 161
Miradouro da Alagoa da Fajãzinha 242
Miradouro da Boca do Inferno 81
Miradouro da Caldeira 186, 188

Miradouro da Caldeira de Guilherme Moniz 257
Miradouro da Eira 131
Miradouro da Fajã da Fragueira 222
Miradouro da Fajã do Conde 309
Miradouro da Fajã do Ouvidor 216
Miradouro da Fajã Redonda 257
Miradouro da Ilha Sabrina 82
Miradouro da Ladeira da Velha 137
Miradouro da Lira 179
Miradouro da Lomba do Vasco 77
Miradouro da Luz 279
Miradouro da Macela 61
Miradouro da Pedreira da Tia Raulinha 57
Miradouro da Praia 279
Miradouro da Ribeira das Cabras 192
Miradouro da Ribeirinha 182
Miradouro da Rocha 126
Miradouro da Rocha dos Caimbros 307
Miradouro das Cumeeiras 77
Miradouro das Lagoas 296
Miradouro da Terra Alta 158, 160, 165
Miradouro da Vera Cruz 126
Miradouro da Vigia 86
Miradouro da Vigia das Baleias das Feteiras 84
Miradouro do Barreiro 53, 91
Miradouro do Cabeço das Pedras Negras 181
Miradouro do Caldeirão 319, 320
Miradouro do Caminho Florestal Monte Brasil 261
Miradouro do Caminho Novo 86
Miradouro do Carapacho 279
Miradouro do Furado 137
Miradouro do José Furtado 126
Miradouro do Neptuno 179
Miradouro do Pesqueiro 125
Miradouro do Pico da Velha 204
Miradouro do Pico do Ferro 103
Miradouro do Pico do Milho 105
Miradouro do Raminho 236, 237
Miradouro do Ribeiro Seco 180
Miradouro do Sítio do Portão 321
Miradouro do Ti Domingos 131
Mistério da Prainha 153
Mistérios Negros 244
Moinho da Achada 270
Moinho da Ribeira da Alagoa 291
Moinho de Vento das Fontes 273
Moinho do Félix 127
Moinho do Frade 143
Moinho do Ilhéu 303
Moinho do Mourricão 171
Moinhos 136
Moinhos da Ribeira Funda 128
Moinhos do Crim 128
Moinhos do Januário 123
Montanha do Pico 146
Monte 143, 305
Monte Brasil 260
Monte da Guia 178
Monte Queimado 178
Morro de Castelo Branco 198
Morro Pelado 215
Mosteiro 289

N
Nascentes da Rocha de Santo António 89
Nascentes de Santo António 88
Nordeste 71
Norte Grande 216
Norte Pequeno 192, 194, 211

P
Panasco 58
Parque da Furada 159
Parque da Grená 103
Parque de Lazer da Casa da Guarda 307
Parque Eólico da Graciosa 274
Parque Eólico da São Jorge 219, 225
Parque Florestal das Sete Fontes 204
Parque Florestal de Água Retorta 111
Parque Florestal de São João 172
Parque Florestal do Cabouco Velho 183
Parque Florestal do Capelo 191
Parque Florestal Luís Paulo Camacho 305
Passagem das Bestas 256
Pedreira 116
Pico 138, 146
Pico Alto 46, 47, 50
Pico da Caldeira 48
Pico da Cruz 76
Pico da Esperança 214
Pico da Lagoínha 238
Pico da Quebrada 261
Pico das Camarinhas 82, 83
Pico das Cruzinhas 261
Pico das Éguas 80
Pico da Vara 120
Pico de Mafra 74
Pico do Facho 260
Pico do Gaspar 245
Pico do Juncal 250
Pico dos Bodes 108

Pico dos Remédios 78
Pico do Zimbreiro 261
Pico Queimado 92
Pico Timão 275
Piedade 160, 167
Piquinho 46, 50, 146
Poça da Dona Beija 105
Poça das Mujas 171
Poça do Bacalhau 292, 300
Poça dos Tremoços 263
Poça Simão Dias 216
Pocinho 143
Poço Azul 125
Poço da Ribeira do Ferreiro 288
Poço da Velha 319
Poços de São Vicente Ferreira 91
Ponta da Caveira 310
Ponta da Fajã 300
Ponta da Ferraria 82
Ponta da Ilha 166
Ponta da Restinga 276
Ponta Delgada (Flores) 298, 303
Ponta Delgada (São Miguel) 70
Ponta de Rosais 205
Ponta do Mistério 243
Ponta do Norte 42
Ponta do Queimado 237
Ponta dos Capelinhos 195
Ponta dos Rosais 204
Ponta Ruiva 302, 305
Portal 222
Portal da Fajã 312
Porto da Barra 272
Porto da Boca da Ribeira 182
Porto da Casa 320
Porto da Lomba 312
Porto de Cima das Feteiras 85
Porto do Calhau 143
Porto Formoso 136
Povoação 70, 106, 108
Praia da São Mateus 272
Praia da Viola 130, 131
Praia da Vitória 232
Praia de Água d'Alto 100
Praia de São Mateus 274, 276
Praia do Lombo Gordo 116
Praia do Norte 190, 192
Praia dos Lobos 65
Praia Formosa 49, 56, 59, 60
Prainha 61

Q
Quinta das Rosas 144

R
Relheiras de São Brás 264
Relva 86
Remédios 98
Reserva Florestal de Recreio da Prainha 155
Reserva Florestal de Recreio do Monte Brasil 260
Ribeira da Areia 210
Ribeira da Praia 100
Ribeira da Salga 126
Ribeira de Santana 65
Ribeira de São Tomé 230
Ribeira do Aveiro 55
Ribeira do Cachaço 125
Ribeira do Estreito 115
Ribeira do Guilherme 118
Ribeira do Meio 231
Ribeira dos Barqueiros 308
Ribeira dos Caldeirões 122
Ribeira dos Pelames 107
Ribeira Funda 128
Ribeira Grande 70, 94
Ribeira Nova 152
Ribeira Quente 106
Ribeira Seca 66, 94
Ribeirinha 161, 180, 183
Rocha da Fajã 294
Rocha da Fajã Grande 297
Rocha da Relva 86
Rocha das Feteiras 84, 85
Rocha do Cascalho 86
Rocha do Chambre 247, 250, 254
Rocha do Padre do Norte 129
Rocha dos Bordões 289

S
Salto da Cidreira 134
Salto da Farinha 125
Salto do Cabrito 94
Salto do Cagarrão 113
Salto do Prego 108, 111
Salto do Raposo 64
Salto do Rosal 103
Sanguinho 108, 112
Santa Bárbara 42, 45, 49, 52, 92
Santa Cruz da Graciosa 267
Santa Cruz das Flores 285, 305
Santa Luzia 148
Santa Maria 36
Santana 149
Santo Amaro 158
Santo Antão 231
Santo António 88, 208
Santo António de Nordestinho 120
Santo Espírito 52, 54
São Brás 264
São João 172
São Jorge 200
São Lourenço 53
São Miguel 68
São Miguel Arcanjo 153
São Roque do Pico 139, 151, 153, 156
São Sebastião 262
São Tomé 228, 230
São Vicente Ferreira 90
Serra Branca 274, 282
Serra das Fontes 275
Serra de Santa Bárbara 254
Serra Devassa 79
Serra do Cume 265
Serra do Morião 257, 259
Serra Dormida 274
Serra do Topo 219, 224
Serreta 236

Sete Cidades 76
Silveira 172

T
Tanque Velho 157
Terceira 232
Terra Alta 159
Terra Velha 43
Topo 230
Trilho das Barrosas 302
Trinta Reis 102
Túnel da Grota 98
Túnel do Pico da Cova 98

V
Velas 201
Vila do Porto 37, 60, 65, 67
Vila Franca do Campo 70
Vila Nova 317, 320
Vinhas dos Biscoitos 240
Vista do Rei 77
Vulcão dos Cinco Picos 256

Z
Zona Balnear da Foz das Coelhas 124
Zona Balnear do Caisinho 159
Zona Balnear do Frade 133
Zona Balnear do Portinho 170
Zona de Lazer do Dublhu 264
Zona de Lazer dos Fogos 142
Zona do Verdelho 142

Cover photo:
Fajã Grande in western Flores.

Frontispiece (page 1):
View from the old whale-spotter's lookout at Ponta dos Rosais (São Jorge) across the canal towards Pico (Walk 62).

Photo on pages 34/35: In the highlands of Pico.

All photographs are by the author.

Cartography:
105 walking maps with a scale of 1:50,000 and 1:75,000 as well as 10 overview maps with a scale of 1:150,000, 1:200,000, 1:400,000 and 1:3,500,000; © Freytag & Berndt, Vienna

Translation:
Tom Krupp, updates translated by Billi Bierling

Serial number: 4818

The descriptions of all the walks given in this guide are conscientiously made according to the best knowledge of the author.
The use of this guide is at one's own risk. As far as is legally permitted, no responsibility will be accepted for possible accidents, damage or injuries of any kind.

5th updated and extended edition 2025
© Bergverlag Rother GmbH, Munich
ISBN 978-3-7633-4847-3

We heartly welcome any suggestions for amendments to this walking guide! Please send an email to: **leserzuschrift@rother.de**

ROTHER BERGVERLAG · Keltenring 17 · D-82041 Oberhaching
tel. +49 89 608669-0 · rother.de